MY RIVER HOME

MY
RIVER
HOME

A Journey from the Gulf War
to the Gulf of Mexico

Marcus Eriksen

BEACON PRESS, BOSTON

Beacon Press
25 Beacon Street
Boston, Massachusetts 02108-2892
www.beacon.org

Beacon Press books
are published under the auspices of
the Unitarian Universalist Association of Congregations.

23   8 7 6 5 4 3 2

This book is printed on acid-free paper that meets the uncoated paper
ANSI/NISO specifications for permanence as revised in 1992.

Composition by Wilsted & Taylor Publishing Services

Library of Congress Cataloging-in-Publication Data

Eriksen, Marcus
  My river home : a journey from the Gulf War to the Gulf of Mexico /
Marcus Eriksen.
    p. cm.
  ISBN-13: 978-0-8070-7276-9 (paperback : alk. paper)
  ISBN-10: 0-8070-7276-1 (paperback : alk. paper) 1. Mississippi River—
Description and travel. 2. Eriksen, Marcus—Travel—Mississippi River.
3. Rafts—Mississippi River. 4. River life—Mississippi River. 5. Mississippi
River—History, Local. 6. Soldiers—United States—Biography. 7. Persian
Gulf War, 1991—Personal narratives, American. I. Title.
  F355.E68 2007
  917.7—dc22   2006031399

For the loved ones
who suffer in the
wake of America's
soldiers coming home.
The ripples of war travel far.

CONTENTS

INTRODUCTION

Another dead goat surfaces twenty feet outside my newly acquired Iraqi tent, two months after the end of the Gulf War.
Stumbling about before the sun rises, I check the wind direction.
Five miles away, oil fires burn. With the wind blowing west, the
thick clouds of black smoke will engulf us in darkness, black-
ening my nostrils by day's end. The shifting sand, windblown
across the battalion perimeter, reveals the ghastly carcasses of
long-dead sheep, chickens, and that goat.

Moments ago, hundreds of flies were gathered on the ceiling
of my tent, their bodies immobilized by the cool desert night.
How many can I kill before the morning heat wakes them to
swarm? The decomposing bodies of dozens of cows and camels
—shot by Iraqis in the suburbs of Kuwait City—created a
plague of insects. The air is putrid. The flies swarm by the billions and blend in with the gray clouds of burning oil.

Everyone's asleep or at least motionless. I've got fire watch
at 0600 hours, which means that Lance Corporal Tomas and I
have four hours of guard duty. We will sit in a sandbag bunker
and guard a nonexistent gate on a nonexistent road against a
nonexistent enemy. We seemingly do not exist either. Forgotten
on a tiny rise in the desert, dubbed Hill 99, we wait for rescue
from this 115-degree, godforsaken slaughterhouse landfill in the
abandoned suburbs of Kuwait City.

"Tomas!" I yell. "You ready?"

"Yeah," he grumbles.

Yesterday, forty marines, out of the approximately six hundred in our battalion, languished in the sick tent with IVs stuck

in their arms. Until a few days ago, Tomas was one of them. He's got the little red pinprick in his forearm from the intravenous rehydration.

We shuffle through the dustlike sand to the bunker. Stuck in the hole since 0200 hours, Corporal Saenz and Corporal Banks crawl out and walk away like passing strangers on a busy street. The inside of the bunker stinks like chew. Saenz's addiction to tobacco has left a small puddle of spit-soaked sand. Tomas and I crawl in and sit on the still-warm sandbag seats, the puddle of chew between my feet.

The wind intensifies with the rising sun. We climb outside the bunker and stand with our M-16s slung over our shoulders and goggles covering our eyes. Scorched air hurls sand in our faces. The sides of the biggest tents hover horizontally and flap noisily. Some marines wander around. A few wait in line for an empty seat on the shitter box placed in the middle of our perimeter. The box has two seats, allowing two marines to crap back to back. No walls, no privacy. The box gets moved every day as a new hole fills.

"I hate this place," I mumble.

I am farther from southern Louisiana than imaginable, far from the bank of the cool Mississippi River that shaped my youth. Everything is far away. The expectations I had of the Marine Corps at the age of seventeen are as inconsistent with the reality of the Gulf War as the Kuwait desert is from the swamp in St. Charles Parish, where life exists in every drop of water. I loved the Marine Corps. I wore fatigues my senior year in high school and a red tee-shirt emblazoned with the Marine Corps bulldog, to advertise my early enlistment. I was certain I made the old vets in my neighborhood proud. As a reservist I was able to attend the University of New Orleans. Maybe I would become an officer, or a civil engineer with the Corps of Engineers building levees on the Mississippi River, like my mother did.

The Gulf War would change everything. I would return home, marry a college sweetheart, and divorce her a year later. Choosing books over a bottle, I would spend a decade hiding in libraries earning a PhD in science education, shackled to the security of self-imposed solitude. I sought to recover the freedom I had lost and to understand the bitterness and anger that engulfed me. A month before graduation in 2003, the U.S. invaded Iraq. Everything changed again.

It was unfathomable that Iraq would become a target after 9/11. Young men and women were going to die. I joined millions marching through the streets in protest. I spoke at rallies, on the radio, and in campus forums. I was a greater warrior than ever before, but haunting memories of the Gulf War resurfaced. The faces of dying Iraqis captured after a tank battle ahead of our convoy and countless charred faces from the Highway of Death intruded on my thoughts day and night. I remembered everything in excruciating detail. I remembered the marines in my platoon. I recalled their faces and their personalities, as well as a promise to one marine to return to New Orleans on a raft down the Mississippi River.

Months after the beginning of the Iraq War, I built a raft and launched it into a quiet stream in northern Minnesota to begin a five-month journey, two thousand miles through ten states to the Gulf of Mexico. I justified the trip to others as a documentary film project, yet I knew that I was fulfilling a promise to myself made long ago in a sandbagged bunker in Kuwait. And perhaps, more importantly, this was a chance to reconnect with America, find forgiveness, and reclaim my life.

"The whole way down...from start to finish," I say to Tomas a few hours later in our sweltering bunker.

"Yeah. The whole thing. Where's it start?" Tomas asks.

"I dunno. It doesn't matter. In Canada I suppose," I reply. "We'll build our own raft...outta empty barrels or somethin'!"

Lost in the idea of an American adventure down the Mighty Mississippi, we waste away the hours of fire watch. Despite the heat and wafting stench, our minds float free under sweet-smelling skies, down a cool, flowing river. For days we remind each other of our audacious plan.

"The Mississippi's like thousands of miles, ain't it?" Tomas says, pausing to contemplate another logistical question. "We'll have to catch fish or somethin'."

"Yeah, those big two-hundred-pound river cats!" I reply.

We sketch out the details. It's a divine plan, a promise to ourselves, something to hope for. We ignore the grit of Kuwaiti sand between our teeth. A boiling sandstorm causes our bodies to sway with each gust, while a muddy mixture of sweat and dust puddles in the wrinkles of our faces and necks. The ping of sand against our green-tinted goggles is so loud we can hear it echo through our heads.

Decisions are made quickly. We will need giant paddles to outrun river barges, oil drums to float with, and a collection of fishing poles and lures to catch our dinner.

We kick the sand around a bit. In our minds, we are on our way to New Orleans. We are on the river floating by small towns. We are somewhere other than this graveyard in the desert, lost to the rest of the world.

We are the "Lost Battalion" of Hill 99.

We would willingly trade our M-16s for paddles. We are dreaming of a river home.

1

HOMEWARD BOUND

Well I built me a raft and she's ready for floatin',
Old Mississippi she's calling my name.
Doobie Brothers, "Black Water"

A blanket of stars hints at clear skies for the start of my 2,300-mile journey down the Mississippi River to the Gulf of Mexico. The Gulf War and Lance Corporal Tomas are twelve years behind me. It took that long to make good on a promise to myself to travel the river. I could not find him, despite phone calls to everyone with the last name Tomas in Louisiana. Time is fleeting, bones get older, and life's responsibilities can sometimes make your future not yours to decide. I'm single, childless, and can leave my job and apartment in less than an hour. Now is the time to go.

A morning mist floats over the calm surface of Lake Itasca, Minnesota, dissipating with the rising sun. Save for the splash of a jumping fish or the soft whistle of an unseen loon, it's quiet. I touch the water with my open palm so that I can feel what I see.

I stand in the shade of tall pines on the east bank of the lake as my raft—rolling on scavenged lawnmower wheels—launches itself clumsily into the cool, still water. The pontoon raft is designed to be stable and unsinkable. Each ten-foot-long, rectangular pontoon is filled with 116 plastic two-liter soda bottles stacked four rows high. A driver's seat from a junked Ford Mustang is bolted between the pontoons. A ten-speed Schwinn bike, transformed into a pedal-powered paddle wheel, is positioned in front of the seat. In order to enhance this mode of propulsion, I included a pair of homemade oars.

"Here we go!" I say softly.

Tony Peck, a documentary filmmaker, records the occasion. Tony will only stay a few days, but he'll return to film in St. Louis, and later in New Orleans, provided I make it that far. Tony and I first worked together creating an educational video about a dinosaur expedition. We survived three months of thunderstorms, golf-ball-sized hail, constant vehicle breakdowns, a buffalo stampede, and skydiving from ranch planes in Wyoming. Our greatest disaster came when I accidentally ignited a two-acre fire while using a cutting torch in a dry, windy field. We braved these foul-ups so that we could stick a thirty-foot triceratops dinosaur, sculpted with steel and a few real bones, into a local historical museum, displayed alongside covered wagons, rusty farm equipment, and an impressive collection of early-twentieth-century angora chaps.

Here we are together again, in northern Minnesota.

I paddle through a marsh of wild rice on the northern edge of Lake Itasca to a thin barricade of granite boulders, which marks the beginning of the Mississippi River. Nearly half a million annual visitors come here so as to be able to boast of having jumped across the Mississippi River.

A dozen tourists photograph, film, and finally just stare as I struggle to drag the raft across a swath of boulders. The water exits Lake Itasca through a ten-foot-wide, six-inch-deep stream that will grow to be a half-mile wide and two hundred feet deep at river's end. This massive watershed drains 42 percent of the

United States, including all or part of thirty-one states. At its mouth, 198 million gallons of water pour into the Gulf of Mexico every minute. The water I splash through in Minnesota will take three months to reach the Gulf, descending 1,475 feet over 2,237 miles. Of course mileage is approximate. A well-placed beaver dam can turn a field of switchbacks into a small lake. A meander may become a closed loop if erosion creates a cutoff.

I pretend to know what I'm doing. The first major obstacle in the river is a two-foot-diameter log only twenty feet downstream. Several tourists help lift my raft over the log, while Tony films everything.

"Just a few months of this and I'm done," I shout. The ankle-deep river is barely noticeable. The river ahead disappears into a tall pine forest. I imagined a swift, deep river that would easily carry me onward. Dozens of downed trees create a nearly impassable barrier. At times the stream narrows to only two feet across and two feet deep as it whisks around stumps and boulders. I drag the raft over logs and across gravel beds for the entire first mile.

"I just gotta suck it up and tough it out," I think. I continue this self-deception, telling myself that the only real obstacle that can keep me from success is the failure of my own determination, perseverance and stamina. Sometimes a plan gets in the way of ignorant bliss, but the result of poor planning is now evident.

"Finally, some deep water!" I yell to Tony. The river enters a marsh of waist-deep water surrounded by tall grass, crowded with submerged logs, and thick with stench-filled black muck. The celebration is cut short as I float up to the first beaver dam. Thin, fresh-cut pine saplings and long grass have been woven into an impressive natural barrier. The raft seems to catch every protruding stick as I ratchet it across the dam. On the other side of the dam, the water level drops two feet. There is no current. I stand on the raft and push-pole my way, inch by inch. The river is now an overgrown pond, dense with algae and other aquatic plants. The floating flora, seemingly intent on thwarting my progress, snags and entangles the pontoons.

By the early evening we arrive at Gulsvig Landing. Blood is running down my ankles from dozens of cuts and scratches. Two miles in seven hours—at this pace I should arrive in New Orleans in three years.

The entire Mississippi River is mapped by the Army Corps of Engineers and the Minnesota Department of Natural Resources (MDNR). The Lower Mississippi (LM) begins at mile 0 in the Gulf of Mexico and ends at mile 950 in Cairo, Illinois, at the confluence of the Ohio River. The Upper Mississippi (UM) begins at mile 0 in Cairo and ends at mile 850 just north of Minneapolis, Minnesota. The MDNR provides recreational maps from Minneapolis upstream 500 miles to the headwaters at mile 1,337 UM in Lake Itasca. I'm at mile 1,335. I have 2,235 miles to go.

"This is insane!" I say. Tony films my desperation. "There's no way I can drag this thing another mile."

"C'mon, you made it this far," Tony says. "That's two miles that are forever behind you." He's encouraging me to continue beyond reason for the sake of the documentary. At least that's my perception, and it's pissing me off.

"What if you get rid of everything but the pontoons? Just tie them together," Tony suggests. "It'll be like a canoe."

I stare dumbfounded. "Like a canoe?"

The raft is back in the van. We're on our way to Bemidji, pronounced *beh-midge-ee,* the first town on the Mississippi River, sixty-three miles downriver from Lake Itasca. I've already driven over three thousand miles to get here, and spent a greater number of dollars to make this trip possible. The thought of failure is nauseating. For two days we consider our options: dump the raft, trade for a canoe, lash the pontoons together to make a pseudo-canoe, or pack it in and go home. Despite the promise I made to myself twelve years ago, my first day on the river might be my last.

~

Standing between the legs of a blue ox the size of a bull elephant, I wait for the Bemidji Visitor Center to open. A two-story Paul Bunyan towers above the parking lot. Larry Young, a proud Bemidjian and executive director of the Joint Economic Development Commission, arrives to open the doors.

"Why don't you rent a canoe?" he suggests. He also knows where I can get one.

"What should I do with the raft?" I say. That's when I meet Miriam Smart, a volunteer at the Visitor Center.

"You can tie the raft to our dock," she says, graciously interrupting our conversation.

Over the phone I meet Timothy, a Swedish Chippewa canoeist, naturalist, and river guide. "Sure I've got a canoe for ya," he says.

I'm left speechless by the rapid outpouring of hospitality. I will store the raft in Bemidji while I canoe the remote headwaters. Then I'll come back for it when I reach deep water.

The following morning, I meet Timothy at Gulsvig Landing. Timothy's blond hair and blue eyes are contrasted by a beet-red sunburn. He's brought a canoe. It's a brand-new, seventeen-foot, plastic two-seater.

"My grandfather was a Gulsvig," Timothy says. "He owned this land. We farmed and collected berries and wild rice on this river alongside the Chippewa-Ojibwe people. This time of year you'll see Chippewa people collecting wild rice from here to Little Falls."

With childlike enthusiasm, Timothy affectionately tells stories about collecting wild rice and finding eagle feathers. He says that if you listen closely, the river will talk to you. He hands me a little birchbark canoe as a souvenir. He would like to be a chief someday, likely the whitest chief in Ojibwe history.

He and Tony help push my loaded canoe into the river. They stand at the water's edge as I slowly drift into the lethargic current. Tony films my departure. The shallow river meanders through a marsh of tall wild rice that bends with the weight of ripened grain that falls with the slightest touch.

"Remember, when you lose the river in the old beaver dams, stay to the left!" Timothy yells. We wave desperately to each other. Then I am alone.

AUGUST 22, 2003—COFFEE POT LANDING—MILE 1,330 UM

Gulsvig Landing lies fifteen miles behind me. I feel empty, exhausted, yet I'm smiling. This is such a different river from what I know. In southern Louisiana the Mississippi River is a giant monster caged behind high levees. It boils and sucks whole trees into oblivion. It churns angrily and sweeps you under if you venture too far into it. As a young boy, I would join my friends on jaunts across the levee and strip down to underwear for a swim. We never went farther than where the tips of our toes could still touch bottom. Even in the shallows, the current held our ankles until we kicked ourselves free. Here in Minnesota, the river touches you softly, invites you to meander with it, yet each new trickle whispers a warning. The river, drop by drop, is becoming more powerful.

The sound of rushing water from a forest stream brings clear water into the river, and a chance to wash off the evidence of the day's mudslinging in the old beaver dams. I'm covered with black mud, and patches of duckweed decorate my hair, shoes, and shorts. Naked, I rinse off in the small stream and think, "The raft would definitely have been impossible."

Estimated to be a century old or more, these beaver dams turn the river into a half-mile-wide braided marsh. There are logs everywhere. The dams barely rise above the water, yet they effectively divide the tiny stream into small pools with multiple flowing exits.

I follow the elusive current wherever it appears the strongest. I drag the canoe through waist-deep black mud hidden by a veneer of translucent, slow-flowing water. I wrestle myself free of the mud with the aid of dangling branches from young birch trees.

Then I reach into the foul muck to retrieve my shoe.

I unload the canoe and turn it on its side in order to pass through the tangled brush. Clearly, this is vindication for my argument with Tony about the impossibility of the raft, or any version of it, making it through the headwaters.

"Go left," I say. I chase the strongest current for much of the afternoon. Another five miles past the old beaver dams, I reach Coffee Pot Landing. I've got one souvenir from the day, the skull and a femur from a lost housecat. I'm one femur short of a pirate's emblem.

Coffee Pot Landing is a primitive campsite maintained by the MDNR. They have created an impressive system of camp facilities every twenty to twenty-five miles along the river for five hundred miles to Minneapolis. Built to protect canoeists from intense weather, Coffee Pot Landing features a small, three-sided log shelter. My sleeping bag, mat, and a rolled up sweater fit into the only dry corner of the shelter. I open cans of chicken soup, string beans, and fruit cocktail. Eaten cold out of the cans, it's a fine meal. It's raining hard, and thankfully I'm doused in mosquito repellant. They buzz incessantly no less than six inches from my head, lulling me to sleep.

AUGUST 23, 2003—IRON BRIDGE LANDING—MILE 1,299 UM

A morning of quiet switchbacks under swirling clouds and occasional rushes of cool wind precedes five hours of intense thunderstorms and howling winds. With strong gusts from the east, I inch backwards between strokes of the paddle. I question the wisdom of my persistence with each crack of lightning. Then when the storm ends, I enter a deceptive maze of floating mats of vegetation, consisting mostly of cattails and wild rice. These floating islands, ranging in size from a Volkswagen Beetle to an eighteen-wheeler, move with the wind and not the current. Waving strands of algae are the only indicators of the current's direction. The algae stops moving, and I lose the current and any indication of where to find the river.

The marsh stretches for more than a mile in all directions. For four hours I retrace my path to where the river was still a river and explore different routes through short stretches of open water and rice paddies that inevitably lead nowhere. I climb over the floating islands. Some support my weight. Others give way, and I drop into a morass of mud and rotting plants that comes up to my chest. At one point, after an hour of chasing a trickle in the direction of a break in the tree line, I enter another lake with a current that confusingly flows against me.

"Where's the goddamn river!" I yell. I'm frustrated beyond my normal tolerance. This is only the third day on the river, and I'm again on the verge of surrender. I have not only lost the river, but the river has lost me.

I think I hear a voice. "Hello?" I mutter, pausing for a moment to listen for an answer. "Who's there?" I yell. Nothing. I endure another hour trying to find a way out. I never stop paddling. Adding to my intense frustration, I discover that I'm back in the same place I was hours ago.

I climb over twenty-foot-wide mats of cattails, hoping that the river will suddenly reappear. The river teases me with wisps of current that appear between the floating roots. I hear voices again. I'm certain this time.

"HELLO!" I yell as loud as possible, trying not to reveal my desperation. As quick as I can move, I head in the direction of the muffled voices, hoping to see another human being. Suddenly, five men in three aluminum canoes pop into view. Before I can open my mouth to speak, one of them asks the one question I don't want to hear.

"Where's the river?"

The worst part is that I have stumbled upon the one group of people who shouldn't be lost: North Minnesota Boy Scout Troop 17. And unlike me, they have a Global Positioning System and topographic maps. They have a better handle on where we are than I do—but anyone would, at this point. Here I sit, a former U.S. marine with a Ph.D., rescued by the Boy Scouts of America! Still, I am relieved. At least we are lost together.

We travel together, moving like pseudopods from a giant amoeba, the canoe with the least resistance pushing forward through the thick marsh. For two hours we probe in different directions in search of the elusive river. Stan, one of the two troop leaders, is in the lead canoe. He blazes a trail through a sea of blooming lilies, and then the river gloriously reappears. The Iron Bridge Campsite is within our grasp, thirty-one miles from where my day began.

We find enough dry wood to build a reasonable fire. Darkness comes before the scouts erect their tents. The fire illuminates their tired faces. A barrage of mosquitoes is kept behind us, on the dark side of our bodies, only attacking exposed skin in shadows.

"You were in the Marine Corps, huh?" I ask. Stan wears a camouflage cap with the Marine Corps emblem stenciled on it.

"Yup," he says with a smile. When two former marines meet, they typically begin by identifying their unit and years served. They automatically resume a mental program of camaraderie. I particularly enjoy this deep sentiment and ignore the battlefield function of this type of training.

"So, what do you think of this war?" I ask, referring to the Iraq War, which officially ended two months ago, yet is already claiming far more American lives during occupation than invasion.

"Well, at least the politicians let the military do their job," Stan says, while munching on rice and beans. "They didn't mingle in the middle like in Vietnam." Stan served in the Marine Corps during the late 1980s, and barely missed the Gulf War in 1991. We talk about the Gulf War with sheltered opinions at first, slowly taking measure of each other's perspective.

Ted, the other troop leader, is the last to join us by the fire, having made sure that everything is set up correctly for his scouts. Troop 17 is enjoying its second summer on the river. Last year, they completed the first thirty miles. They'll complete more than fifty miles this year, and another fifty miles next summer.

"We're gonna keep coming back every year," the youngest scout says, adding, "We should finish the whole thing to New Orleans by the time I'm forty-seven."

They will take breaks from their plan. The oldest scout will complete high school this year, before joining the Marine Corps. The two younger are not far behind. They are enamored by the culture of military service. It is a rite of passage, a duty, and a badge of courage that they want to wear on their chests.

Eager to become uncommon men, they absorb their identity from heroes. I can see it in the subtle ways they emulate Stan and Ted, both veterans. They follow their own words with a careful glance to measure approval. Otherwise, they exude confidence. They yearn to be warriors.

The mosquitoes give no relief. We're all exhausted and soon escape into our sleeping bags. The next morning I quickly load my canoe. As the scouts emerge from their tents I push off from the misty bank. "Thanks for everything!" I yell. In a few days we will cross paths again.

I take advantage of the morning coolness and leave them to their glorious adventure. I'll soon return to Bemidji, the first town on the Mississippi River, only fourteen miles away.

2

WARRIOR'S ENCHANTMENT

MAY 1985—SIX DAYS OUT OF HIGH SCHOOL
I've never seen the Louisiana swamp from the sky. The sun's
shattered reflection bounces through the trees as it rises from the
watery forest floor. "The Mississippi River really does wander
for miles in both directions away from New Orleans," I think.
Leaving Louis Armstrong International Airport, I can see my
neighborhood disappearing quickly through the window. Everything I know is now a shrinking microcosm of security and
youthful carelessness. I'm on my way to the Marine Corps Recruit Depot (MCRD) in San Diego.

It's my first time in a plane that I can remember. On the journey west I see my first desert over Nevada, first mountain over
California, and a lasting glimpse of the Pacific Ocean before
touchdown. Signs in the San Diego International Airport point
to a sweltering gray bus, where I sit with other young men,
mouths closed and eyes kept on the back of the head of the person seated in front of us, as instructed.

Entering MCRD, I take my place on a trail of yellow footprints stenciled on the ground. I begin my dissolution. Civilian
clothing is packed in a single cardboard box and numbered. Everything gets numbered. All of us assume our new first name:
Private. The line for haircuts doesn't stop moving, evidence of
the barber's skill and the simplicity of the rapid front-to-back
movement of the shears, reducing the look of our heads to that
of an oversized grape. All scars become evident. Nicknames
quickly take shape. "What the hell happened to his head?"
someone whispers. "Blender-head."

Stripped of our external identities in one day, it will take another three months to strip our minds of individuality and instill
a deep sense of pride, loyalty, discipline, and unquestioning sacrifice. On the first night, in the dark squadbay, we sink into our
bunk beds, men without a clue about the future, stunned by the
novelty of the present, our sense of self skyrocketing away from
the past.

I am a product of my culture—blue-collar, suburban Louisiana
—raised twenty miles outside of downtown New Orleans, surrounded by sinking tract housing. Three miles farther away, I
could peer over the St. Charles Parish line into virgin swampland.

On boiling summer weekends, I would join a small troop
of gangly youths for the hike down Veterans Boulevard to the
swamp. Anthony and I were the same age. Little Richard was
the stereotypical fat kid, and Sam and Dave, our younger brothers, completed our gang. In our backpacks, we carried canteens,
peanut butter and jelly sandwiches, pocketknives, a fishing kit,
a pillowcase for snakes, and a snakebite kit lifted from Woolworth's department store. Once over the levee, a dirt mound
that keeps the swamp from flooding suburbia, we would follow
a pair of train tracks that extend deep into unexplored territory.

At the age of fourteen I killed my first alligator along those
tracks, while standing waist-deep in slick swamp mud. My ma-

chete penetrated its skull. I felt horrible, but at least we ate it. Killing animals never amused me, but hunting is part of my culture, and is unquestioned, at least until experienced. The Louisiana license plate reads "Sportsman's Paradise." We ate what we killed, except for the poisonous snakes. They were beheaded and skinned. Sam skillfully rolled the snakeskins around sticks. His backpack would fill with a dozen little scrolls of scaled skin waiting to be stretched, salted, dried, scraped, trimmed, then nailed to the inside wall of our clubhouse. Among stacks of aquariums filled with live snakes and turtles and walls covered with that reptilian tapestry, we would spend countless nights sharing cookies, soda, and stories about what we would grow up to be.

In a few years, four of us joined the Marine Corps, and five years later, we found ourselves in a convoy headed to Kuwait City.

"Get the fuck up."

"Sit the fuck down."

"What are you looking at?"

"Why are you crying?"

Private So-and-So is bawling. I never see him again. Another Private So-and-So just got knocked in the chest. He stays down. Another Private So-and-So stands his ground. Four barking drill instructors (DIs) hurl themselves in his direction. The private is huge, muscular, and about to be reduced to a puddle of subservience as a lesson to the wide-eyed spectators.

The DIs take turns yelling. "Do you want to hit me?" "Give it a shot, shithead!" "Just try it, you goddamn, piss-face, monkey fucker!"

Only five minutes earlier we were sitting quietly on the floor in our squadbay, when four unknown DIs marched in with ceremonial precision. They slowly turned to face us. In a flash, without any pretext, all hell broke loose.

My platoon of roughly eighty terrified recruits huddles in the squadbay, a giant rectangular hall with three rows of bunk beds. We are outfitted with tennis shoes, camouflage pants, and sweat-shirts with our platoon's number, 2058, stenciled across the chest with black shoe polish.

"Holy fuck! We got a little mamma's boy. Go ahead, cry like a little baby," one of the demons says to Private Who-Cares-As-Long-As-It's-Not-Me, who is on his knees sobbing loudly into his open hands. "Shut your pie hole!" the DI screams down at him, just above his head. "Where the fuck do you think you are?"

Another DI chimes in, "What makes you think I want a piss-poor piece of shit like you in my Marine Corps?"

The poetic profanity rolls off their lips with precise annunciations that pump jolts of fear through my body like an un-expected firecracker. We run in circles, failing to obey the intentionally contradictory commands.

"Push-ups. Up, down, up, down, up, down . . . faster!" the DI says as fast as the words can coherently exit his mouth. This is "thrashing," an instrument of punishment, or amusement, in-volving rapid exercise with frequent changes in the kind of exer-cise performed. A typical thrash may begin with push-ups, move on to running in place, sit-ups, and side-straddle hops, and often end with a few humiliating acrobatics. "Dead bug" means on your back with your arms and legs in a vertical position. "Eat dirt" is literally what it says. We are thrashed incessantly. Even-tually, after a few weeks of hourly thrashing, the DI only has to say "Begin" or "On your face" to cause the private to thrash himself.

"Sir, Private Eriksen requests permission to speak, Sir," I say.

Dialogue with a DI begins and ends with "Sir," and the first sentence is always a request to speak.

"Speak," the DI says dismissively.

"Sir, Private Eriksen requests permission to make a headcall, Sir!"

"Go away," the DI responds to my urgent request to use the bathroom. I really have to pee at this point, but pissing off one of my DIs is a greater evil than pissing in my skivvies.

"Sir, yes Sir!" I say, before I wobble away.

Peace comes when the lights go out. We practice the "Marine Corps Hymn," much to the dismay of our tormentors, who promise endless thrashing for misspoken verse.

"Wake up! Get up! Get your rags on, girls, and GET OUT OF MY SQUADBAY!" The last half of the sentence is yelled directly into the face of Private Guitowski as he scrambles out of a deep sleep to platoon formation in less than sixty seconds. DI Sergeant Lentil monitors his stopwatch. The entire platoon swarms down three flights of stairs and gathers outside the chow hall. Grasping our belts, blouses, and our unlaced boots, we get dressed in formation. Day after day, we make it to the chow hall in under sixty seconds, still half-asleep.

I am the bastard child of a failed romance in England. My parents had a wonderful affair that turned into a chaotic, cross-cultural yelling match that lasted a few weeks shy of a year. My mother returned home to Iceland. When I was two, she was wooed in a bar by a young punk in the U.S. Air Force, and we were swept away to a promised better life in New Orleans.

In a humid delta, overgrown with creeping vines that grow before your eyes, my mother and I ended up in the roach-infested two-bedroom wooden house of my stepfather's parents, Grandpa Sydney and Grandma Bella. Their dark, sticky furniture always smelled musty. The newspaper-covered hallway kept the two dirty little poodles from crapping on the torn linoleum floor. In the backyard, nearly a hundred chickens kept the ground barren. A minority of turkeys strutted about. In the front yard, a rusted 1950s sedan, perched on concrete blocks, served as dry storage for hay to feed the old pony that kept the front lawn partially mowed. We lived in that house until I was four.

My earliest memories of my stepfather are in the new brick home he and my mother purchased in a suburb built on re-claimed swampland. I remember wandering down the hall, cry-ing, because my mother was screaming. I turned the corner to the living room and saw my stepfather hovering over her. She was crouched in a ball in the opposite corner by the door. He was kicking her, but stopped when he noticed me. In a moment of compassion or shame, he allowed her to get up so that she could carry me back to my room. My brother Dave, a year old, was in the crib next to me. They divorced the following year.

My stepfather remarried and moved to Mississippi. Because we lived in Louisiana, child support recovery was nearly impos-sible for my mother. Mississippi could have been another planet in terms of legal communication between Southern states in the 1970s. We still visited my stepfather on random weekends.

Waveland, Mississippi, with silt-laden Mississippi River wa-ter lapping its sandy beaches, was a dream for a child. We could walk to the beach in an hour with fishing poles and crab nets in hand and bathing suits under cut-off jeans. We couldn't see our feet beneath the muddy water as we waded into the Gulf. Al-ways fearful of stepping on stingrays, we treaded water when-ever possible. The dirty water, spewed from the Mississippi Delta, left a weird, disgusting film of dark green slime around our mouths and noses, as if we had been eating guacamole. In the woods near the coast, we built forts on the concrete slabs where houses had stood before Hurricane Camille carried them to sea in 1969.

Every Fourth of July a parade wound through Bay St. Louis, Mississippi. Standing on the edge of a street covered with crushed oyster shells, I awaited the first cars in the parade mak-ing their way around the corner, their image distorted by the waves of heat off the concrete.

Pretty girls rode in bright-colored antique cars covered with flowing paper ribbons in patriotic colors. Instead of a marching band, a flatbed truck would roll by bulging with people singing some '70s hit.

Then came the old guys in little cars. Their sputtering go-kart engines drowned out our yells. They threw unwanted Halloween leftovers, like peppermints and gum. They wore little hats with little tassels. They wore silver and gold medals, rows of multicolored ribbons, and shiny pins and insignia plucked from the uniforms of bygone days.

I earned gold and silver stars in school for good behavior, but these guys got medals. I wanted to touch the purple hearts and bronze stars. "They must have done great things," I thought. I wanted one of my own.

My stepfather and his second wife lasted less than five years. He started a fishing business running crab traps throughout the Mississippi delta. It quickly failed.

Homeless after a year living in his car, he moved into the abandoned New Orleans home of his dead parents. My stepfather died drowning in his own saliva somewhere in a VA hospital. Among the empty whiskey bottles and molding carpet, my brother found letters addressed to him, each more unapologetic than the last.

DI Sergeant Lentil, a large black man from New Orleans with a bite bigger than his bark, is sufficiently annoyed with my existence. "Who's from New Orleans?" he asks.

Officially I'm from Kenner, twenty miles outside of the city. "Sir, Private Eriksen is from New Orleans, Sir."

"What part of town, Eriksen?" he asks, surprisingly polite.

"Sir, Kenner, Sir," I say.

"That's not New Orleans! You lying shit!"

Combat training takes place at Camp Pendleton, located between Los Angeles and San Diego. We throw grenades, hump the hills around the base, crawl under barbed wire, and don and clear gas masks in the gas chamber. Tear gas provides DIs with endless amusement, as blinded recruits with ill-fitting masks burst out of the chamber with two-foot-long strands of mucus swinging from their noses.

We climb Mt. Motherfucker—an endless, dusty, forty-five-degree slope—in the dark. DI Sergeant Lentil yells, "Where are you, ERIKSEN!"

"Sir, right behind you, Sir!" He's breathing heavy like a panting pack mule. I slowly pass him. He's pissed. I can barely catch my breath. My heart wants to jump out of my chest. Predictably, on the top of Mt. Motherfucker, I thrash.

Days later we return to MCRD to begin our third and final month of boot camp. We spend hours daily marching across the parade deck. Eighty recruits march with one loud, thunderous footstep. We are being perfected.

I was sixteen and still catching snakes. It was the twelfth one I'd caught that day that bit me. I'd whittled a walking stick with a forked handle, which I could easily flip around to pin a snake. Each of us sculpted his own. The fork is wide enough to fit over the triangular head of a cottonmouth or copperhead. Eleven live snakes lay motionless in our ice chest, suspended in a state of temporary hibernation due to the chunks of ice keeping the cooler at winter temperature. Our gang won't kill these. We catch them with no purpose in mind, perhaps acting on a primitive fascination.

Four of us rolled out of bed at 7:00 a.m. and met at the nearest street corner thirty minutes later, decked out in our latest Goodwill fashions and vintage military surplus gear. Fortunate to have two much older brothers in the Marine Corps, Anthony and Sam have been given genuine military goods, including C rations, which are canned meals phased out soon after Vietnam in favor of lighter, dehydrated "Meals, Ready-to-Eat," or MREs.

After a three-hour walk with many unplanned detours, we

eventually scaled the solid steel wall that divides suburbia from the unspoiled, virgin swamp. Moss-covered cypress trees dominated the landscape. We would spend the entire day on the other side until the hoot of great horned owls reminded us of dusk fast approaching. The whine of cicadas would serenade us on our tired walk home. Entire summers would waste away with days like these, but this day was different. Dave, Sam, and Anthony saved my life.

I pressed the forked end of my walking stick tightly against the neck of the cottonmouth. Its jaws opened wide, exposing white flesh and backward-curving fangs. I firmly grasped the snake by the back of the head and raised it into the air.

"Got another one!" I yelled. My friends ran toward me with their sticks in the air, dragging the ice chest behind them.

To our amusement, we had discovered that a reptile on ice becomes slow and stiff but doesn't die. A cold snake is like a stiff twig, easy to manage and interesting to watch as it slowly warms in the sun. I'm sure that the snake doesn't much care for the rapid change in temperature. We only put the poisonous snakes on ice. The king snakes, gopher snakes, and garter snakes slither in separate pillowcases.

The last cottonmouth was no different than the others: about two feet long, hissing loudly, with a flicking tail and pungent, musky smell. My brother opened the ice chest as I stretched out my arm to drop it in. The snake quickly wrapped itself around my wrist just as I released my tight grip. In a flash its head whipped around and its fangs sank into the flesh of my hand. The venom burned like a hot knife—fire in my veins. I flailed my arm up and down, but the snake wouldn't let go. It pumped its venom into my blood. As soon as its ammunition was discharged, we both fell to the ground.

The snake slithered away, but my brother caught up to it and killed it in retribution. He jumped to the suburb side of the wall and ran for help. I lay in shock. Sam and Anthony fumbled for the snakebite kit we never thought we'd need. The kit contained two suction cups, a razor, and a piece of string. Anthony sliced across the bite marks with the razor. Sam placed the suction cups over the wound. The cups quickly filled with a substance similar to apple jelly. We assumed it was poison.

My brother returned in the back of a fisherman's pickup truck. Within twenty minutes I was sitting in a fire station with my arm, grotesquely swollen to unimaginable proportions, submerged in a bucket of ice. In and out of consciousness while waiting for an ambulance, I could see the looks of terror on their faces. We are brothers, a pack of courageous fools, destined to be friends forever.

After I'd spent four days in the hospital and two months at home recovering, my brother and I secretly met Sam and Anthony at the street corner at 7:00 a.m. for another jaunt to the swamp. I caught my biggest cottonmouth ever, a six and a half footer! Had I kept its skin, it would have been a contender for the Louisiana state record.

"I need a volunteer for the Smokers," DI Sergeant Lentil announces after mail call. Smokers are boxing matches between platoons. One recruit with boxing experience from each platoon is pitted against another. Four matches between eight platoons are set up on a crisp morning two weeks before graduation.

"Sir, Private Eriksen has been boxing for years, Sir," I say, eager to volunteer. Actually, I've only spent a few months messing around in a gym, without ever hitting another human being. I inform him that I've got a prize record with a dozen fights and only one loss in the last two years of fighting. He buys it. He secretly hopes I get knocked out.

On the morning of the fights, I sit in a Quonset hut with the other recruits, all of whom are donning headgear and wrapping their wrists with bandages. I'm matched with a young fighter with more real fights than the number of fights I lied about. We warm up and work the bags until we're called to fight.

An outdoor boxing ring surrounded by bleachers is packed with roughly six hundred soon-to-be marines. The first three fights end quickly. The young jarheads roar each time a punch lands, cheering the brutality. We hate on command. I climb into the ring swearing to pummel this guy. I don't care that he is like me. I just want to hurt him. We pound on each other in quick, one-minute rounds. By the middle of the second round I am covered with blood. I can feel it flowing out of my nostrils and into my mouth. DI Sergeant Lentil is laughing. I can hear the crowd cheering my failure, my defeat.

I'm checked out and give the OK. Someone yells, "Fight!"

"Just swing," I tell myself. "Just beat him. Beat the shit out of him."

My opponent, Private Who-Gives-a-Rat's-Ass from some other platoon, stumbles. I'm not sure if I'm hitting him, but he's flailing backward. He falls and stops moving. I knocked him out! I was swinging my arms like a madman, like a little girl, but I must have hit him enough times.

"OohRah!" The battalion of recruits in the bleachers is screaming.

"Marine Corps!"

"Marine Corps!"

"Marine Corps!" I'm yelling at the top of my lungs. Days later, I am summoned to carry the battalion flag for graduation.

As young teenagers, my brother and I often met Anthony and Sam at the corner after school. Sometimes we were joined by Little Richard. We would plan afternoons of war games complete with toy guns and real "Rambo knives." The handles of our knives, with embedded compass, screwed off to reveal a hollow chamber for storing matches, fishing line, hooks, and other miniature bits of useless survival gear. We each had one. Mine had a six-inch black blade and a camouflage handle.

In our neighborhood, veterans surrounded us. Anthony and Sam's older brothers were veterans from the Marine Corps. Mr.

Clyde across the street was a navy vet, and so was Mr. Jim next door. Sometimes Mr. Jim's cousin, Mr. Carl, visited. He was in the army and went to Vietnam. A couple of times I spied on them sitting together on the back porch at night. Mr. Carl was sobbing about something.

I had learned that the Vietnam War was a bad thing for a lot of innocent people, and that soldiers who went there to do good things were treated like dirt when they got home. I was determined to be a good soldier for them.

We dominated the neighborhood as we patrolled through nearby fields with our plastic rifles, setting up ambushes and swinging on ropes strung up to the tops of willow trees. A nearby private elementary school provided ample opportunity to engage in afterschool urban warfare, as well as rewarding us with footballs and Frisbees found on the roof. We called our little troop "The Bad Explorers." In our childish hearts we dreamed of avenging the wrongs committed against Vietnam veterans. We played our war games on weekdays and sneaked over the parish line to collect snakes on weekends. We hiked for miles through swamp, hunted, fished, and trespassed on school property, construction lots, and junkyards. We were home and in bed by 9:00 p.m.

In high school, I joined Air Force Junior Reserve Officer Training Corps (JROTC). With my long hair, big ears, and awkward-fitting blue uniform, I thought I looked really slick. Recruiters from all branches of service would stroll down the hallway trawling for us. The Marine Corps recruiter wore his dress blues, a uniform that was far superior to anything else I had seen. He was brilliant, untouchable, like the surface of the sun. He gave us posters and stickers with which to cover our walls. I counted the years, months, and days before I turned seventeen and could drag my mother into the recruiter's office to sign on the dotted line.

We sneaked into theaters to see our heroes in our favorite

films: *Deer Hunter, Apocalypse Now,* and *First Blood.* They defined patriotism, honor, sacrifice, and masculinity. Eager to make the veterans in my neighborhood proud, I was determined to serve my country. I wanted to be a warrior, just like them.

Tomorrow, I will be a marine. DI Sergeant Lentil gathers the platoon for today's feature film, *The D.I.* Perhaps he's wasting time on a day of nothing to do but wait for tomorrow. Maybe he's attempting to validate tradition, which seems more likely, since the entire platoon is rolling in laughter at how the drill instructors of the 1940s bark, growl, curse, walk, and act in every way like the tough bastards that have molded us into marines. No one can sleep, despite having already sung our nightly chorus of the "Marine Corps Hymn," followed with a loud "GOODNIGHT, SIR!"

Fireworks ignite beyond the squadbay windows. From my top bunk on the third floor I have a view across the parade deck, over the obstacle course, over the runways of San Diego International Airport and civilian neighborhoods, to the evening show in the skies above Sea World. I have come to enjoy the evening ritual. I can see a few other recruits with their heads lifted above their pillows to get the full view.

For me, tonight's show celebrates my new identity. I will return home with the ideology of unquestioned obedience to the Marine Corps. The indoctrination is extraordinarily effective. I am a loyal son. The Marine Corps can do no wrong.

Dangerously arrogant and convinced of the superiority of the Marine Corps, I reenter the world.

"Don't touch my uniform!" I yell.

"Get that dog away from my shoes!"

My brother has mistakenly put my cover, or hat, on his head. "What the fuck makes you think that I would give you permission to do that?" I bark at him. In the mirror, I see a miniature

DI with one little red stripe on his shoulder, a clean high-and-tight haircut, and far more attitude than purpose.

The Marine Corps Reserve Unit in New Orleans, on the southern shore of Lake Pontchartrain, is not the Marine Corps I know. The reservists act soft, skirt regulation haircuts, and arrive to weekend drill with hangovers. But I can't shake boot camp. I stand at attention with my eyes on the back of the head in front of me.

I've joined a platoon of infantrymen led by Sergeant Hernandez, whose appearance is akin to the Tasmanian Devil. His running songs exude humor rather than cadence. For kicks, he forces the platoon to lie on their backs for close-order drill.

"Forward, march!" he growls with laughter. We look ridiculous, like synchronized swimmers in grass.

"Platoon, halt! About face!" Now our faces are nuzzled directly into the dirt. We are a platoon of stooges. Two-thirds of these marines in STA (Surveillance and Target Acquisition) Platoon will not be around when we are activated for the Gulf War five years from now.

I join the color guard. I'm one of four marines in dress blues who present the American flag at NFL games. I eagerly seek every opportunity to wear my dress blues uniform. On November 11, 1986, we march ceremoniously into a rented banquet hall to celebrate the Marine Corps's 211th birthday. The battalion commander speaks of tradition, honor, and sacrifice, then says, "1986 Marine of the Year is . . ."

I'm handed a small metal plaque mounted on faux-wood particle board, engraved for ten cents a letter. I am the marine in the posters on my high school bedroom wall. I am the twinkle in an old vet's eye. I am a warrior.

3

TRAVELER

"What's a brat?" I say. I've been whisked away to a neighborhood potluck picnic with barely enough time to shake the duckweed out of my shorts. This is "Minnesota friendly," complete with eight different variations on pasta salad and meaty casserole.

"Brat? You never heard of bratwurst?" Tim says with a puzzled look on his face. "It's a sausage packed like a hotdog."

In polite defense I respond, "Ever heard of boudin?" We engage in a five-minute discussion about sausages from our respective parts of the country. It's a warm, dry, sunny day, the kind of day I'll relish in the months ahead. I gorge myself on brats, burgers, a little of each pasta salad, and a hefty dollop of cherry ambrosia for dessert.

It was a six-hour journey this morning from Iron Bridge Landing to Bemidji. The river meandered through marsh and old-growth hardwood forest, complete with an inexhaustible supply of fallen trees to portage. One slippery trunk marked my first, though not my last, full-face plunge into the Mississippi River.

The slow river, brown like tea from tannins leached from fallen leaves, suddenly becomes green like pea soup as it enters Lake Irving on the south side of Bemidji. The oxygen-deprived water, caused by an algae bloom, sends a few thousand little fish belly-up. This is where I left my raft three days ago, tied to the dock of Terry and Miriam Smart.

This morning, as I paddled across Lake Irving, I began to recognize the back of their house and the dock I had tied my raft to. The raft wasn't there.

I noticed bundles of plastic bottles strewn about their backyard. The raft was actually half-sunk in the lake, shipwrecked on the bank with long strands of algae draped over the pontoons. Terry caught a glimpse of my canoe coming in and greeted me on the dock. He explained everything, with a chuckle ending every other sentence. He used phrases like "piss and vinegar" and garnished every other sentence with bar-room adjectives.

The powerful storm I endured earlier also struck Bemidji with forty-two-mile-per-hour winds and high waves. The two-liter plastic bottles, duct-taped together in bundles of eight, blew out of the raft and floated across the lake. Terry Smart, donning hip-waders, rescued the bottles. His son Andy pulled the listing raft to the bank.

There was little time to assess the damage this morning. I helped load lawn chairs and a barbeque pit into Terry's truck. I was starving and luckily a bounty of pasta salad awaited.

"There's a recycling center around the corner," Terry says, signaling for me to hop in the truck to go dumpster diving. There are fourteen missing bottles I need to replace.

Terry admires the raft, but secretly he thinks I have a low

probability of making it from Bemidji down the river. He's got his own boat, a sailboat, in the garage, with a crack in the hull thanks to a lightning strike a few years back. His garage is necessarily larger than his house in order to accommodate the multiple, simultaneous projects in the works. We talk shop for a while. Mostly I ask the questions. We get along well.

Quickly we pull two dozen bottles out of the dumpster and rip the labels off, then a quick stop at Terry's bar for a few beers to go. Terry built the Keg & Cork Pub by hand three decades ago and recently passed it on to his son-in-law. Terry keeps his tradition of cooking soup for the Monday lunch crowd. If you're ever in Bemidji, Minnesota, stop by the Keg & Cork around noon. Ask for Terry's soup of the day. Let one of his twenty-plus recipes surprise you. He remarks to the bartender about the soup he'll bring this week, and then we're off.

The picnic ends by midafternoon. A couple of Terry and Miriam's friends take up chairs around my raft. Tim and his wife, Kim, have brought a couple of six-packs to fuel the conversation.

"Well, ya just can't call it *The Raft*," Kim says. I explain that Tony and I deliberated for weeks and came up with *The Recycled River Rover*. Everyone pauses and stares for an eternal moment.

"You call it what?" someone finally chimes in. I agree it's dumber than dirt, but it's the best I've got.

The sun sinks below the tree line. In a few short months, Terry and a hundred other Bemidjians will drag their icehouses onto the lake to fish through two-foot thick ice. They'll fish there for months. To stave off cabin fever, the town will bust a giant hole in the ice for the celebratory "Plunge," whereby brave souls jump in for kicks. Another festive winter event is turkey bowling. Our conversation seems to hang on the contrast between these last days of summer and the rapidly approaching fall/winter season.

"Can you keep the ice behind you?" Miriam asks with sincere maternal concern. (She will follow my progress down the river and become one of the few good friends I'll keep in touch with along the way.)

"I figure I'll make it to New Orleans by Christmas," I respond, but I really have no idea. It's becoming a common question, so I just give the same answer.

"Why don't you call it the *Bottle Rocket?*" Kim says proudly. She's been silent for a while, perhaps contemplating the plausibility of a few different contenders.

"The *Bottle Rocket?* I like that!" I say with sincere enthusiasm. I tell them my bottle rocket story. Twenty years ago, my brother had trusted me to put a dozen bottle rocket fireworks in his back pocket. I told him that if he ran really fast after I lit them they wouldn't hurt. They blew off his pocket, burned a hole through his pants and underwear, and put a little raspberry on his butt. Everyone is staring again.

No one vetoes the name. With the last drops of beer, we christen the raft *Bottle Rocket,* each person repeating the name with approval.

The next day is spent repairing the *Bottle Rocket.* Holes are drilled into the aluminum frame of the pontoons above and below each column of four bottles. Wires are tied to the pontoons and around the neck of each bottle. Terry insists on driving me twenty miles downstream past the first dam, to take a look at the condition of the river.

"This is as low as it's been in years," Terry says, trying to plant the idea in my head that I should hang on to the canoe for a while. "You're not gonna get much help from the current," he adds. The shallow river is more akin to a hundred little streams weaving between thousands of basketball-sized boulders. I'm easily convinced.

The next morning, I put the raft in the back of a horse trailer borrowed from the editor of the *Bemidji Pioneer,* after a brief interview. The trailer and my raft will stay in Terry's driveway for a few weeks. I paddle away from their dock loaded with a minimal amount of gear.

"Don't forget to stop at the city dock in Lake Bemidji," Miriam says. In fifteen minutes of paddling I arrive at the Bemidji Chamber of Commerce via the river. Terry and Miriam are already there. Larry Young, executive director of the Joint Economic Development Commission, offers me souvenir bobblehead statues of Paul Bunyan and Babe the Blue Ox on behalf of the people of Bemidji. Terry hands me a Keg & Cork mug and tee-shirt. Another canoeist and his son will paddle with me across Lake Bemidji. I cannot imagine hospitality greater than this.

It takes three hours to reach the bridge that Terry and I peered over yesterday. Terry is there waiting to help me portage the canoe around the dam. He hands me a bowl of his bean soup and a handful of crackers.

"You'll do just fine." We wave to each other until the river bends.

The river widens and narrows in gentle undulations. My paddle combs through long strands of bright green algae that gracefully wave in the current. There is so much algae that I cannot see the rocky bottom. I stand in the canoe and push-pole against the exposed boulders, easily negotiating a path. The sun is warm. I'm still awestruck by the warmth from people in Bemidji. I haven't felt so much kindness in a long, long while.

AUGUST 1990—UNIVERSITY OF NEW ORLEANS— IRAQ INVADES KUWAIT

In Kennedy International Airport, the marquee listing international flights bound for and returning from Kuwait City displayed a long list repeating "cancelled." August 2, 1990, the beginning of the end for the dictator of Iraq. People who'd hoped to board planes for Kuwait were milling about with desperate faces. I'd just returned from another month traveling overseas on my own dime.

Transportation to Kuwait City would resume in six and a half months, via U.S. tanks, armored personnel carriers (APCs), and thousands of other allied vehicles in massive convoys riding on the heels of a defeated foe. As the threat of war in the Persian Gulf builds, I returned to the University of New Orleans as a full-time geology student.

"Hey, Rusty, what do you do when your brake pedal is kinda spongy?" I asked my roommate.

"You gotta bleed the brakes," Rusty said. "I'll show ya." His thick Southern Mississippi accent painted his words. He was kind, always smiling, always giving.

We're both in the backyard. He's under my truck. "Okay, press on the pedal now!" he yelled. He fixed my brakes sooner than I could have located the release valve on the brake line.

One month later, driving back to campus through a thunderstorm, I saw Rusty's car wrecked on the opposite side of the freeway circled by a dozen vehicles with twirling lights. Minutes later I walked into the house and was told bluntly, "Rusty is dead."

Richard, the fat kid in our childhood gang from the old neighborhood, was in the car with Rusty while driving in a downpour. The car spun and slammed sideways into an abandoned van on the shoulder of the freeway that had not been there an hour earlier. Later, in the hospital, Rusty's parents allowed me into the room to see him. His eyes had been removed for donation. He was cold, silent, but still giving. Richard was in the hospital with a twisted left arm, which had been trapped under Rusty as he passed away. He described the slow departure of Rusty's soul. We cried for a while.

Six weeks later, on Monday, November 20, 1990, the recorded message said, "Sergeant Eriksen, report to your duty station for orders." I called my brother, David, who already knew and was quickly getting his life in order. I called Richard, with his arm in a sling, who was already packed. Within five days we would all be on the way to Camp Lejeune to retrain for war.

On Day One, I moved all of my belongings out of my apartment and into my mother's home for storage. On Day Two, I dropped out of the University of New Orleans. It was late in the semester; therefore, I was able to earn grades for all classes. Biology required a bit of bargaining, until reluctantly, the professor gave me a B, followed by a chorus of "Take care" and "Good luck!" from the classroom audience. In the vertebrate paleontology lab, I had been in the middle of a project mounting a skeleton of an opossum. I tied a note to the tiny shoulder blade that read "Gone to War."

On Day Three, I joined Sergeant Sellers on the roof of his house with several other marines from STA Platoon. He and his wife had just bought a house and ripped the roof off a week earlier. We all brought hammers and worked through the day to lay tarpaper and shingles.

"Are you packed yet?" Slam!

"No. When do you think we will ship out?" Slam!

"Why the hell are you asking me? We're not even gone yet." Slam! The roof went up quickly as guys from the platoon came and went. That night the marines dominated Cooter Brown's, a local bar, for a final bash in New Orleans. I called Melida, an old college sweetheart, with the news of our activation. By that afternoon we were dating again, and in a few weeks we would become engaged to be married.

On Day Four, back in the old neighborhood, the parents of all the kids going off to war surprised us with a party. My brother, Sam, Richard, and I were marines in the same company, but in different platoons. Ricky next door was an army corpsman. We were many years from our days of catching snakes along the parish line.

Richard was still talking about Rusty, and would think about the accident while we were training in Camp Lejeune. The pain in his arm was overshadowed by his deep sorrow. He was spared the experience of the Gulf War. He returned home before we packed our seabags for Saudi Arabia.

We were eating cake decorated with "Bless our Boys." Mothers were crying and men gave out tight-lipped handshakes. The next day, the marines reported to the Drill Center. My mother cried openly. Her only family, her two sons, was going to war.

I was twenty-three, a sergeant in United States Marine Corps, a squad leader in STA Platoon, and on my way to the Persian Gulf to fight for the liberation of a country that most people couldn't place on a map, or hadn't even heard of. In the weeks between the weekends of reservist duty, I had attended college, but I'd received a better education with my passport. Between school semesters and my one-weekend-per-month reserve duty, I traveled.

In Dachau, Germany, the site of a Nazi concentration camp, I met an old man returning to Europe for the first time since his Dutch family had been released from a prison camp at the end of WWII. The gates of Dachau were ornamented with metal images of barbed wire and twisted bodies and the words "Never Again." He allowed me to walk with him through the prison, now a museum, as he recalled life in a concentration camp. He had lost most of his family there. We stood by the ovens where thousands were burned after being hung by rope beneath the rafters only a few feet away. He wept alone, but still asked me to walk with him. So I did, and absorbed every precious memory he shared.

In Turkey I spent two weeks in a small village on the Black Sea. After surviving a motorcycle accident, I was befriended by a family and invited to join them at a mosque. The inside of the mosque was empty except for hundreds of small carpets completely covering the floor. We were greeted by the mullah inside. They motioned for me to remove my shoes. The ceiling was tall and curved. Beneath the curve of the giant dome, a few small windows allowed sunlight to illuminate the padded floor. The Koran was laid open in front of the mullah, while we knelt before him in a single row. He sang from the Koran, pausing between sentences. He sang the words as if he were wailing at a funeral or calling his sheep to come home. I could see the others on either side of me. Their hands were in their laps. Their heads were in their hands. It reminded me of kneeling for communion.

In Geneva, Switzerland, I walked through the United Nations building. For a couple of bucks I picked up a copy of the International Bill of Human Rights, which was far more comprehensive than the Bill of Rights my nation drafted two centuries ago. I was so impressed by the idealism that I later made copies and left stacks in the building stairwells of my university.

Traveling is its own university.

When I stepped down from the plane onto the tarmac in Saudi Arabia, I had already been to a dozen other countries. I had begun to understand the cost of war, the commonality of faith, the ideal of human rights, and the sorrow of death. It would be immensely difficult to dehumanize another people, a key ingredient of warfare. I had learned a great lesson: Beware of traveling, you may grow to respect the ones you're supposed to hate.

4

A NOVICE IN UNFAMILIAR TERRITORY

Nature is beneficent. I praise her and all her works.
She is silent and wise. She is cunning but for good ends.
She has brought me here and will lead me away.
Johann Wolfgang von Goethe

AUGUST 27, 2003—STAR ISLAND—MILE 1,262 UM

With talons opened wide, a bald eagle hovers high above Cass Lake, making minor adjustments with single feathers to steady its position. In elegant slow motion, both wings curl behind its back before it plunges into the water. Saberlike claws pierce the silvery skin of its next meal, gently lifted and carried away.

Such grace is a sharp contrast to my battle against waves whipped to a frenzy by a brisk wind on a shallow lake. I've seen a dozen eagles already today, but none on the hunt. Each time the river bends, it unveils the next scene with unsuspecting wildlife caught in the usual act of doing nothing.

The waves lap against the bow of the canoe and splash inside. There are a couple of inches of water sloshing across my feet. Minnesota is the land of ten thousand lakes—actually 11,842 lakes of ten acres or larger, according to the Minnesota Department of Natural Resources. Cass Lake is the sixth largest, and one of the few that absorbs and releases the Mississippi

River. In the center of Cass Lake is Star Island, and a campsite, according to the soggy MDNR map in my lap. There is a lake named Windigo within Star Island. It's one of the few examples in the world of a lake within an island within a lake.

Approaching the island, I can see the beach and the presumed location of the campsite. Someone has beat me to it. There are two canoes. No, three canoes. Three aluminum canoes. Two are tied together. It's Troop 17! Four days ago we were lost in a marsh fifty miles from here.

"Well, look who showed up!" Stan says, helping me drag my canoe, a quarter full of water, out of the waves.

Ted is warming stones in a cast-iron pot over glowing embers. The three other young scouts have been busily laying tarps over the frame of a sweat lodge erected by previous visitors. As dusk approaches, we all strip down to skivvies, climb into the sauna, and sit in a circle around a pile of hot stones. Stan drips water on the sizzling stones, creating steam. We barely break a sweat while Ted tells a story about the Great Spirit that eats beets and pisses red in the river so that future canoeists in the bog don't get lost. An hour ago I was battling a headwind as water began to fill my boat, now I'm half-naked in a sauna with a bunch of boy scouts.

Later, around the campfire, we talk about knots. It is the longest conversation I've ever had about knots. The Boy Scouts of America foster independence, leadership, honor, heterosexuality, and kinship with nature. We talk about the beaver dams, muskrats, bald eagles, the flow of the river, and the waves that brought us here.

Then someone mentions the MDNR. The Minnesota Department of Natural Resources, both loathed and respected, is responsible for implementing government regulations regarding use of public lands. Locals love to hate and hate to love the MDNR. Stan begins his story, "A MDNR agent was after some Indian boys for the fish they were catchin'. Well, the boys got a jump on him and stuffed a rock bass in his butt."

As if startled from sleep, I respond with an inquisitive, "A what?"

"A rock bass. A fish. They had to take him to the hospital and everything."

The youngest boy scout chimes in enthusiastically, "Yeah, they got spines in their fins, so ya can't pull 'em out." There's not much else to talk about for a few minutes.

I remember that the oldest boy scout will finish high school this year and join the Marine Corps. "What's your MOS (Military Occupational Specialty) going to be?" I ask, interrupting him from making dessert.

"I'll be a radar operator," he responds.

"That's more useful training than being a grunt," I reply. He puts the cast-iron pot back into the coals, but this time there's cake batter inside. Building a Dutch oven is another boy scout skill. He's making a big chocolate cake. I think they get a badge for it.

Stan and I resume the conversation from four nights ago about Iraq, and then Ted joins us. The young scouts are fully enthralled with our every utterance, with what they perceive to be elder warriors recalling stories of battle in distant lands.

Ted asks, "You must have some interesting stories about being in the Marines."

"I can tell you about the time a dozen of us had liberty in Memphis for a weekend, drank away all our money, and came back with nothing but an Elvis tapestry."

One young scout's eyes widen. "Yeah, tell us that one!"

I can smell the cake and the chocolate icing being spread over it.

Ted seems worried I'll say something immoral. He narrows his question. "How about your experience in the Gulf?" I tell them brief summaries about the Gulf War, while stuffing cake down my craw. I tell them about the souvenirs I picked up, the wildlife that lives in that desert, the men I served with, and the Iraqi army that fled Kuwait City on the road to Basra, but didn't make it. I keep the conversation clean, somewhat neutral, and completely honest. Ted seems content.

Everyone appears contemplative. Were the young scouts expecting stories of hand-to-hand combat, or carrying the wounded over my shoulder while firing my rifle to take a hill? Perhaps they were wondering how much of the warrior ethos is myth?

We return to the current war and the rationale behind it. We exchange what we think and what we know. Finally, Ted concludes, "What we need is new leadership." I couldn't agree more.

The following morning I quickly gather my gear. Sleepily, one of the young scouts stokes the glowing embers of last night's campfire. They're in no hurry. Today is their last day. They will be picked up on the other side of Cass Lake. They all stand along the shore as I paddle away. We wave and exchange good wishes.

"You be careful now," Ted says loudly.

I yell, "Travel well, my friends," my own little silly catchphrase that I'll use again and again on this river journey, as though I were Daniel Defoe's Robinson Crusoe sailing away into my own fictional life.

Lake Winnibigoshish, much larger than Cass Lake, is the largest body of water the Mississippi River flows into and out of. The tree line disappears on the other side as the earth's curve hides the opposite shore beyond the horizon. The MDNR maps indicate that it's twelve miles across the lake, eighteen miles if I hug the shore on the southern end. I compute the rowing time in my head. It is windless, cloudless, and the water is smooth as glass. I choose the shortest distance between two points. Such deception invites a fool. The folks in Bemidji warned never to cross Winni. Two years ago on a crisp April morning, two men, hoping to travel the entire river, ended their journey here. They died when their canoe capsized and the cold, early spring snowmelt stole their lives. I begin to paddle with steady determination.

It's smooth paddling almost half the distance, four miles out. A calm wind in my face quickly creates one-foot waves. They are manageable. I keep going, but the wind doesn't stop, and the waves seem to grow exponentially larger.

I count each stroke of the paddle. In my head I've decided that each thousand strokes is half a mile. Water is pouring into the canoe. Shadowed by clouds and cooled by wind, I am shivering from the spray of cresting waves.

"What the hell am I doing here?" I ask myself. "This is dumb. You've got yourself up to your neck in trouble." It's a fool who takes an uncalculated risk, but also one who takes no risk at all. Today I am clearly the former.

There are two choices: turn around and hope that I can ride the waves back to where I came from, or continue on to the near shore, three miles ahead. I make the unwise choice to continue against the wind and the waves. Actually both choices were bad, based on an initial dumb idea. Soon the crests of two-foot waves are splashing over me. I'm soaked. "Don't stop. Don't stop. Keep going—985, 986, 987...." I'm still counting strokes with a strange comforting confidence, as if the numbers will equal certain success. In reality, I'm making little progress and my endurance is fleeting. Another wave dumps a couple of gallons into my canoe.

Jeff almost passes me by on his way back to his dock after an unsuccessful, rained-out morning of fishing with his wife and young son. He saw a dark smudge amid the white froth created by the turbulent waters. That peculiar contrast would be my salvation.

"What are you doing here?" he says, his tone implying that I'm an idiot. "I had no idea what that was on the water." He's surprised to see a canoe out here in this weather. His boat is the only one I've seen since I began across the lake hours ago. We

haul my drybags, paddles, canoe, and my souvenir Wilson basketball found floating in the river yesterday, into the back of his
boat. It takes twenty minutes to get to the elusive tree line on the
eastern shore of the lake that I so eagerly and desperately begged
the gods to let me reach. Jeff is a retired navy pilot. He takes
great joy in reminding me how often the navy has to rescue
marines. I don't care, grateful that I was found floating in my canoe rather than facedown in the water.

New rule: No more crossing big lakes.

The river widens and narrows, forming large, shallow, marsh-
filled lakes. Yellow stalks of wild rice bend over with the weight
of ripened, purple grain. The seeds are dispersed by the river, in
search of fertile soil.

I'm not alone here. The Chippewa people travel in pairs in
their canoes. One stands in the rear push-poling the canoe
through the wild rice, while the other, seated in front, gathers
the grain.

The traditional method of gathering the grain requires two
short sticks, like a broom handle cut in two. One stick is used to
pull a bundle of the stalks into the canoe, while the other stick is
used to whack the purple grain off the plant and into the boat.
After a few hours on a good day, one pair can fill their canoe
with three hundred pounds of wild rice.

"How long have you been doing this?" I ask the sunburned
man standing in the back of the canoe. A heavyset man with
dark glasses and a cowboy hat sits in the middle, knocking grain
into his lap.

"Every year since I was a kid," he says. "We do it only for a
few weeks, then all the rice falls off."

I'm now paddling alongside their canoe. "How do you get
the grain out of the sheath?" They each take turns describing the
process, seemingly content to have an audience. They will eventually earn eight bucks a pound after processing the rice. Soon

they exhaust this patch of marsh and move across the river. We part company. I will canoe past a dozen other native people ricing the river, as they have done for centuries. I leave them to their traditions. I have no other business here.

Wildlife continues to amaze and humble me. I am an intruder into the headwaters, not the first nor the last, but I invade a wilderness that is indifferent and unforgiving.

A family of three river otters fiercely barks a quiet "gamph, gamph" and follows my canoe until I'm out of their territory, reminding me that my presence is temporary. Beaver dams line the bank, which is now too wide to dam across. Another bald eagle leaves its perch as I nudge around a bend. A badger swims in front of me, later a fox scrambles up a steep riverbank. Schools of large fish swim beneath me. Thousands of red-winged blackbirds cast shadows over my canoe. Swallows glide above the water and leap over me. Wild ducks thrash in the river ahead.

I intrude here, yet in time I may earn my place on the river.

On a calm, cloudless morning I easily accomplish a dozen miles before noon, lazily riding the current with a few paddles on either side to keep me parallel to the river's edge. On the east bank I notice an animal, a dog, pacing slowly. She's unable to cross a tangle of dead trees and branches on either side of a hundred-meter stretch of the steep bank she occupies.

I almost pass her by, but out of the corner of my eye I notice her slow movement and then watch her stumble into the river. She weakly climbs up the bank again. I turn and paddle toward her. As I approach, I notice footprints, thousands of footprints everywhere along the river's edge for ten feet up the steep bank. She's been here for days, maybe weeks. She is a beautiful husky. Her fur is thick and matted, and her eyes are sunken deep into her skull. I can feel her ribs as I lift her light body into my canoe.

She climbs to the front of the canoe, but not before crapping by my feet. "C'mon now," I say softly, as I lay my hand on her shoulder. "You're gonna be okay. I'm not going to hurt you." She sits, attempts to howl, but it's only a raspy gargle. She lies down quietly.

"Don't die on me now, Little Mutty." I amuse myself with the play on words referring to the Southern slang for the Mississippi River, "Big Muddy."

An hour downstream I spot a family of four on a Labor Day picnic. "Hello!" I yell. The two boys come running down to the floating dock with their father close behind.

"I've found this dog lost on the river." She has a collar. There is a number on a little blue aluminum tag, I explain, but I can see the man's reluctance to get involved.

"Yeah . . . I don't think we can do anything," he says in a slow monotone. "Ya know, there's a ranger station down river a ways. I'm sure they'll be open tomorrow."

I remember a Mark Twain quote I once read: "If you pick up a starving dog and make him prosperous, he will not bite you. This is the principal difference between a dog and a man."

Then comes the mother. With natural maternal compassion, she glares at her husband and says, "We WILL take care of her."

The mother makes a call on her cell phone to the number on the tag and discovers that it's a pet service that's closed for the holiday.

"We'll take care of her," she assures me. "Don't you worry."

I can't help thinking about that dog and the simple mistakes that perhaps we both share. The dog and I are intruders into raw nature, sharing ignorance in a place we know little of. Like me crossing Lake Winnibigoshish, this dog would have died, not from starvation or cold, but for stupidity, for blatant ignorance.

The common perception of "nature in balance" is wishful and foolish. The truth is that nature is more akin to an incessant, selfish, tooth-and-claw struggle for survival that passes no judgment. The behavior of the river current, the cold of the air and water, the rain and sun, and the voracity of mosquitoes are somewhat predictable facts of the river, but not yet to me. In time I will know my place, my abilities and limitations. I will re-set the balance in my favor, actually: I will learn to compete. I will become part of a system, an inseparable entity that strives for existence like everything else.

FEBRUARY 24, 1991—WESTERN BORDER OF KUWAIT, MOMENTS BEFORE THE GROUND WAR

Our platoon is split. Three 4-man teams sit on a sand levee along the Saudi Arabian border overlooking Kuwait. The other three teams are waiting in humvees a mile away. We will not see each other again until we get to Kuwait City. Somewhere on the near horizon, beyond two minefields, Iraqi troops are dug in.

The ground war hasn't officially started yet. We're impatient, bored with watching and waiting. There is nothing to the east but endless desert and dark, distant clouds of black smoke. A quarter mile into Kuwait, an abandoned, single-story yellow building, not more than three hundred feet in diameter, breaks the otherwise endless, barren vista. It blends into the horizon and would likely go unnoticed from a dozen miles away. There has been no activity near the site since we've been here.

"Who wants to go check it out?" Four of us gather for the short trek into Kuwait for our own prewar offensive. Locked and loaded, we clear a few abandoned Iraqi bunkers along the way before blasting through the gates of the compound. The bars in the window give it away as a prison. The steel doors swing open to a concrete courtyard, surrounded by empty rooms littered with helmets and AK-47 rounds. Sergeant Sellers, Lance Corporal Crawley and I perform a few room clearings, as we practiced in Camp Lejeune, with lots of yelling and screaming.

"All clear!" Sellers yells. Now we play. Saenz unloads a hun-dred rounds from his SAW (squad automatic weapon) into a giant metal and glass bookcase. The tracer rounds burn bright red in the brick wall. I'm popping cans off the shelves with my M-16. Sellers finds a Soviet-issue grenade, smaller than ours, green, about the size of a kiwi. He tosses it into an abandoned bunker. When the dust from the explosion settles, we climb into the hole. The effect is an impressive distribution of pinholes in the corrugated tin roof, like the bright spots on the ceiling in a planetarium, but with laser-like beams of light cutting through the dusty interior.

We swagger away from the prison compound having expelled a few rounds of lead and testosterone. Walking back to the Saudi Arabia/Kuwait sand levee, we wander by a fifty-five-gallon oil drum, half buried in the sand and rusted through on one side. Inside, a skinny greyhound is curled. "What the hell is that dog doing here?" Crawley says. Sellers fires one shot over its head. The dog screams across the desert followed by several three-round bursts from Saenz's SAW. It doesn't belong here. It is an intruder. It will die here.

Returning to our secure position, we tell our adventure to eager eyes and ears hungry for a departure from the endless wait. Some of the marines are huddled around the PRC-77 radio listening excitedly to the beginning rain of artillery strikes against the Iraqis only two kilometers away.

We are a standing army that cannot stand for long. Collectively, we are impatient, charged on aggression, and strangely confident, perhaps relieved by the perceived "turkey shoot" ahead. But one by one, plagued with uncertainty, we submit to the machine that brought us where we don't belong. Without each other, we would surely perish.

This desert appears barren and so void of novelty that we anticipate the night, when we might have shooting stars and fighter planes to count. In moments of surprise we learn that the desert is alive beneath us. Carving a foxhole in moist, beachlike sand,

I invade the home of a legless lizard. I have severed its tail with a vertical slash of my entrenching tool on the inside wall of the foxhole, revealing two tiny passageways, with a strange head sticking out of one. The lizard disappears, leaving its tail wriggling on the floor of my hole, like the dismembered tails of green anoles I used to catch in Louisiana.

Saenz would later find an Egyptian spiny-tailed lizard and bring it back to the platoon for show-and-tell. Its two-foot-long muscular body stood defending itself against our curious prodding, until our boredom warranted its freedom. One morning I found a complete articulated skeleton of a desert monitor lizard, which I mailed, free postage, to a paleontology professor at the University of New Orleans. It arrived safely, but "with a mild odor," he wrote back.

For sport we matched mice with scorpions in sand pits. One marine found a strange palm-sized arachnid with a pair of giant mandibles. Teased with plastic spoons, it could crush or perforate the plastic with each bite. A preserved specimen of this nocturnal predator, called a solpugid, or camel spider, would eventually make it back to the United States, having been stuffed into a plastic candy dispenser with a dozen alcohol swabs squeezed into it. A couple of scorpions and a giant dung beetle would make it home the same way.

One night I awoke to the sensation of something scratching the skin of my inner thigh. It had crawled into my sleeping bag and then, remarkably, up my pants leg. There were only a few choices to resolve this event that had turned a deep sleep into instant terror.

"Could it be a scorpion inching toward my crotch?" I asked myself. Option 1: Wait for it to turn around. Option 2: Smash it. Option 3: Jump up, drop trousers, scream like a little girl. Those jarheads around me awoke to the shriek of a marine scared of a giant beetle.

Camels wander aimlessly about. Few moments are more terrifying than being on a front-line observation post at 3:00 a.m., the only one awake, believing that the four legs you see in your night-vision goggles are two Iraqi soldiers inching closer to your position. It takes time to learn the landscape, to understand what it takes to survive in a completely new environment, both natural and cultural.

The desert offers us quick lessons in wildlife and warfare. Those little wires sticking above the ground are not to be touched, same as the scorpions that sometimes fall into our foxholes. Drink a lot of water when you wake up, throughout the day, and before you hit the sack, otherwise you wake with a headache. Be careful of domesticated camels—there's no such thing. *"Irfaa idak, ana jundi Amriki"* means "Put your hands up, I'm an American soldier." We are quickly learning how to survive in this strange, dangerous, unforgiving landscape.

How did we get here? What did we believe about our country to make us join the Marine Corps? Will we die? If not from a stray round or shrapnel, or one of the buried mines waiting ahead, then will our ignorance be the cause of our demise? None of us has seen the enemy. None of us has seen their weapons or knows their tactics. How do they fight? Do they leave booby traps behind? How many of us will return home in bags and boxes? Our platoon commander, Staff Sergeant Honeydew, a decorated Vietnam veteran with a Navy Cross, reiterates an old saying: "If you survive the first month, you'll probably make it home." Which of us will not be so lucky?

The desert is alive. Everything struggles to hold on to its piece of ground, to protect itself, to obtain its own resources for survival.

Two weeks after the hundred-hour war ceased, a strange little purple flower blossomed, pushing its way through the soot-covered sand. It was evenly distributed every few feet as far as one could see. A natural history of trial and error sculpted this flower to persist here. In the face of us, regardless of us, ambivalent toward our dirty little war that blackened the world around us and littered the landscape with rusted exoskeletons of tanks, armored personnel carriers, and military vehicles of all kinds, those seeds proceeded to march to their own time. As a reminder to us of the common destiny of all living things, they sprouted, bloomed, and then withered away.

5

MEN OF STA PLATOON 3/23

In time this commerce increased until it gave employment to hordes of rough and hardy men; rude, uneducated, brave, suffering terrific hardships with sailor-like stoicism; heavy drinkers, coarse frolickers in the moral sties like the Natchez-under-the-hill of that day, heavy fighters, reckless fellows, every one, elephantinely jolly, foul-witted, profane, prodigal of their money, bankrupt at the end of the trip, fond of barbaric finery, prodigious braggarts; yet, in the main, honest, trustworthy, faithful to promises and duty, and often picturesquely magnanimous.
Mark Twain, Life on the Mississippi

The Surveillance and Target Acquisition Platoon is the eyes and ears of the battalion command and the snipers. There are six 4-man teams and four pairs of snipers. We all carry M16A2 rifles, except for one marine in each team who carries a SAW. Everyone's got four grenades and at least two hundred rounds of 5.62 ammo. The guys with the SAW carry more. The sniper teams share one M40A1 rifle with a 10x Unertl scope. The pride and joy of the sniper teams is the new fifty-caliber sniper rifle that can punch holes through cinder-block walls from a kilometer away.

Six of the snipers are Mormons from Salt Lake City, Utah. Sergeant Hicks even went on a two-year mission to spread the Mormon word. "How can you guys carry high-powered rifles?" I ask, prompting him to grumble and walk away. I never get an answer.

I am a team leader, Sergeant Eriksen, with three other marines by my side: Corporal Langston, Corporal Saenz, and Corporal Banks. They call me "Tree Hugger" because I bring up environmental issues on occasion.

Banks is a year younger than I am. He graduated from the University of New Orleans with a degree in business administration, which is a far cry from his childhood near housing projects in New Orleans. His mother managed to send him to a private high school, where few other African Americans attend. He is wise, faithful to everyone, and keeps his spirit nourished with his Bible and his love for his wife-to-be. He will marry when he gets home, open his own business, and begin a family.

Langston is organized, sanitized, and rather efficient in the way he goes about things. He's small in form with blue eyes, but makes up for size with wit and a strong determination to make it big when he gets back home to New York.

Saenz is a muscular, green-card marine from Honduras. "El Hulk." He wears black face paint under his eyes and carries the SAW. I would trust him on all that matters most. He cannot fail me, but he's nuts. And dirty like a pig. He's quite unlike the gangly marine I met three years ago, naïve to the field and often quiet. He once got lost while on patrol training in Camp Lejeune. For two days he and another marine survived on swamp water and acorns.

We've trained together for years, but only on weekends and two weeks each summer. We get along well enough to protect each other more than we fight each other.

One summer, a few years before the Gulf War, while running a training patrol in the backwoods of an army base in Arkansas, at 3:00 a.m., we stumbled upon an ancient, overgrown graveyard abandoned in the middle of nowhere. Half of the headstones had fallen over. We patrolled right through it.

"I really don't think we should be here," Langston said.

We huddled in the center of the cemetery while I read the map under the red glow of my flashlight. A tall, vertical headstone hovered above us.

"You almost done figuring out where we're going?" Banks asked.

I shone the light on the headstone and began to read the text. A poem was etched above the name and dates of the deceased buried under our feet. I read it first to myself before copying it in a notepad. I then read it aloud.

> Stop dear friend as you pass by,
> As you are now so once was I,
> As I am now soon you shall be,
> Prepare for death and follow me.

"This ain't right. This ain't right," Langston said excitedly. I could see the whites of Saenz's eyes. He was in silent agreement with Langston. I had almost finished writing when Saenz leaned against the headstone behind him.

"Slam!" The headstone fell to the ground with a loud thud. Saenz left the ground like a cartoon character spinning his legs in midair. Without a word spoken, without a moment of hesitation, no need for instruction, we all bolted in the direction from which we'd come.

Secretly, we enjoyed the shared fear, the natural rush, panic, sense of strength in numbers—like kids running from a home run that broke a neighbor's window, like wolves in a pack, our natural way, but with boots and rifles.

After a week lost in Arkansas, one squad of STA Platoon embarked on two days of liberty. Eight marines, six cases of cheap beer, a rented minivan, and Graceland on our minds, we commandeered the cheapest motel in Memphis. We returned broke, drunk, and stinking of cigars. The only evidence of our indulgence was a portrait of young Elvis on a three-by-five tapestry.

Before leaving for Saudi Arabia, STA Platoon spent one month in Camp Lejeune, North Carolina, retraining at the rifle range,

gas chamber, and plywood city, where we practiced urban warfare tactics. We left the U.S. on Christmas Day.

The whole platoon congregated in one room on Christmas
Eve to celebrate our last moments stateside. Everyone contributed food from care packages they had been hoarding but
had no intention of taking overseas. We tossed a football
around. The football became a pound cake, followed by a box
of cookies, M&M's, jellybeans, and brownies flying across the
room. I managed to hit Sergeant Sellers in the face with a soft
brownie, in retaliation for being stunned by a peppermint. The
next morning we were gone.

After a ten-hour layover in JFK, a refuel stop in Rome, and
a night flight over Mecca, we eventually landed near Camp 15,
an inland base camp in the northern desert of Saudi Arabia. It
had been established four months previously when Colin Powell
convinced the Saudi government that 250,000 Iraqi troops were
massed on the southern border of Kuwait, prepared to invade
them next. The spy satellite photos of the buildup were so secret
that even the Saudis were not allowed to see them.

AUGUST 30, 2003—SOUTH OF GRAND RAPIDS, MINNESOTA— MILE 1,184 UM

Thirty-nine miles is a fine reward for a full day of canoeing.
Small Minnesota river towns serve as landmarks to reach by
day's end, with the promise of a warm meal and maybe a
shower. I can get provisions, then trek to the local greasy spoon
for the daily special. Interestingly, it's pork half the time.

As I paddle under a walk bridge, an old man yells to me,
"How far ya goin'?"

"Gulf of Mexico!" I yell skyward into blinding sun, having
stopped paddling for the conversation.

"Not much current," he adds, pausing on his walk while I
float under him. "I haven't seen it this low in all my life."

Compared to the headwaters, this current is not too bad, but
I don't know what the river is like during the spring snowmelt,

or during nondrought years. I've chosen the driest month in the driest year to begin my adventure. The *St. Paul Pioneer Press* reports that this summer is the ninth driest August in the 113 years that the National Weather Service has been collecting data. Only 1.12 inches of rain have fallen.

The fellow continues, "I built a cedar-strip canoe last year, but I'm afraid to take it out on account of all those rocks."

"Yeah, it's kinda shallow!" I yell back, having floated nearly out of hearing range.

"Good luck!" I hear him finally say over the soft trickle of water.

People are exceedingly gracious—could be sympathy. I meet dozens of campers, usually curious about my trip and usually cooking something. On the afternoon of my ill-fated attempt to cross Lake Winnibigoshish a few days ago, I dragged my canoe to an empty campsite near the Winnie Dam, where that lake becomes a river again. Within less than an hour of arrival, I was enjoying a hamburger, German potato salad, and cookies, thanks to Judge Andy Krohn and his wife on holiday from Missouri. It's another example of a day of hell becoming heaven.

"November first, that's when you want to be south of Missouri," Judge Krohn said, pronouncing his home state "Mazurah." "That's first frost," he added.

In the small town of Pallisades, at mile 1,090 UM, a retired couple practically force me to eat a plate of beans and a slice of pie. That's where I meet Tom and Denny. Tom, Denny, and I talk over a campfire for a few hours, sharing stories, politics, beer, and choice words about mosquitoes. We talk about the state of the world and come to agree and disagree evenly. In summary, Tom says, "Goddamn French. Just a bunch of surrender monkeys." Denny says, "I accept defeat. Those in power do not care about the rest of the world or the future." I conclude, "Renaissance or revolution, change is on the horizon." Having deemed ourselves worthy travel partners, we decide to stick together. We take off early the next day to make the cool morning miles.

Tom and Denny are the Cheech and Chong of the river, cousins in their late forties on a midlife reunion/adventure meandering lazily down the Mississippi, with no attention to time or a particular destination in mind, their comfortable accommodations neatly packed in a single two-person canoe. Tom sold his company for a two-year, cross-country tour of America's national parks in a new mobile home. Denny is a nurse, professional gambler, and former eco-warrior, who can whip up a mean batch of potatoes au gratin from scratch. They pack a large tent, air mattress, stove, pots, pans, plates, utensils, ice chest, portable table, several jugs of water, and two large backpacks into their canoe. Tom has a fresh can of cheap beer within reach at all times. Denny, a foot taller and a few pounds heavier, serves as both navigator and ballast. They wear their straw hats, sunglasses, and a thick layer of sunscreen. Their canoe barely rises above the water.

For a couple of hours I paddle far ahead so that I can have the joyful surprise of spotting animals before they spot me floating around a bend. I discover that wildlife sightings are inversely proportional to human sightings. The human footprint is more apparent with each mile. The shallow river south of the Blandin Paper Mill Dam in Grand Rapids, Minnesota, exposes artifacts of the river's recent cultural history in shades of wet and dry mud. A monotony of countless tires is broken by a lawn chair, then a mattress, washing machine, and one vintage potbelly stove.

Four miles south of Pallisades, Minnesota, near mile 1,078 UM, there is a 1953 Chevy wagon permanently parked in the river. It's rust brown with broken windows. I sit on the roof for lunch, and later pry the chrome Chevrolet nameplate off the dashboard—always the collector. I don't see many eagles.

County Road One crosses the river at mile 1,059 in Aitkin, Minnesota. Twenty feet before the bridge, there's a railroad track sticking out of the bank. The shallow river exposes a pile of gray ballast stones. A row of decaying wood pilings juts out vertically along the bank, barely above the water, indicating where a landing must have been.

Below my canoe I spot thick metal bands draped over an assemblage of rusted metal parts, as if a large wooden crate had spilled its cargo here after rotting in the mud. I reach for a corroded wrench, then a few oversized chain links that look like belt buckles. There are several foot-long sections of chain with five-inch metal spikes attached to each end.

In a month I will share my river junk with a historian in the National Mississippi River Museum and Aquarium in Dubuque, Iowa. "Hey, where did you get those log chains?" he will say. The chains with spikes were once used to bind hundreds of logs into enormous rafts, which would be floated downriver to sawmills in Minneapolis, St. Louis, or any of the other big towns along the way.

I continue to scavenge the river bottom for the tools of the trade of early river rats in the Northern Territories.

Tom, Denny, and I find a state campground south of Aitkin on the edge of the river. We pitch our tents on buried railroad ties where the riverfront railroad once roared. The steamship landing is gone. It's all buried beneath a manicured lawn and a sewage treatment plant next to the campground that buzzes all night and illuminates our tents.

It's a mile walk to Main Street, where the ornamental red brick façade of small-town America still dominates storefronts. In the local diner I get the special: pork patty, mashed potatoes, and your choice of vegetable. I order it twice. I thumb through a stack of local history pamphlets borrowed from the deli counter.

The town of Aitkin became a strategic steamboat landing on the Mississippi in 1870, when the Northern Pacific Railroad surveyors determined that the first accessible point to the Mississippi by rail from Duluth, Minnesota, was this spot. The men who were privileged to work on the steamships signed on for months or even years, leaving home behind them. Thousands of people and tons of freight were carried by steamships like the *Fawn,* the *Irene,* and the giant sternwheeler, the *Andy Gibson,* which sank somewhere south of town.

In the morning, I depart a few hours ahead of Tom and Denny. The morning mist is thick. It hangs in the air and splashes on my cheeks as I paddle through it. Trees lining the riverbank emerge as gray shadows, slowly taking form, and then regaining their lively hues as I paddle near them. I imagine steamboats navigating on this narrow river, no more than two hundred feet across.

At mile 1,057 UM the muddy bank is exposed, revealing a strange pattern of parallel beams, like the ribs of a whale turned belly-up. They look like a row of giant toothpicks jutting from the mud. They suddenly register in my head as the ribs of a ship, a steamship! It is the *Andy Gibson.*

The large, clumsy *Andy Gibson* successfully navigated through snags and shoals, once setting the speed record for round-trip service from Aitkin to Grand Rapids, a three-hundred-mile journey, in under four days. Many ships of that time were incinerated down to the hull or blasted to toothpicks by sparks flying out of the smokestacks or overheated boilers. The *Andy Gibson* suffered a less traumatic fate, without drama or excitement. Retired from service in 1892, the heating system and the remainder of the machinery salvaged, the hollow steamship sank slowly into the mud. The *Andy Gibson* is now a sunken hull robbed of its elegant garnishing. Abandoned, it died unnoticed, like most things. Nothing is left but waterlogged planks, beams, and a few twisted steel bars. I remove a nail from a piece of the hull rising out of the water—a nail hammered in more than a century ago, likely by some old salt or young gun eager to make his mark on the world.

DECEMBER 27, 1990—CAMP 15, SAUDI ARABIA

We've just arrived in country. The Seabees are busy building dozens of plywood barracks, the size of four-car garages, on still-wet concrete slabs, for the thousands of marines that seem to arrive daily. They build a dozen more in the two weeks we are there. We scavenge/borrow half a dozen pallets and a few sheets of plywood for a New Year's Eve fire. After jokes, songs, nonalcoholic beer, and roasted peanuts, Sergeant Sellers and I lay a plywood bridge across the flames for the platoon to run across. The Seabees had their own fire, perhaps not as celebratory as ours, setting barrels of human feces and diesel fuel ablaze.

The command quarters and the chow hall are a quarter-mile walk across hot sand. Once you slip past the armed gate, life becomes more civilized. The roads are paved, you can get a cold soda, and Arnold Schwarzenegger has donated an entire weight-lifting gym to the base.

The big orange sun quietly sinks through a dust-filled horizon framed with distant minarets and the rising flames from the latrines, but soon the lullaby of call to prayer will be accompanied by the incessant drone of fighter planes and bombers overhead. Saddam Hussein ignores the final deadline to retreat. In less than three weeks after our arrival, war begins.

On January 17, 1991, at 5:00 a.m., I awake to the words of the president of the United States justifying the beginning of the Gulf War. Overhead, contrails cross the sky in parallel formations pointing north to south, indicating the endless sorties dropping their payload on Kuwait and Iraq. Our battalion has left Camp 15, establishing a perimeter near the southwest border of Kuwait. STA Platoon has been given the mission to maintain observation posts north of the battalion, nearest to the Kuwaiti border, nearest to the dug-in Iraqi army.

"You're in the safest spot being out there," says Staff Sergeant Honeydew, the platoon commander, offering illogical reassurance. "If we get overrun, they'll just pass you by and head for us in the rear."

Our mission is simple. Each four-man team will spend forty-eight hours in two shallow, camouflaged foxholes quickly excavated a mile beyond our front line. We will be inserted by a humvee that will not stop to let us out, for fear of giving away our location. We will have a radio, spotting scope, night-vision gear, and loaded weapons. Report any enemy movement.

Banks and I pair together, leaving Saenz and Langston to each other. Each pair takes four-hour shifts all day and night. Our foxholes are only a hundred feet apart, so that we can shout back and forth. We share these days and nights watching the northern horizon. Most of the time we sit, read, or stare at nothing. Always waiting for something to happen. This is the sum of life for now.

"You hear that?" Banks gets my attention with a shove. It's his turn to take watch. I'm trying to make up for lost sleep. I sit up and peer out of the hole like a gopher. There's an endless column of tanks making a beeline for our position.

"Are they ours?" I ask Banks. Through the binoculars he can make out the upside-down V that symbolizes the allied forces. Besides, he can recognize the front-view silhouette of the A-1 Abrams tank speeding closer to our tiny burrow.

"Well, get out and wave!" I say, as I join him climbing out so that we can all see each other.

"A million miles of desert and they have to pass fifty feet behind us," Banks calmly announces. Langston and Saenz have the same idea. We wave. They wave. Roughly twenty tanks go by.

Hours later, "Whatcha makin? More cocoa?" Banks asks.

"Yup," I respond, without looking up.

Every four hours, Banks and I yell to Langston and Saenz. "It's your watch!" They take forever to get up. "Come get the radio!"

Off to the east, a high-pitched whaaaaaaaaa can be heard growing louder.

"What the hell is that?" I say, laying my M-16 across my arm.

Banks recognizes it first. "It's a motorcycle." The rider doesn't see us. Quickly we recognize the uniform.

"How did he get a job like that?" I say with astonishment. He's a messenger traveling between command posts. He's got the bike opened full throttle. He's racing across the desert on a straight line to his destination. I wonder if this flat desert looks any different at fifty miles per hour than from the inside of a foxhole?

"You disgusting motherfucker!" Langston screams. "Get out! I don't care where you go!" he howls, while Saenz laughs loudly. "It's not funny. You're a nasty human being. Just go."

Saenz and Langston are the odd couple. Saenz doesn't bathe. He has defied the rule of funk, which states that after three weeks of not bathing one reaches terminal filth and simply cannot get any dirtier. New dirt just falls off. If you can tolerate this level of poor hygiene, then there is no need to shower again. The rule of funk does not apply to Saenz. He attracts flies and burns your nostrils with a putrid smell that is unique to him alone.

"I said get out! I'm tired of it!" Langston yells. Saenz is laughing hysterically. Moments earlier, unbeknownst to Langston, Saenz squatted and relieved himself in a small pit latrine dug only a foot away from the edge of the foxhole they share. The latrine collapsed, sending Saenz falling backward onto the sand and the contents of the latrine sliding into the foxhole onto Langston, where he had been comfortably sleeping.

"You marines know why we are here?"

Captain Dustin, our company commander, and also a civil lawyer in the civilian world, has decided to call a company formation to discuss the seriousness of the looming ground war. Sixty marines from Communications Platoon, Motor-T, and Supply, as well as the cooks and half of STA Platoon are standing in a horseshoe formation around him. STA Platoon holds him in low regard as a competent grunt officer.

"The enemy is near. We train for this day. We must... blah, blah, blah," he begins his monologue. His lazy eye is starting to wander in unpredictable directions.

"Does anyone know where north is?" He asks an obvious question.

A dozen hands point north, while mine points intentionally in the opposite direction. Half of the marines chuckle, while the other half watch Captain Dustin turn red. Seemingly confused, he yells, "Come here, motherfucker!" He attempts to grab me, but succeeds in only a push. I follow him out of formation. Once my back is to him he gives me a shove and orders push-ups. After five minutes I'm back in formation, staring at him intensely, while he continues his motivational speech.

This is where the Reserve fails. There is no adequate system for testing leadership among the ranks without sustained active duty. Unfortunately, the only sustained active duty for the reserves is combat, not the best time to test your officers. Reservists do harbor an indignation that comes with college education and prolonged civilian comfort. These effects cause unwarranted critical thinking among NCOs and a sense of civilian entitlement that conflicts with the unquestioned obedience drilled into our skulls in boot camp. Captain Dustin finally asks for questions or comments.

I raise my hand. "Sir, I pointed south intentionally to relieve some of the stress around here. Of course I know where north is. STA Platoon runs OPs to let you know what's happening up north. Sir, I know there's danger ahead, but don't worry. I'm behind you all the way. I would walk into a hail of bullets at your command. We're in this together, all the way."

It would have been nice if I had actually said this, but what really comes out of my mouth is, "Sir. Since we are within artillery range of the enemy, will this be our last company formation?"

After an uncomfortable pause he explodes in a fury, dismissing everyone except me and First Sergeant Jones. "First Sergeant! You deal with him," Dustin cries out before storming away. Jones was a grunt in Vietnam. He eases the tension with a half-smile and an empathetic explanation of Dustin's plight.

"Just leave the man alone. He's got enough to think about," Jones says. We continue shooting the shit about the days ahead, and he unloads a few stories about what Vietnam was like.

That night Captain Dustin posts a guard outside his tent. "What the hell is he so worried about?" someone in STA Platoon asks. Fortunately, marines are programmed to be loyal to command and dutiful to the Corps. Marines don't frag their officers. In a few days Captain Dustin and I privately iron it out. It's a one-on-one rehash of his earlier pep rally. In the end it all comes to nothing.

"Twenty-nine," Sergeant McKeehan says to me first thing in the morning.

"Fifteen," I respond. We count the days that we've put in overtime. Our contracts with the Marine Corps ended soon after the ground war, but once you're in country there's no going back.

McKeehan has a wife and a job as an Alcohol, Tobacco, and Firearms (ATF) agent waiting for him in New Orleans. "I can't believe they pay me to do what I do," McKeehan says of his job conducting drug raids in the city. He and his team of agents wear black masks when they bust down doors of suspected dealers. He's the point man with the battering ram. He always has the platoon enthralled with his stories.

It has become unequivocally clear who the natural-born leaders are, and McKeehan stands out. He skillfully delegates work and never sits idle watching others. His judgment and expectations are clear. He's confident, trustworthy, and faithful to the men in the platoon. We're both squad leaders, yet I would gladly follow him into battle.

~

The men of STA Platoon were all so different, but through common experience we knew each other, at least a side of each other that knew our own brand of suffering. We shared a moment in our nation's history, and our personal histories made us more than common men. Yes, we were rough and hardy men; heavy drinkers, reckless fellows, every one; profane, always broke by the end of the weekend, fond of barbaric finery, dreaming of something else, somewhere else; yet for that time in the desert, when called upon, we were honorable, moral in judgment, faithful to each other, trustworthy, and at times the best-looking bunch of grunts in the Corps.

6

FAST WATER, SUBMERGED ROCKS, AND LAND MINES

"Bless this journey down the river. Carry him safely to his next destination as he puts himself in your hands," Timothy says. "To the north and south we bless this river. To the east and west we ask you to watch over him. We thank you."

He looks at me pointedly and says, "No one has ever tipped over after my tobacco blessing."

"That's fine with me," I say.

Timothy, the river guide who rented a canoe to me weeks ago, is standing in the river up to his knees performing a tobacco blessing he learned from the Ojibwe-Chippewa elders in Bemidji. He crushes a cigar in his hand, holding the pieces of tobacco tightly in a fist above my head. He releases bits of it onto the raft and into the river.

A few hours ago, I was still enjoying the canoe on the upriver side of Potlatch Dam in Brainerd, Minnesota, knowing that soon I would be reunited with the *Bottle Rocket*. The canoe was new when Timothy gave it to me, but you'd never know it by the scarred underside that I had dragged through the shallow headwaters, over beaver dams, and across gravel beds. I called him a week ago to arrange for the return of my raft, which now sits on the downriver side of the dam, waiting to dip its pontoons into the river again.

Tom and Denny quietly help stabilize the raft in the water. We've been camping and canoeing together for a week. They've been anxiously awaiting a formal introduction to the *Bottle Rocket*. They're not saying much now, perhaps out of awe, but likely they are politely withholding their doubts.

All of my gear is stuffed into plastic milk crates tied to each corner of the raft. "Here's some chokecherry jelly from this summer season," Timothy says, handing me a small mason jar he canned himself.

"And this . . ." he says, pausing to hand me a plastic bag with a flat fish in it, "is smoked walleye." He also presents me with a box full of cookies and trail mix from friends I made in the Bemidji Visitor Center.

Bits of tobacco are still floating in the river as I row into the middle. The current is slow and there's a slight headwind to battle, but the river is deeper and wider. I'm hopeful that the raft will make it from here. Besides, I'm way over budget, having rented the canoe for three weeks. Tom and Denny are by my side for the seven-mile journey to the next campsite.

A group of five other canoeists passes by. They witnessed the tobacco blessing, and paused long enough to gawk at my raft and snicker. They quietly pass me by and snicker again. Tom and Denny are supportive of my diligence and will support me beyond my expectations, although, at this moment, they are not impressed by the surprisingly slow pace of my raft—and neither am I.

It takes the remainder of the day to reach the next MDNR campsite. To our dismay, the five canoeists have arrived first. They commandeer all of the flat ground and steal the only bench. They don't say much. They greedily surround the only fire pit. They are obnoxious, drunk, and loud for most of the night.

Tom, Denny, and I set up our tents on a relatively flat trail leading away from the campsite. Denny skillfully cooks up sausage and beans on a kerosene stove. My crank radio crackles with news of good weather tomorrow. Then the radio cuts to a speech by the man in the White House.

"Good evening. I have asked for this time to keep you informed of America's actions in the war on terror. . . . I will soon submit to Congress a request for eighty-seven billion dollars. . . . We are serving in freedom's cause, and that is the cause of all mankind. Thank you, and may God continue to bless America."

"Hmmm?" Denny says with punctuated enthusiasm.

"Did he say eighty-seven billion?" I ask, for clarification.

"Yeah, I think so."

We chuckle in disbelief at the astronomical proportions of that demand on ordinary taxpayers. During his eight-minute speech, he managed to insert the word "free" or "freedom" into his monologue twenty times—Operation Iraqi Freedom, for the free freedom seekers from the freedom-loving freedom fighters. "Monkey logic," I say to Denny.

Denny replies, "Being free is not as important as believing that you're free."

We share a little more music from the radio and a few chosen words for the camp hogs, and then Tom, Denny, and I wander off to bed.

Even moist toilet paper stuffed in my ears doesn't drown out their shrieking laughter. "Shut the fuck up!" I grumble in a tone only audible to me. It's more for my own comfort. I manage to hibernate in half-sleep for a few hours until all is finally quiet.

Six weeks from now, I will meet one of the obnoxious canoeists, Dan, south of Davenport, Iowa. He will see an article in his local newspaper about my progress. Dan will remember the consensus around the campfire on this night. "We put your chances of making it down the Mississippi River at zero," he will say. He will gracefully eat his words, then hand me a beer. But for now, here in Minnesota, Dan and his fellow canoeists are keeping me from much-needed rest.

In the first waking moments of the day, as dreams slip away, I begin to take notice of my senses: the glow inside the tent, the restrictive sleeping bag, the persistent ache in my lower back. It takes a couple of minutes to remember that I'm now spending my days floating on plastic bottles, and not in a canoe.

I feel a mixture of excited anticipation and worry. The mild stress caused by a preponderance of unknowns is a bittersweet stress that can simultaneously be blood-pumping and nauseating. It takes longer for me to pack the *Bottle Rocket,* since my precise canoe packing strategy is no longer valid.

Tom and Denny are emerging from their tent as I prepare to shove off. "Okay guys, I'll see you downriver," I say.

"We'll see you in a couple hours or so," Denny replies.

"Take care now," Tom adds. "We'll catch up to ya."

A gentle headwind pleasantly cools the sweat on my face. My jovial mood takes a downward plunge as the wind escalates, nearly matching the force of my forward movement. The brisk headwind is my nemesis. I long for the river to meander in the opposite direction so that the breeze will be at my back. I curse the river when it straightens against the wind. The raft is almost stationary in the middle of the river, as if anchored to the rocks below. Tom and Denny creep up to the side of my raft.

"This wind kinda sucks, huh," Denny says rhetorically.

By noon the sky is overcast and the wind is temporarily calm. Tom and Denny tie themselves to the front of the *Bottle Rocket,* with the idea that they can help tow my raft. Rowing ferociously, I'm trying to keep slack in the rope to ease their burden. They tow me for two hours. It begins to rain. I try to convince myself that this is progress.

"Cut him loose!" Tom yells. Suddenly, the river is faster. Whitecaps form in places where the river narrows. The elevation of the land is dropping. Sometimes the river widens into pools of slow-moving water, and then it narrows again, forming instant rapids over large boulders. Tom and Denny are barely floating above the waterline, because of the weight of their gear and themselves. Tom is the point man in the front seat of the canoe. He sees it all firsthand. "Cut him loose!" he yells nervously.

"It's getting kinda scary," Denny calmly says to me, while untying the towrope. Car-sized boulders stick out of the river-bed. They paddle away and soon engage rapids ahead.

The *Bottle Rocket,* rigid and inflexible, seems to handle the current well, but shudders and crackles loudly when it slams into a submerged boulder. Bottles are sticking out. A dozen wires have popped.

"Let's stop soon!" I yell to the guys. The riverbed is a wide swath of boulders, with the river continuously dividing and converging. They're busy negotiating a different path of the river. Around the next bend appears an island the size of a football field. We drag the canoe and raft onto the rocks before wandering the boundaries of our new campsite.

"Hey, what's this stuff?" I say to Denny, pointing to a strange oily substance splashed onto a few trees. I investigate the texture with my fingertips, and then smell its rank odor. Denny does the same.

"I don't know. Maybe it's grease or somethin'," he says.

"Here comes a boat," Tom says. A plump white guy, decked in camouflage from head to toe, wobbles up to our camp. He's got a bucket filled with foul-smelling restaurant leftovers.

"Ya know I'm baiting for bears here," he says with a healthy dollop of Minnesota-friendly in his voice. He starts pouring the slop onto the horizontal trunks of fallen trees about a hundred feet from our tents. He withdraws a spray bottle and begins squirting the surrounding trees. The same odor from my fingertips now hovers in the air around camp. Whatever is in that bottle is also on our hands.

"What's that stuff?" I say.

"It's bear scent," the hunter says matter-of-factly. Denny and I simultaneously grab a handful of leaves to wipe the scent from our hands.

The bear hunter adds, "Didn't you guys see all the bear tracks?" We look down to see a traffic jam of bear footprints leading to and away from the baited logs, scented trees, and our tents.

The hunter will return in a few days with a tree stand and a rifle, and will sit perched in his stand until the bear returns. With the skill of a predator, a warrior marksman, he will hover above the wild bear feeding on restaurant garbage. He'll train his scope on his powerful foe and release a single round from twenty feet away.

Despite the hunter's poorly veiled desire for us to go somewhere else, there's no chance that any of us would suggest getting back on the river now. We relax on Bear Bait Island for the night, but not without the occasional look over our shoulder for uninvited guests.

FEBRUARY 20, 1991—BORDER OF KUWAIT AND SAUDI ARABIA, ON THE EVE OF THE GROUND WAR

"Goddammit! That motherfucker went behind the berm!" The voice crackles through the receiver on the PRC-77 radio. Half of STA Platoon is still sitting on the sand levee, peering into Kuwait from the Saudi side of the border. Three of us are crowded around the radio receiver, while the rest of the marines around us probe excitedly for updates.

"What's happening now?" one marine hovering behind me

says. "What did he say? Did they get 'em?" We salivate at the sound of combat going on around us, frustrated not to be there. Officially, the ground war hasn't started yet.

A few seconds later the voice corrects fire: "Shift left! Shift left!" Bang, boom, then a whistle as two more artillery rounds soar over my head. Over the radio, elation explodes—"I got some! He's history!" Another fortified Iraqi bunker has been obliterated, like shooting fish in a barrel.

After a day of heavy artillery, the Iraqis crawl out of their holes in the sand and stagger about with little white paper pamphlets held high above their heads. Two dozen POWs, with empty sandbags over their heads, rumble by in the back of a five-ton truck. Another hundred tired Iraqi soldiers surrender and fill a barbwire pen on the Saudi Arabian side of the sand berm.

I help distribute MREs to them. I take one of the pieces of white paper out of a soldier's hand. It's a little smaller than a dollar bill, with a cartoon image of an Iraqi soldier having two thoughts, drawn in bubbles: fight and die in one bubble, surrender and see your family again in the other.

Written in Arabic and English, it's an example of PSY-OPS, or psychological operations, intended to discourage the will to fight. Dropped from the sky by the billions, it will be the salvation of these soldiers.

On the other side is a list of instructions on how to surrender, a do-it-yourself guide to not getting shot. The last line states, "If you do this, you will not die."

Unfortunately, no one has told STA Platoon what a surrendering Iraqi soldier looks like. We'll figure it out by trial and error, or maybe we'll each find our own little list of instructions on white paper blowing across the desert.

The POWs are tired and hungry, yet seemingly thankful to see the end of their participation in the war. This army of men in rags looks like the B-list of draftees, young and old, with inconsistent uniforms, some of them wearing dress shoes or sandals, fatigues or blue jeans. They exhibit poor hygiene and a surprising willingness to lay down their weapons.

STA Platoon is eager to cross over into Kuwait. The air is filled with a grotesque overconfidence in light of this inferior enemy. We call the edge of the battlefield, where opposing armies are close enough to wave to each other, the Turkey Shoot.

Young men in fierce repose are eager for combat action and to earn their medals for being there. Everyone wants the fight, regardless of the foe. "Let me shoot one," pleads Private First Class Wurst, fresh out of boot camp, before Sergeant Hillman sets him straight. Our blood pumps loudly. We are restless on the eve of the storm.

FEBRUARY 23, 1991

When the time comes to move into Kuwait, there's no grand entrance, no triumphant charge, no bugles, and no battle cry. There is silent confusion with incessant shifting of vehicles and people, as the ground offensive, in the form of massive convoys, begins to coalesce. It hints at the oncoming chaos. I sit in the back of a five-ton truck with twelve marines from STA Platoon and eight Iraqi prisoners. I'm not sure why they are here, but I imagine it's because no one knows what to do with them. A young lieutenant from the battalion command yells a bit of useless direction: "They're only with us until we get rid of them." The Iraqi men smile cautiously. They are uneasy, and quickly follow eye contact with a nervous smile or a light chuckle. They are our surreal guests of honor.

"What the hell are you worried about? It's over for you," Corporal Grant belts out, only half joking.

We are apathetic toward the Iraqis, which is worse than hate. To hate someone requires good emotions betrayed. But there is nothing. They are objects, a little less than human. This will make it easier to kill them.

We are dangerous strangers. While their war has ended, ours has just begun. Our bravado hides our anxiety. Our future is now uncertain, as well as how we will endure this war. The risk of death, the gamble with fate, makes one's own behavior unpredictable. I wonder, which of us will die, cry like a scared child, or surprise everyone with natural courage, leadership, or bravery? Weeping, laughing, hating, killing will not be ours to decide.

"What are you looking at?" I say to the filthy, middle-aged man in torn patent leather shoes. He smiles. There's nothing much to say to a man who only moments ago might have shoved a bayonet through my neck if given the chance, so I think. I know he has sufficient reason to hate me. He has suffered. He has seen his own people die. He is the one who looks skyward to fighter planes and bombers going to and from his homeland. He is the turkey being butchered. I've no idea what to say to an enemy who just sits there smiling nervously. Saenz offers one of them a cigarette. I give the man a pouch of dehydrated strawberries from my MRE.

"He's not drinking from my canteen," someone blurts out.

In less than an hour, our eight Iraqis are transferred to the massive pool of thousands of prisoners formed somewhere along the convoy in the middle of an empty desert.

Thin little wires protrude a foot above the sand. "Keep your arms in the truck," someone calmly suggests. We are passing through the first minefield. The wires sprout from the sand randomly for about three hundred yards in front of us. To the left and right they appear to have been sown endlessly. They look like a winter wheat field long after harvest, when only a few random stalks still stand above the dirty snow.

The convoy is color-coded. We are blue. Blue ribbons dangle from mirrors and antennae to mark vehicles. Blue barrels mark our entrance into the minefield. The entire convoy converges on a single set of tracks meandering around the wires. The truck tires drop into the ruts and slowly inch along, like a rollercoaster car slowly climbing to the top, clicking along the rails. The light-colored sand in the fresh tracks contrasts with the black soot that covers everything else.

I can see the wires, clear as day, when we enter the minefield. "What good are they when you can see them?" I think. Soon after exiting the first minefield, we enter the second. An American M1-A1 Abrams tank is disabled ahead and listing to one side. Its right track is blown apart.

"Hey, is everyone all right?" someone yells to a marine standing on top of the tank. He shakes his head side to side as we pass them by. I sit silent, with my body leaning toward the center of the truck rather than to the side. Everyone's quiet. Slowly we creep along.

For hours the convoy moves slowly, swaying with the contour of the rutted sand beneath us. The horizon glows below black skies. Rain falls lightly for most of the day. Oil and water soak our clothes, and soot fills our nostrils and coats our throats. The minefields are now a memory. At times the convoy is stretched thin, giving us time to pause. Hundreds of prisoners stagger in a loose formation a few hundred yards away.

"Well, that's good to see," Banks says, adding, "Less for us to deal with."

Three four-man teams from STA Platoon bounce around in the back of a five-ton truck somewhere in the middle of the convoy heading due east for Kuwait City. We are sleep-deprived, and strangely, we are starved for novelty. We anxiously wait, but there is nothing but emptiness.

Then something new appears, jutting out of the sand, like a whale breaking the surface of the ocean. An incinerated Russian-made T-72 tank is half-buried with the turret popped up like the lid of a soup can. It's black, rain-soaked, and smells like a wet campfire. A bright red, white, and blue bumper sticker, which someone ahead in the convoy stuck on the body of the destroyed tank, reads, "Don't Mess With The U.S." Next in the sideshow appears another destroyed tank, then an armored personnel carrier, and on our left, a jeep. The destroyed jeep has something lying next to it. I stand and quickly recognize the paralyzed form.

"Hey look. A body!" I yell. The five-ton comes to an abrupt halt. Every marine looks up, and out we go. We all jump out of the truck, all twelve of us, plus the driver, for a glimpse of our first victim. The convoy will not notice the delay, with the next vehicle a couple hundred yards behind us.

We encircle the Iraqi soldier who has been blown twenty feet from the fireball that incinerated his jeep. We stand around the dead man in an unintentional moment of silence, a moment of wonder and curiosity.

"Damn that's fucked up," someone says slowly in a muffled tone.

We are soaked from the rains that have been pouring on us over the past twenty-four hours. The body has been washed, cleansed of blood. Our minds are busy etching the experience in our heads for endless dreams and bouts of future contemplation. No one says a word more.

No "OohRah!"

No "Got some camel jockey, rag head, hadji motherfucker!"

No "I wanna join the turkey shoot!"

Nothing but silence.

The man is lying on his back with his arms outward as if crucified. His eyes and mouth are wide open. His moustache is neatly trimmed. His feet are tucked under his buttocks as if he tried to stand one last time, fell to his knees praying, and then fell backwards. His back is arched. His intestines have spilled out of his abdomen and lie across his waist.

His arms had been flailing about in the sand making angel wings, like the ones children make in snow.

"It doesn't look real," Langston says. There's a long pause.

Someone adds confirmation, "Like a wax dummy or some-thing." Our average age is not more than twenty-one. More si-lence. We walk away, leaving our innocence standing around the fallen enemy like ghosts.

The difference between the infantryman and everyone else is the memory from the senses. For a grunt, an enemy soldier isn't a silhouette through a scope, or a greenish glow on a video screen. Dead men on a battlefield are sensed. They imprint their ghastly image, their smell, and their silence. It's like staring wide-eyed into a light bulb, and then turning away and having the image of the filament burned into your retina. But the battlefield image lingers much longer. We learn that the enemy has a face. The enemy suffers. The enemy dies. It could easily be one of us.

Corporal Madden is climbing over the charred remains of the jeep. "Check this out!" he says, holding the metal remains of an AK-47 in the air. Everyone welcomes the distraction. We all climb back in the five-ton and marvel at his trophy with envy. I want an AK-47. So does everyone else. Behind us, the next truck stops for the sideshow. They begin pouring out of their ve-hicle. They're standing around the corpse, repeating our lesson for themselves.

"Get out! Get out of the truck!" Sergeant McKeehan barks above the echo of a single artillery round that lands a hundred yards away. The five-ton turns right abruptly and stops. We pour out of the truck and rapidly dig in. Humvees and other trucks returning from the front converge onto our position. A hasty perimeter is assembled, much like a wagon train. There is a gentle rise ahead of the convoy. Beyond that we can hear the explosions from artillery and tank rounds.

Our eyes are fixed on the crest of the rise, only a klick away. "Saenz! You ready?" I yell. We look at each other with strange smiles on our faces. We dig shallow pits, deep enough to hide be-low flying shrapnel. Twelve marines sit half-buried with wide

eyes and warm triggers, responding more to instinct than training. But the Iraqis don't come. Another round splashes down a
klick away. Every marine in sight ducks simultaneously, the precise reaction seemingly choreographed. Many of us look at each
other in acknowledgment of how quickly we've learned to survive. American tanks engage Iraqi forces dug in west of Kuwait
City. The Iraqis accomplish nothing. Their futile attempt at defense is nothing more than a few random volleys of artillery.

"What's going on?" Sellers yells. "Who's got a radio?"
There is no one to ask, besides one another. We wait. Soon engines start. That's our cue to get back in the truck. The convoy
forms and we take our seats. Then comes the black rain. We
wear our new, plastic-wrapped, British-made chemical warfare
suits for warmth, and our Vietnam-era ponchos to keep somewhat dry. We inch closer to the amorphous front line, then dig in
again while the tank battle rages on.

A CH-53 Sea Stallion helicopter lands abruptly, first arching
skyward till almost vertical, then turning slightly before dropping to the ground. Cases of tank ammunition pour from the helicopter. The trucks that come in to collect it also deliver dozens
of injured prisoners. They arrive with blood-soaked bandages,
many missing arms or legs. They lie in the sand surrounded by
razor wire.

I stand gazing at them as if in a museum. One of them is lying dead with his mouth open. A young man sitting next to him
slowly rocks back and forth, grasping his thigh. The rest of his
leg is missing. His bandages and pants are soaked red. His boy-
ish face stares at me. I hover over him. "I am supposed to hate
you," I think. "You are the ones that murdered in Kuwait, raped
women and pulled infants from incubators. That's what CNN
said."

He stares at me as if he's squinting to see a ship on the horizon. His lip curls and his eyebrows turn upward in the center as
if he harbors a burning question or vengeance. I don't know

what he wants. I can't tell if it's rage, fear, or pain. His stare is penetrating my head. He wants something badly. He is skinny and has no facial hair. He is young, maybe sixteen. His stare turns into a defiant scowl, like that of a hero moments from being slain, ready to accept martyrdom. We stare at each other. I turn away first.

So many of them have died as our bombers and fighter planes attacked precise and imprecise targets: civilians, soldiers, unlucky bystanders on bridges. So many will die in the Shiite and Kurdish rebellions that will rise and fall after the war. So many will die in the decade of sanctions to come when medicine and food become scarce commodities.

Every Iraqi citizen mourns a dead relative. No Iraqi citizen is without loss, someone dead at the hands of an Iranian, an American, or their own bastard brutal dictator. At this point, Iraqi soldiers are surrendering or dying, or dying while surrendering. Few are fighting.

Black clouds suffocate the sky. Specks of oil rain down on us and make us filthy. One last round of random artillery explodes nearby. Sand, steel, and human flesh move through this desert with varied velocity. Otherwise, there is nothing here.

We'll stay here for half the night. The three teams of STA Platoon dig in. We dig our individual fighting holes, our shallow graves. In my hole I bury myself. I bury my sorrow until my temples throb.

"This is not right," I mumble angrily. "This is not right." Then I shout, "Get some sleep while you can." I don't know if anyone hears me. With the last glow of daylight below a swirling black sky, I fumble for my pen and journal.

FEB. 25, 1991

We crossed over the Saudi berm, over miles of desert and two mine fields. We saw hundreds of trucks, tanks, bulldozers, APC's and refuelers. Also along our route we saw hundreds of POW's marching along. We finally were kicked off the vehicle to guard an ammo dump. They were also unloading injured POW's here. Some were missing arms, feet and blood everywhere. I do not feel victorious. It is now dark with many distant fires illuminating the horizon. An occasional arty. round comes in.

FEBRUARY 26, 1991

The tank battle is over. Rain extinguished the burning vehicles. Crawley and I are alone, walking up to the overstretched convoy halted in the middle of a quiet battlefield. We've been out for a stroll, our own tour of what's left. It is an endless landscape of horizontal nothingness, broken only by abandoned or destroyed Iraqi tanks, armored personnel carriers, and bunkers randomly spread out around us. The battlefield is an empty playground for idle marines anxious for something to do.

"Hey, look at 'em," Crawley says, pointing to the rest of STA Platoon a hundred yards away wearing gas masks. "Do you think they're fucking with us?" Sellers and the rest of the platoon give the arm signal for a chemical attack. With their arms stretched outward, they repeatedly bend both forearms skyward 90 degrees, as if posing for a Mr. Universe contest.

"Put your mask on," I say to Crawley. This is not the time to second-guess anyone, but it is quite feasible that we're the butt of a joke. We walk toward them with another souvenir AK-47 to add to the pile.

The convoy has been stopped for several hours. In these moments of endless, restless wait, we have kept ourselves busy amassing an impressive collection of Russian-made Iraqi weapons. Corporal Madden abandoned his burned AK-47 in exchange for his choice of new ones. Those Iraqis who survived the night have surrendered empty-handed, leaving their equipment intact. One vehicle was even left running. Strangely, the AK-47 rifle is losing its charm in light of the machine gun, mini-mortar, rocket-propelled grenade launcher (RPG), and the prized sniper rifle.

Some of the tanks are nothing more than smoldering exoskeletons that quickly begin to rust. There was a turret from a destroyed Russian T-72 tank upside-down in the sand, surrounded by charred, unexploded ordnance. I tiptoed around the craters, corroded grenades, and tank rounds to get to the tank itself. It was morbidly like being a kid in a candy store. It's all for the taking. In a pit the size of a swimming pool was a Russian-made BMP-1 Iraqi armored personnel carrier, abandoned with its back doors wide open. Blankets, uniforms, letters home, ammunition, and weapons spilled onto the sand. I climbed out smiling, with an RPG in my hands.

However, at this moment, Crawley and I are walking back to the other STA teams in our chemical suits and gas masks. "Hey, what's going on?" I say to Sellers. He mumbles something and shrugs his shoulders.

Conversation is difficult, as is anything else one might attempt to do while suited up for chemical war. Warfare in a chemical suit is like trying to ride a bicycle in a gorilla costume. We're just standing there waiting for something to happen. We gaze at our cache of weapons, each trying to figure out how to get them home.

McKeehan comes back with word from the radioman, "Take 'em off. It's a false alarm."

After we've wrestled with our suits, Corporal Banks turns to me. "Hey, you still taking those pills?" he asks.

"I guess so," I reply. A week ago, Sergeant Paden, our platoon sergeant, distributed packs of little white PB pills (pyridostigmine bromide) to every marine.

"They say this stuff is experimental," Paden says. Every four to six hours we take a pill so that when Iraq launches chemical weapons, like sarin or soman, we will survive a few minutes longer.

No one knows what the side effects are, or the combined effect this drug has with the seventeen immunizations we received in Camp Lejeune, or with caffeine, nicotine, DEET, depleted uranium, or smoke from oil fires. In the years ahead, pyridostigmine bromide will be linked to Gulf War syndrome. Thousands will suffer nervous disorders, skin disease, insomnia, confusion, ataxia, depression, persistent headaches, and loss of memory.

McKeehan has tossed his pack of PB pills to the ground. "I ain't takin' this crap." Several other marines do the same. We've already devoured half of the pills. We've been guinea pigs long enough. Banks tosses the unused half of his pills to the ground.

"I figure that if chemicals rain down on us, no little pill is gonna make my life worth livin'," Langston says, emptying his pockets of the vile prescription. I dig in my rucksack for my pills. I feel like a sucker. I dump them in the pile with the rest. It's a triumphant display of dissent, which each of us savors.

We climb back in the truck, filthy, wet, covered with specks of oil, stained black from the charcoal-lined chemical suits, and tired of being carted around the desert as spectators.

FEBRUARY 27, 1991

The monotonous horizon is now rural farmland. Corrugated tin fences follow worn gravel roads. Shrubs and palm trees grow next to gray brick houses. A few tall concrete buildings stand prominently against the black sky. The convoy stops. We leap from the truck when we get the order to secure the southern flank of our position. I gather my team to patrol a nearby farm.

"Saenz, I need you in front of me," I yell. He's got the SAW. Langston takes point. Banks is taking up the rear. Sellers and McKeehan lead their teams to start their patrols in other directions.

"You see anything, Saenz?" I say. The farm is abandoned. Animals have been shot and are covered with flies. Suddenly, behind us, less than a quarter mile away, the sky illuminates with a five-story ball of fire.

Everyone is running like mad to where we last saw each other. "Where is Sellers?" McKeehan yells. A hundred yards away a dozen marines are hauling in fifteen Iraqi soldiers who have just surrendered. In the direction of the flames, we can see at least three humvees. They're the TOW (Tube-launched, Optically tracked, Wire-guided missile system) teams, engaging enemy forces along a tree-lined compound. A BMP-1 armored personnel carrier, hit by a TOW missile, is now sending off secondary explosions from its own ordnance, while thick black smoke pours out from its top hatch.

Sellers is running toward us from the direction of the flames. "The rest of our platoon is with Captain Alberts," he yells while catching his breath. "We gotta get there now!" It's a frenzy of action as we grab our gear and souvenirs from the truck, and hustle to climb on board with the other three STA teams. As the battalion begins its assault on Kuwait City, STA Platoon, finally united, rides ahead sitting on the tops of humvees.

When we move, Elvis leads. Sgt. Sellers has unfurled the Elvis tapestry STA Platoon acquired years ago while on liberty in Memphis. It's our flag, resurrected on a pole firmly attached to the roof of the lead humvee as we roll into Kuwait City, Elvis's young peachy cheeks becoming freckled with oil specks from burning wells.

Suburban Kuwait City is a cinder-block maze of light-colored walls and single-story buildings. This place is eerily abandoned. The battalion moves slowly. Captain Alberts is in the vehicle ahead. He's got the voice of the battalion commander in his ears. We slowly roll down empty streets and alleys, making our own trail across open lots and empty courtyards. Our bodies sway with each irregular contour of the ground, as if riding a horse back home. We seem to be the only ones here.

"Look at that guy!" Banks hits me on the shoulder and points. I've got my binoculars trained on a man in civilian clothes, standing on top of a grain elevator, waving a giant flag.

"He's waving a Kuwaiti flag," I say to Langston. I've got Captain Alberts on the radio: "We've got a friendly on the right flank, three o'clock. See him up there?"

"I've got him. I'll let 'em know in the rear," Captain Alberts replies.

The man is waving his flag high above the convoy. The top of his head is the highest point as far as I can see in all directions. We must be an awesome sight. There are thousands of marines converging on Kuwait City, the First Marine Division from the south and the Second Marine Division from the west. It's an endless trail of American tanks, APCs, five-ton trucks, and countless humvees. We are here to replace the fourth largest army in the world with the first.

My message passes through the ears and mouths of at least five marines. My voice to Captain Alberts, his voice to someone in the battalion command, battalion command to one of the line company COs, that CO to a platoon commander, then into the ears of young marines with their fingers tightly wrapped around their triggers. Something gets lost in translation. A barrage of gunfire erupts. Glowing tracer rounds ricochet off the metal tower. I don't know where the flagman is now, but he certainly is not on the tower.

We stop rolling just before sunset. Vehicles with thermal sights stare down streets and alleys. I sit on top of a humvee, peering out across a field of short, green grass. The desert rain has brought the otherwise desolate landscape to life. I'm on watch for two hours while my team sleeps.

The night is pitch-black with no moon or stars. The only light comes from oil fires on the horizon and a glow over Kuwait City. Through thermal sights, the world is blood-red, except for warm-blooded creatures. They glow pink or white, reflecting the intensity of their body heat. Two mice appear as pink dots bouncing around, like the white dots that bounce above the words to a sing-along song on TV. To my amusement, they bounce and crawl toward each other. When they finally collide, they leap in opposite directions.

The wildlife show is interrupted with news that the president of the United States has called a cease-fire. At that same moment, thousands of Iraqis are fleeing in futility a dozen miles away, as bombs pound their retreating convoy. Army units are engaging a dysfunctional Republican Guard in southeast Iraq. Allied forces are celebrating swift victory in every place where there is a radio. Saddam Hussein is thanking his lucky stars that he still exists. A futile Shiite rebellion begins its own genocide. In the morning, the sun shines on the Third Battalion, Twenty-third Marines and our first day of occupation on a tiny rise in the desert known simply as Hill 99.

7

THE RAT KING

Pick it up and put it in your pocket, or somebody else will.
Stan Ridgeway, "Pick It Up"

SEPTEMBER 10, 2003—BEAR BAIT ISLAND, MINNESOTA—MILE 985 UM
The *Bottle Rocket,* bruised but still floating, requires mainte-
nance. I push two dozen bottles back in place and rewire them.
I'll need thicker-gauge wire, which I can buy in the next town.
Little Falls, Minnesota, is eighteen miles, or two days, away.

The elevation of the river continues to drop. I did not expect
to see rapids on the Mississippi River. At times it widens to two
hundred yards, then narrows to less than a hundred feet across,
pouring over a crumbling landscape of rounded boulders of
all sizes, covered in dark algae, only inches below the surface.
SLAM! Another boulder has appeared from nowhere. They're
completely camouflaged against the dark background of the
river bottom.

I learn quickly from the river's brute lessons. As with duck-
ing incoming artillery, fear evokes fast learning, although the
knowledge is shallow and reflexive. The river behaves differ-
ently depending on the speed and depth of the water. I learn to

avoid a flat surface with short, choppy ripples, which signals shallow water. I steer my raft in the direction of fast-moving, light waves, where the deepest pools are.

SLAM! "Aw, crap. Where did that come from?" I grumble. Another incoming round for a slow learner. The raft plows into a refrigerator-sized boulder. The two aluminum pontoons are no longer on the same plane. One is bent slightly upward.

The river widens to nearly a quarter mile across, with several islands in the middle. Tom and Denny choose left, following the forked stream along the east bank. I hug the west bank to follow a deceptive current that eventually becomes a trickle through a shallow gravel bed. Tom and Denny, hidden behind a long island, have come upon a braided stream over a shallow sandbar.

I'm stuck. I've got to drag my raft to deeper water. When fully loaded, the *Bottle Rocket* weighs roughly three hundred pounds. If I jump down between the pontoons, I can grab the frame of the paddle wheel with one hand and a leg of the seat with the other, then dead-lift the raft and lunge it forward two or three feet at a time. I could belly-crawl faster than this. It takes more than an hour to cross fifty yards. My ankles are cut and bruised on both sides from sliding between rocks and under the pontoons. Tom and Denny appear far ahead around the island. I wave my hand in a motion that signals "Keep going." They understand that I will meet them at the next MDNR campsite.

Arriving hours behind them, I pitch my tent and stagger off to slumber. Two wheels have fallen off the raft, more bottles are sticking out, wires are broken, and what was aligned on the raft is now skewed. I should have kept the canoe.

"If I make it to Roscoe Island by noon, then I can probably get to town by nightfall," I whisper. Before emerging from my sleeping bag, I have already figured out how long it will take to get to Little Falls at the pace of the previous day. I'll make it if nothing goes wrong. Tom and Denny finish packing and get an early start.

Surprisingly, the river has deepened to the point that I cannot see the bottom. It's also much faster. In some stretches, the white-capped waves send me howling down a gauntlet of rocks with thick plants whipping the sides of my raft. I try my best to keep the raft straight. If the raft turns to the left or right, the current will surely knock the bottles out of the pontoons and I will certainly sink. I regret my prayers for a deep and fast river.

Ahead, I see three dark silhouettes wandering around on a gravel island. There are Canadian geese standing motionless around them. As I approach, I see they're wearing hunter coveralls and have shotguns slung over their shoulders. They wander around their decoys as if they're looking for lost keys.

I row aggressively against the current so that I can reach their island before the river sweeps me away. One of them climbs over a pile of boulders and grabs the corner of one of my milk crates. Together, we haul my raft a few feet up the bank of the island. We're on the south end of Camp Ripley, an Army base that borders the west bank of the Mississippi River. There are random booms of artillery to remind us.

"You see any geese up from where you comin' from?" one of the young men asks.

"Yeah, about twenty or so were on a sandbar watching me drag my raft for a while," I say. "I'm sure they flew this way." Their ears perk up at word of geese on the move. They haven't seen a thing all morning. The hunters called in late for work to take advantage of the early goose season. Apparently, there are too many Canadian geese in Minnesota this year. They are a public nuisance, as they deposit tons of crap on sidewalks and golf courses, which justifies the early hunting season. But in the absence of geese on this gravel island, in this cold drizzle, these men hunt for rocks.

"I guess you guys aren't from Camp Ripley," I say, in the tone of a question.

"Nope. There's no one left," one of them replies.

The middle fellow, with the single-barrel shotgun slung over his shoulder, adds, "They've all gone to Iraq or somewhere else." They take turns describing how the town's strip bars and liquor stores are closing their doors 'cause the troops are gone.

"You guys didn't sign up?" I ask, hoping one of them might continue the conversation about Iraq.

The third guy chimes in, "Somebody's got to take care of home. Besides, who wants to go over there and get killed anyway?"

One of them hands me a rock, a piece of agate. "These things are pretty rare," he says. "You can sell 'em. This one is the biggest one I've found in a while." He insists that I keep it, adding, "If you keep it wet you can really see the designs and colors." I can't refuse his precious gift. They help push my raft back to the edge of the river. Despite the rapids, I want to keep going.

One man has a two-foot-long, corroded metal spike in his hands. "You know what this is?" He's testing me with a smile.

"No, but I'm sure you do," I reply, with a hint of sincere curiosity.

"It's a log peavey," he says proudly. "You see, there would be a long wooden handle attached to this spike. Loggers used it to push logs around. It's an antique." He found it half-buried in the gravel. He offers it to me. I'm amazed that the river still holds such treasures. I hesitate less than a second before accepting the souvenir. It's a fine object to add to my collection of river artifacts, even though it adds at least five pounds to my raft. After a helpful push, the current swiftly carries me away.

With my best effort, the *Bottle Rocket* averages seven miles per day. It's an improvement compared to the first day leaving Lake Itasca, but at this pace I'll arrive in New Orleans in nine months, or some time around June 15. Before then, the river will ice over all the way down to southern Iowa. I'm ignoring the obvious fact that the raft is failing me. I dream of the canoe, which averaged twenty-three miles each day.

I am fatigued after hours of negotiating incessant rapids and the frequent collisions with subsurface obstacles. I attempt to steer the raft around giant boulders while the river carries me, often against my will. Tom and Denny have likely arrived in Little Falls, and are busily gathering supplies and portaging their canoe around the dam.

I see the town almost a mile ahead. The river widens, becomes shallow, but the current is unbelievably fast. The water pours over an enormous sandbar that extends from bank to bank and continues downriver for several hundred feet. I'm dragging the raft through the middle. In some places it is only a few inches deep, then suddenly it drops to several feet. I watch the raging current of sand instantly bury my feet where I stand. It migrates along the river bottom, and quickly piles against the pontoons whenever the raft gets stuck. The raft lunges forward when it enters the deep pools, nearly escaping my grasp, until it hits the next shallow spot.

I've got one of the oars pointed downward as a lever against the sandbar. In a flash, I watch the raft slam into the next shallow bed. The oar, driven into the sand, launches itself out of my hand, out of the boat, and into the river. The circular, handmade oar-ring slowly slides off the floating oar and quickly sinks into the haze of rushing sand.

Rowing, my only means of steering the raft, is now impossible. The river is quickly pulling me toward the Little Falls Hydroelectric Dam that is now clearly visible, less than a quarter-mile downstream. I rapidly pedal the paddle wheel and try to steer with one oar. I grasp a brick protruding from the footing of a train bridge. There I sit, with soaked clothing and bleeding ankles. At this moment, the trip seems more doomed than ever before.

SEPTEMBER 11, 2003—LITTLE FALLS, MINNESOTA—MILE 967 UM

The current is dead behind the footing of the train bridge, except for the small whirlpools spinning against the bank. The shoulder-deep water permits me to tiptoe the raft to shore.

It is drizzling. I'm tired, miserable, and trembling from the cold.

"It could be worse," I think. Could it be worse? I sit on the flattest rock. "This is impossible," I think. "Just stupid." I cannot quit, though. I have purposefully shared my optimistic plans about my fantastic journey with friends and family in preparation for moments like these. I use my own pride against myself.

I remove the remaining oar-ring from the raft, sling my drybag over my shoulder, walk up the bank, and begin hiking toward town.

Two hours of walking and inquiring with town folk about my dilemma land me in a machine shop. I tell the machinist about my raft and show him the remaining oar-ring. "Give me another two hours and I'll make you another one," he says. Another customer, Kevin Schroder, an eclectic entrepreneur who is waiting to pick up a custom-made part for his tractor, asks, "Instead of waiting here, how about lunch?" He looks like a middle-aged Paul Bunyan with overalls and a red-and-black checkered, long-sleeve shirt.

We drive through intermittent swaths of forest separating fields of corn and wheat. The short gravel road to Kevin's house winds past his cornfield of one acre, his apple orchard of one tree, and his vineyard of one vine.

Barb, his wife, is standing in the doorway as we pull up. "Just in time," she says. "It's on the table."

It's another meaty Minnesota casserole, and this one tops Bemidji in terms of creative combination. On the bottom of the pan lies a thick layer of ground beef, covered with green beans, smothered with cream of mushroom soup, and finally topped with Tater Tots. Kevin insists I dig in first. Besides, he's working on his appetizer of sliced tomatoes coated with granulated sugar. It all goes down well, chased with a hefty bowl of vanilla ice cream.

To ward off lunch-induced drowsiness, I take a guided tour of the farm. We drive past the garage, around the henhouse, past hibernating farm equipment in hues of rust, to the log pile out in the pasture. Kevin touches the teeth on the giant circular blade of his newest project. "I'm gonna mill my own lumber." He waits for my reaction as if he's just delivered a punch line.

"That's quite ambitious," I say, imagining that it's probably cheaper to buy a board than make your own.

"You see that tree over there. I can probably get five hundred board feet out of it."

He is a multidimensional jack-of-all-trades with a survivalist bent. In order to be a good father and husband, and meet the measure of a man, he must know that he can independently care for his family. He's a farmer, lumberjack, mechanic, and a truck driver by trade. He doesn't grow his own Tater Tots, but he could if he wanted to.

We drive back into town, where the machinist hands me my original part and two replacements. "I made you an extra one just in case." Kevin drives me to the train bridge where I left my raft.

It's now my turn. I show off my river souvenirs.

I proudly show him the log peavey I received from the duck hunters, the log chains I dredged from the river, and a handful of rusted nails from the wreck of the steamship *Andy Gibson*.

I've attached the cat skull and a few turkey feathers to the bow of my raft, along with the Wilson basketball and the chrome Chevrolet nameplate from that intact 1953 Chevy wagon upriver.

Kevin is as impressed with my boat and collection of river junk as I was with his farm collection—a combination of sporadic interest, low-level boredom, and secret moments of envy.

We pleasingly recognize our shared interest in purposeful, if not personal, junk collecting.

We load my raft into his truck and portage to a boat launch on the other side of the dam. It begins to rain again. We exchange addresses and part with a wave and good wishes.

It's a short distance down the river and up a tiny stream to the Pine Creek Campsite where Tom and Denny are camped. It's still drizzling when I find their empty tent erected on the bank. The campground is closed for the season, but Tom and Denny have found an unlocked shower room and a mostly empty one-room log cabin built by the WPA in the 1930s, which only contains a couple of picnic tables and a bulletin board announcing the park's past summer schedule of nature hikes and evening events.

I lay my sleeping bag in front of the stone fireplace and reignite the half-burned logs. Tom and Denny choose to sleep in their tent with their already inflated air mattress. Steam floats from my socks, underwear, and tee-shirt that hang on the mantle above the fire.

Snug in my sleeping bag, I swiftly fall asleep with my stomach full of casserole and my head filled with gratefulness for the kindness and coincidence that turned a day of failure into a day of promise. In these last few moments of consciousness, I challenge foolish notions of my own independence with thought experiments about alternative outcomes for this day, as if anything I do is really a solitary accomplishment.

It could have gone badly, very badly. Before falling into slumber, I pay deliberate attention to the gift of warmth from the crackling fire.

FEBRUARY 28, 1991—THE DAY AFTER THE GULF WAR

Private First Class Wurst speeds by in an Iraqi jeep, with the horn blaring and marines hanging out the sides. He speeds by again, as the sergeant major, a Vietnam vet, belts out, "Get outta there! Do you want us to shoot you?" The jeep, spray-painted with "He who lives, wins!" comes to a skidding halt in the middle of STA Platoon's corner of Hill 99. The jeep is ours.

I've got an Iraqi army duffel bag, collected/scavenged/looted from an armored personnel carrier, now half-filled with souvenirs. Earlier in the day, I left the bag in the back of a truck amid unknown marines from another platoon. In my brief absence they ratfucked my bag and distributed the contents among themselves. An officer had my Iraqi binoculars around his neck.

"Excuse me, Sir, but those are mine." Surprisingly, he apologized and gave them back. But my compass is gone.

"Ratfucking" is a brute phrase that collectively describes looting, pillaging, trophy hunting, stealing, souvenir collecting, scavenging, and borrowing with no intention to return. The distinction depends on who is watching. By default, ratfucking is a purposeful means to salvage useful gear from someone's junk. Days ago, a damaged humvee along the convoy into Kuwait City was picked clean down to the frame, like road kill stripped by vultures. This is tactically sensible. Gear left unattended is a gift, taken without remorse or hesitation. "Who ratfucked my pack?" one might say in response to a pair of goggles missing from an unbuttoned pouch.

A large deserted Iraqi compound lies quietly a half mile from our battalion's position, on a four-to-five-acre farm surrounded by a tall brick wall and date trees. Inside, there are several one- and two-story brick buildings littered with fifty-five-gallon barrels and pallets of fertilizer. The yard is a rolling landscape of connected tunnels and trenches.

STA Platoon has been given the mission of collecting intelligence on the site, including official-looking documents, maps, and electronic gear. The war is over, so the data is useless, but the mission justifies the trophy hunting. Our officers will confiscate what we find and redistribute the prizes among themselves. We know this.

Two teams enter the compound, eight marines in all. We divide into pairs and begin our search. Sergeant Paden, the platoon sergeant, has joined our patrol. "We know the war is over, but the Iraqis don't," he reminds the teams. "Watch each other's backs."

The trenches are filled with filthy blankets and abandoned weapons. I follow a trench into a subterranean bunker. Light trickles in through a few holes in the corrugated tin roof, otherwise it is dark. I enter when my eyes adjust to the dim light.

"*Irfaa idak. Ana jundi Amriki,*" I yell, just in case.

Nothing.

I yell again into the darkness before climbing in.

There is a half-opened door in the back of the room. I open it slowly and find hundreds of crates of tank ammunition stacked to the ceiling. Crash! Something falls behind me. An instantaneous surge of adrenaline launches my senses into hyperawareness, like those moments near the Kuwait border when that camel on its nightly stroll walked by our distant observation post. It's an intoxicating experience that leaves your hair permanently on end.

"Banks! What the fuck!" I yell. "Say something first." He enters the underground bunker and stares at the cache of ammunition with me. The bunker is enormous, with adjacent rooms and doors leading away from it. On the walls there are maps of Iraq and Kuwait and posters of Saddam Hussein smiling under a black beret. Pieces of uniforms and papers are strewn about the floor.

I walk across the room to a wooden footlocker in the corner. It is filled with hundreds of maps and military manuals. Pictures in the manuals of Iraqis installing mines and firing weapons, along with drawings of patrol formations, give away the story between the pages of Arabic writing. On the inside cover of the manuals there are photos of Saddam and other generals.

I dig through the footlocker to the bottom. A green book with faux leather texture and gold lettering catches my attention. It reminds me of a high school yearbook, with its elegant trimmings. It's written in English. In fifteen brightly colored pages, it showcases six missiles available for purchase for the French Mirage fighter jet. Some Iraqi general visited some military industry convention and collected these documents according to Saddam Hussein's wish list.

Digging deeper, I discover another document in English. This one is like a hardcover telephone book with gold lettering on the cover, reading, *British Defense Equipment Catalogue, 1989.* With this document, the Iraqis could purchase, from hundreds of British and American companies, battleships, tanks, radar equipment, missiles, rifles, artillery equipment, and anything else a modern army might need. My gut reaction, before any contemplation, is shock and shame.

I flip through the pages, looking at photos of familiar weapons for sale. The caption under a photo of a patrol boat reads, "Vosper Thornycraft offers a wide range of surface warships expertly designed to individual customer requirements." The company's phone number is on the bottom of the page. On page 206, "The addition of a 76 mm grenade system to the Helio range now ensures coverage of a large part of the world's need for grenade launchers."

"Pitiful. Bastards making money," I say aloud.

On page 237, "The LAW80 is a light anti-tank weapon with exceptionally high hit and kill probabilities against modern main battle tanks . . . with no noticeable recoil, making LAW80 a user-friendly weapon, which inspires soldier confidence."

"Banks, look at this." He just shakes his head.

We eight marines regroup and show off our booty. Everyone has a shiny AK-47. Sergeant Hicks proudly presents his new bayonet. Sergeant Kip has a uniform lapel showing the rank of a general (he will regret turning in the insignia to the wide-eyed intelligence officer who buried the souvenir in his pocket). There are books, maps, weapons, and hundreds of unopened crates. We need shopping carts.

MARCH 1, 1991—THREE DAYS AFTER THE END OF THE GROUND WAR
With the tip of my K-bar—a knife with a five-inch blade that only marines carry—I try to pry a periscope from the inside of a T-31 Russian-made Iraqi tank. Shaped like a flattened shoebox with multiple-angled mirrors inside, it is interesting enough to warrant collecting.

"They just left it here?" Private First Class Crawley asks, climbing into the tank after me. I sit in the driver's seat, peering through the turret-mounted periscope, still trying to get it loose. I give it up and continue collecting/scavenging. Between my legs, under the seat, I feel a pistol.

"Check this out! Looks like a flare gun," I say, turning to Crawley. He looks at me, smiling from ear to ear, and says, "Oh yeah, look at this." With both hands he displays an Iraqi flag, red with a white horizontal stripe in the middle and three green stars.

"Damn, who said you could climb in my tank?" I say.

The next tank is more rewarding. I pull a shiny AK-47 from behind the driver's seat. This one hasn't been rained on or burned, just polished and wrapped in a towel. I reach under the seat, fumbling around, and discover a pair of green binoculars with the Iraqi army symbol stenciled on them. I pause for a moment, and then realize that I have the exact same model around my neck. Both are American-made.

"Look at this shit," I yell to Crawley.

"What the fuck? Are they the same as ours?" he replies.

Hanging from the steering wheel there is a small leather pouch. I open it and pull out a compass, elegantly designed, made of brass painted black, with a pearled disk floating in the center to show magnetic direction. On the back, below the engraved Iraqi army symbol, in small letters, it reads, "Made in the UK."

The spoils of war are everywhere. Iraqi tanks and armored personnel carriers spill their treasure. Kuwait is for the taking.

~

In another successful day of ratfucking, I've come up with a huge Iraqi tent and a dozen new, plastic-wrapped Russian tank helmets with a flexible cloth covering, built-in headset, and sheepskin lining. The tent, white like the ones the Bedouin sheepherders have, is shorter, cooler, and more efficient in the desert than the olive drab, tall, American-made canvas houses of the Vietnam era. Later that afternoon, I stand in front of the platoon and divvy the Russian tank helmets—it's like tossing doubloons and trinkets at Mardi Gras. Communications Platoon, a hundred yards away, is unloading furniture from a humvee.

My cache of souvenirs is on display around my cot in the back of our new tent. Most of STA Platoon's souvenir weapons have been confiscated, but not before I traded some uninformed jarhead a shiny AK-47 rifle for another British-made Iraqi compass. My personal inventory of war souvenirs includes:

Two AK-47 rifles
Two black berets
Shoulder-carried magazine pouch
Extra canteen and magazine pouch
Iraqi H-harness with belt, canteens, and ammo pouches
Iraqi jacket (new)
Poncho
Yellow flag for guiding tanks
Baton
Two Iraqi vehicle license plates
Red-and-white checkered flag
Prayer rug, prayer beads, and two miniature copies of the
    Koran
Slide rule and hundred-meter tape measure
Conversion chart for tank artillery
Ankle chains for a camel
Kuwaiti and Iraqi postage stamps, coins, and bills
Gas mask
Field periscope

Three shoulder bags
Green helmet
Ammo pouch
Copy of a Palestinian Liberation Organization magazine
Pair of Iraqi dog tags
Beige helmet with crescent (Iraqi corpsman)
AK-47 bayonet
American-made Iraqi binoculars
British-made Iraqi compass
Dome light from inside a tank
British Defense Equipment Catalogue 1989
Document selling missiles for Mirage fighter plane
Two Iraqi field-training manuals
Poster of Saddam Hussein
Dozen Iraqi military maps
Instruction manual for installing mines
Artillery field booklet for calculating fire
Tank field booklet for calculating fire
Iraqi soldier personnel file
A dozen different psychological war pamphlets
Iraqi field radio, which I traded to British soldiers for:
    Green beret
    Complete British desert camou uniform
    British Insignia and patches
Camel tooth
Two scorpions and camel spider preserved in alcohol
Rocks and fossils collected in a quarry in Saudi Arabia

I arrived in Kuwait with one seabag, filled with issued gear. I will leave with three. I am King Rat.

SEPTEMBER 13, 2003—BLANCHARD DAM—MILE 957 UM

The river is deceptively calm beyond Little Falls, Minnesota. After a few morning hours of minor rapids, the river widens to form a quarter-mile-wide lake. Tom and Denny give me a two-hour lead that melts away quickly in the ensuing headwind. Another obstacle, the Blanchard Dam, is only five miles away. A gentle breeze churns light waves that softly lap against the bow of the pontoons, yet the raft barely moves. With each push on the oars the *Bottle Rocket* moves a couple of feet, stops, and then floats backwards. The raft has suffered and survived a lost oar-ring, broken bottles, and a bent frame, and still the river denies me passage.

"Damn! This is stupid." My frustration at my inability to move is exacerbated by my realization that the wind is barely blowing. I should be moving. All momentum is lost to a puff of wind, a tiny ripple, and tremendous drag.

Tom and Denny quickly catch up to my raft and row beside me for almost an hour. They paddle slowly, easily keeping up with my mad rowing. This isn't working. The water is deep, but there is no current. They are glancing toward me, hoping I will recognize the futility of persisting further.

Blanchard Dam is the smallest of the thirty dams ahead. Behind each of these dams there is a lake, called a "pool," that can stretch for miles upriver and miles across. Fifty miles from here there is a ten-mile stretch with two dams and the Coon Rapids. One hundred miles after that is Lake Pepin, which is twenty-one miles long and four miles wide.

"There's a boat launch on the east side of the river before the dam, about five miles from here," Denny says. "Why don't you meet us there in three days?"

Tom and Denny speed ahead, promising to meet me with a truck to remove the *Bottle Rocket* from the river. Reluctantly, I agree to the plan. I neither accept defeat nor express certainty that I'll continue ahead. I am burdened with frustration and exhaustion. I simply don't know what to do.

It takes the remainder of the day and the following morning to reach the dam. For hours I sit, sleep, read, think, and become excessively bored.

A father and son arrive at the boat launch and unload a large cardboard box near my raft. A fifteen-pound snapping turtle crawls out. Early in the morning they rescued the creature as it attempted to cross a local highway. I haven't seen one this big since the massive collection of turtles I kept in my mother's backyard twenty years ago. At that time I had amassed a collection of eleven snakes and ninety-six turtles. This fellow effectively demonstrates the power of its jaw muscles as it clamps down on an inch-diameter stick waved in front of its open mouth.

We talk about collecting things: bottle caps, coins, stamps, leaves, feathers, and rocks. Andy, the father, invites me to a quarry on the riverbank to collect rocks.

"You dig in the mud and you find starulite crystals," Andy says.

"It's one of two places in the world like it," his nine-year-old son, Little Andy, adds. He is obviously eager to follow his dad's example in dress and demeanor. They both wear baseball caps and monster truck tee-shirts. "Yeah, we'll show ya," Little Andy says, repeating, "If you dig in the mud you can find lots of little cross-rocks."

I've been collecting rocks since I was Little Andy's age. In elementary school I would secretly scoot up a two-story drainpipe in order to access the roof above the principal's office. There were bits of gravel up there that I had to check out, in case any of them were worth collecting (I still have some of them today). That rooftop was the only place to collect rocks in the delta of southern Louisiana. One day, a couple of fear-struck teachers caught me shuffling down the pipe with rock-filled pockets. That was my first behavior report. I got a second one that year for beating the crap out of Arthur Hicks. He deserved it for tattling on me for forging my mother's signature on that first behavior report.

Rock collecting followed me to the Persian Gulf. The first

ounce of weight I added to my pack upon arriving in Saudi Arabia was a handful of rocks and fossils excavated from an empty quarry. I used the butt of my M-16 like a rock hammer, to dislodge fossilized clams and snails, and chunks of selenite, a translucent form of gypsum.

On the eastern bank of the Mississippi River, directly opposite the Blanchard Dam, a tiny stream flows out from the rocky shore. Andy, Little Andy, and I kneel in the cool stream, digging into the silvery-green sediment looking for starulite, or crossrocks. The starulite crystal grows in four directions, resembling a crucifix.

It's hot and humid; the sweat drips off my nose. Excitedly, we share our finds, commenting on the size and perfection of each specimen. We employ subjective standards for rarity, value, and beauty. Within an hour I've got my pockets full. Little Andy and I trade our best ones with each other, like baseball cards.

8

CHAOS

Beautiful ideals were painted for our boys who were sent out to die. This was the "war to end all wars." This was the "war to make the world safe for democracy." No one mentioned to them, as they marched away, that their going and their dying would mean huge war profits. No one told these American soldiers that they might be shot down by bullets made by their own brothers here. No one told them that the ships on which they were going to cross might be torpedoed by submarines built with United States patents. They just told it was going to be a "glorious adventure."
Major General Smedley Butler, USMC, War Is a Racket

SEPTEMBER 15, 2003—BLANCHARD DAM—MILE 957 UM

Denny's red, battered 1983 Dodge pickup, with a constellation of scratches and dents on all sides, precedes an advancing cloud of dust as it rumbles down the gravel road to the boat launch next to the Blanchard Dam. I wait till they are almost here before I rise from the reclined seat of the *Bottle Rocket*. I wasn't sure if they would return. Why would a couple of vagabonds on an extended vacation bother to get even deeper involved in my rapidly unraveling plan?

Tom, hidden behind his straw hat and glasses, hands me a breakfast beverage of Milwaukee's cheapest. Denny's tattered shirt and blue jeans advertise what he had for breakfast, probably eggs. "I don't know if it's going to fit," he says with the tone of a warning, adding, "We can try."

I designed my raft with a fifty-two-inch width so that it would fit between the back doors of my Ford Econoline van. In the back of Denny's truck, there's just enough room between the

wheel wells for the pontoons of the raft. Everything else fits between the pontoons or on top, including their canoe, ice chest,
portable table, stove, utensils, gear bags, tent, and inflatable
mattress.

"I think that does it," I say to Tom and Denny. I pause for a
moment, hoping they will suggest the next step. For two days
I've pondered my choices. There aren't any good ones. "Well," I
mumble, pausing again for response. "I guess we can go?" I say,
looking back and forth between them.

Tom looks at me, pauses for a few seconds, and says, "Where
do we go now?"

MARCH 3, 1991—HILL 99—KUWAIT

"We can go wherever you want," my brother, Dave, says from
the driver's seat of the humvee he's borrowed for the day. Third
Battalion, Twenty-third Marines continues to occupy the same
gentle rise in the middle of rural Kuwait. Hill 99 provides a
three-foot vertical advantage above everything else for a half
mile in all directions. The grunt companies and STA Platoon
make up the perimeter. Dave drove around the hill and parked
next to my new Iraqi tent.

There's no point in asking permission to leave, since everyone is somewhere else. I've got a plan for this ride. I want my
brother to witness what I've seen during my earlier jaunts outside the battalion perimeter.

This isn't my first or last time out. The official end of the Gulf
War has not stopped the hunt. The TOW teams, with their own
humvees, have been our wheels. We scavenged the encampments
where the Iraqis had so miserably huddled while their numbers
dwindled with the hundreds of nightly sorties overhead and the
brief, but decisive, transition of occupiers.

Yesterday, Corporal Peterson, one of the TOW team leaders,
and I cruised about town. Donning our new Russian-made tank

helmets, we rumbled through empty neighborhoods looking for evidence of Iraqis. I had my American-made Iraqi binoculars around my neck.

"Check out that tank!" Peterson said. It was empty. Someone had beat us to it, but we played like kids, spinning the turret as fast as we could.

A two-story brick building a hundred yards away had a large gun barrel sticking out of a giant metal door. Inside we found a dozen artillery pieces. I climbed on top of the nearest barrel and jumped from one to the other without touching the ground. Peterson got one spinning around as he rapidly cranked a pair of handles. I hopped in the seat of the one next to him for a chance to duel.

The barrels didn't quite reach, but we got a kick out of slamming them into the wall. It wasn't being a very productive day thus far, with only a few pieces of uniforms found, but on the way home we discovered an abandoned palace. All of the windows were shattered and the marble façade was pockmarked from small-arms fire. Someone had defecated on top of a table. Everything was smashed—every door, every dish, every cup—silverware was bent, the carpet smelled like urine, and a live mouse had its foot caught in a sticky trap. I rested for a moment in a king's chair adorned with gilded lion heads and cherubs. Peterson took the chair.

The way home was long. Children chased us, yelling for MREs. "Give 'em the ones with the pork patty," Peterson said. I ratfucked Peterson's box of MREs for MRE number 11, chicken and rice. It's got a bag of M&M's inside. I put it in my Iraqi duffel bag for later.

We returned to Hill 99. The battalion commander's tent had acquired another lawn ornament from the Iraqis. It looked like a miniature tank with monster truck tires.

Banks had a cup of cocoa warming above a glowing chunk of purple fuel. Everyone was quiet. Sergeant Hillman and Sergeant McKeehan were hovering over the back of the platoon's absconded Iraqi jeep. Behind the seats, under a blanket, was a familiar machine gun. They'd had a successful day.

"Where did you get that?" I asked.

"It was mounted on an Iraqi tank," Hillman replied, adding, "It's a Browning fifty cal. American-made. Can you believe it?"

"I wonder if it shot at us?" I said.

I want my brother to witness the unimaginable. "You're not going to believe this," I say to him. It is the fourth and last time I will visit the road to Basra, Iraq, also called "Highway of Death." They've got it pretty well cleaned up by the time my brother sees it. The only bodies left are the unrecognizable chunks of charred flesh rotting in hard-to-reach places.

The first time I came here was a couple of days after the war's end. I hitched a ride with Sergeant Sharp from one of the TOW teams. There were four of us out on a sightseeing shopping spree. We stopped to survey the damage to one Iraqi compound with scattered armor, deflated tents, and bunkers half-full of sand. That's where I found the huge white tent. Next-door was a small building where the Iraqis had tended their own dead and dying. Dried blood splattered against the light-blue cinder-block wall, reminding me of a tee-shirt design I made in summer camp when I was a kid. A bloodstained, stainless steel gurney lay empty against the wall.

"He who lives wins," I said to the marine standing next to me. I was ratfucking my soul of compassion.

We took the highway north toward Basra, but only as far as the road would allow. There were three lanes flowing in each direction. In a final and futile attempt to leave Kuwait, the Iraqi army had fled north in a massive convoy of over five hundred vehicles occupying all six lanes. The convoy included buses, taxis, limousines, motorcycles, passenger cars, a few military trucks full of weapons, and anything with a running engine, including two or three tanks. Any homeward-bound euphoria in the minds of their youngest soldiers quickly evaporated as hell descended.

In order to stop the advancing/retreating Iraqi army from having contact with the swift U.S. Army, which had already penetrated through southern Iraq, the U.S. Air Force obliterated them.

I stopped counting bodies after a while. Five or six of them, covered with green-and-white striped blankets, were laid in a row like sardines in the middle of the southbound lanes. It didn't smell so bad yet. That came later. I would invite a few marines from my platoon to the site on the second trip, and then again on the third. In a few days it smelled like a blackened steak forgotten on a barbeque pit.

Thousands of hand grenades, tank and artillery ammunition, and RPG rounds, burned and corroded, were strewn across the sand. I tiptoed around them as the voice of reason rang through my ears. "Don't go near 'em. They're like land mines now, set to go off with the slightest touch."

Though I walk through the valley of the shadow of death . . .

I saw the allied forces for the first time. Saudi Arabian soldiers and British forces sifted through the still smoldering debris. We watched each other loot the dead. Sergeant Sharp opened his hand as we stood in the skeleton of a charred bus. "Do you think I can keep these?" he said. Two 1-ounce gold bars glimmered in his palm.

Under an upside-down tank, spray-painted with "THIS SIDE UP" and an arrow pointing downward, I found a bayonet half-buried in the sand, blued from the heat of the surrounding inferno.

I kicked a grenade and watched it roll ten yards away from me. I don't tiptoe through the debris anymore. I didn't care. "I cannot die," I mumbled to myself. A foolish sense of immortality disguised itself as courage. I kicked another. "The war is over. I can't die."

. . . I will fear no evil . . .

A passenger car was sandwiched between a truck full of anti-air artillery cannons and a bus. In the driver's seat, a black ribcage sat open with white-tipped ribs and a chunk of greasy meat in the middle.

"I guess that's a heart," I said to Sharp. The passenger was a stumped torso with the back half of an empty skull still attached and hanging backward, like a bowl. The stub of his penis was pointed upward. Someone before me had found some hair and placed it around his genitals like a bird's nest.

I was sick. "Some fucking joke!" I said aloud.

Another man was lying in the sand unburned, wearing dark green pants and jacket, with his mouth open like many of the others, and his neck arched. The sun reflected off an aluminum dog tag sticking out of his shirt. I couldn't tell how he'd died. I didn't see any blood. Perhaps he was hit in the back. The dog tag was inscribed by hand, with a large A+ in the lower-left corner.

I grabbed it, but it was attached. I pulled the chain around until I saw the clasp. Slowly I unhooked the chain and pulled it gently from around his neck, as if I were afraid I might wake him. The chain caught on his skin, resisting my theft. With one last pull it was free, and quickly I walked away so that no one else would know.

. . . for you are not with me.

Dave and I ride through the Highway of Death down a single meandering path bulldozed through the northbound lane. Most of the bodies are gone, but it still stinks. Allied forces are climbing over and under the vehicles like ants on a dead fledgling sparrow fallen from its nest.

One Iraqi soldier lies prone in the desert a few hundred yards away. In a week of visits I've cataloged the first stages of his desert mummification. His fingertips are shriveled, and his moustache is peeled halfway off his upper lip, flapping in the wind.

We wander around. I walk to the top of a ridge, to an abandoned Iraqi foxhole, so that I can get a full view. The swath of vehicles is as long as it is wide. I try to imagine the chaos as the front vehicles took the first hit. The first instinct must have been to get off the road. The front half of the convoy had no time or place to move, evidenced by the neat row of dozens of incinerated vehicles. What did it sound like? Where did the ones on foot run to? How many of them were completely cremated? Where are the survivors now?

I walk down the hill through the maze of metal mausoleums, across a field of scattered munitions. I kick an ashy grenade. It doesn't do anything. "Fuck this place," I say over and over.

I find my brother. "This is really messed up, huh?" I say in a somber tone. "Maybe I shouldn't have brought him here?" I think.

I shouldn't have brought him here. My own flesh and blood will forever have the memory of this massacre in his head. Little did I know that it would resurface in our dreams of Kuwait and thwart our search for reason and the return of humanity to our hearts.

He replies, "Damn. I'm glad it wasn't us."

"So am I."

But it was.

It takes more than a week for the battalion commander to rein in the wanderlust of his marines. The CO sends a humvee to every tent to gather souvenir weapons. STA Platoon parts with a dozen AK-47s, a few sniper rifles, machine guns, and one mini-mortar. I give up two rifles.

My last joyride into Kuwait doesn't venture far from Hill 99. I've seen enough burning oil fields and dead Iraqis. The novelty of free rein isn't feeling very novel anymore. The marines secretly want the Marine Corps structure to return. We need our checkpoints, PT exercises, and high and tight haircuts.

Less than a mile from Hill 99 there's a walled farm. And on

that farm there are a lot of dead cows and camels lying around. I sit on top of the humvee so that the foul breeze cools my sweat.

"Hey, go over to that camel over there," I say to Peterson, who's driving. There are two other marines sitting in the back. The long neck of the animal is the only discernible characteristic. Otherwise, it's as bloated as the dozens of other cows and camels decorating the football-field-sized green pasture.

"Shoot that one," Peterson says. I've got my Iraqi flare gun loaded and cocked. The metal pistol has a two-inch-diameter barrel, making it look like a cartoon gun borrowed from Yosemite Sam. We are twenty feet away when I let loose a red flare that sinks into the camel's stomach. A red glow pours out of the hole, and a gray cloud lifts off the carcass, but it's not smoke.

The gray camel becomes a brown camel as a swarm of a million gray-winged flies leaves the body and surrounds the humvee. I can hear them bouncing off my goggles. They are landing on my lips. There are thousands of them swarming inside the humvee. I bang on the roof. "Go, go, go!" He's already hitting the gas as I yell.

We retreat to our little hill in the desert among the comforts of our military traditions, while the putrid world outside our perimeter begins to take measure of its destruction. Kuwait is now the domain of worms. We have morning formations, shave regularly, and begin to build a complex of reinforced foxholes, sandbagged checkpoints, and a sand berm around our perimeter.

We figure we're not going anywhere for a while.

SEPTEMBER 15, 2003—BLANCHARD DAM—MILE 957 UM

"Where do we go now?" Tom says again.

"I dunno?" I reply.

Denny suggests the obvious: "Let's look at a map." He points to the image of a little green tree on the map. "That's the

Minnesota Valley State Park. There's a cardroom a few miles away in Shakopee."

I need time to weigh my options of what to do next. First, I need time to figure out what those options are. Fall in Minnesota has arrived quickly, and winter feels close behind. The least of my possessions is time.

It begins to drizzle the moment we arrive at the campsite. When it's not raining, it's hot, humid and the mosquitoes drain your blood supply. When it does rain, it's cold and clammy. I gather some wood from the ground before it is soaked. I pull a dead branch down from an oak tree. With a dry cardboard box, retrieved from the camp dumpster, I get a decent fire going.

For a couple days we sit, sleep, talk, walk, drink, fart, and not much else. Conversations spark and sputter, sometimes dying after a single sentence.

"You can steal more with a briefcase than a gun," Tom blurts out in a stream of consciousness that rests on a single statement. Denny follows hours later with, "God is either the greatest mathematician or the ultimate practical joker."

In the middle of a thunderstorm, Denny and I are sitting in his truck talking about free will. He says, "Life is like the Mississippi River, you can choose to paddle along the east bank or the west, but all rivers eventually flow to sea."

I think only about my raft. It's resting on gravel in the parking space next to my tent. It looks morose and abandoned. "It was an admirable try," I say to myself. I could junk the raft and spend the last of my money to buy a used canoe, or I could just tuck my tail between my legs and go home. I don't want to do either.

"You tried. You tried hard, but it didn't work out. That's okay," Tom says in consolation.

"If you're gonna keep going, you have to somehow make the *Bottle Rocket* go faster and float better," Denny suggests.

I don't know what to do. I can't stand failure.

I decide to take the least plausible, yet preferred, option. The plan, practicality aside, gives order to chaos. I will modify the raft and then reenter the river on the downriver end of Lake Pepin, the last major lake on the river. "No more crossing big lakes," I remind myself. I will jump ahead of a hundred miles of shallow water, two dams without locks, and the Coon Rapids. Lake Pepin is the last impossible obstacle I can foresee. From that point on, I should have deep water and a current. I realize I'm skipping miles, but there's no other sensible choice. I can live with that for the sake of continuing with my raft.

In order to increase speed, Denny advises that I get a sail and lengthen my oars. To increase buoyancy, I decide to fill the space between the plastic bottles with expanding foam, the stuff used to insulate door and window frames. In a local hardware store, with only eighty dollars to spare, I clean the shelves of their supply of the stuff: twelve cans.

It's a sticky mess. All twelve cans fill one half of one pontoon. Six in each would have made more sense. It's an irrevocable mistake. The foam oozes out and hardens into a yellow blob. The little raft looks even more wounded.

"This is really stupid," I think. My budget cannot be stretched any thinner. I need to spray a few more cans into the first pontoon and then fill the second. I need at least eighteen more cans of foam.

"A good day at poker is better than a week at nursing," Denny says.

"Huh?" He caught me off-guard with that one. Denny has been a registered nurse for the past seven years. Long before nursing, he made a living counting cards at the blackjack table, in the days before multiple decks and continuous card-shufflers.

"Poker is really the only game you can win at. You've gotta follow the bad players from table to table." Denny is enjoying the captive audience. "Learn to read other players," he says softly, as if it's a secret. His welcomed outpouring of advice continues:

"With good players you can play a bluff maybe once a day."

"This game rewards patience."

"Wait for the good hand and bet aggressively."

In Shakopee, a small town nine miles north of our campsite, sits the Canterbury Park, a racetrack for horses. There's also a cardroom. Denny's been there before. He knows most cardrooms across the United States. "Let's go play cards," he says.

There are no horse races today, but the parking lot is half-full. I've never sat at a card table. The extent of my experience gambling is the sum of a handful of quarters dropped into slot machines over many years. When I drive through Las Vegas, I usually gas up and visit a cheap buffet, dropping a quarter or two as I walk in and out.

"Patience. Controlled, but aggressive betting," Denny whispers as I sign up for the 2/4 hold'em table. "Play only your good hands." Denny struts off with the cadence of a master.

There are six players and a dealer wearing a red jacket. My hand moves hesitantly across the table before dropping thirty dollars on the green. "I need that thirty dollars," I think. It's my turn to fork up the blind. In hold'em, there's an initial ante that one player lays on the table before cards are dealt. The blind moves to the next player after each game. I lose my first two dollars in the first two seconds.

Denny said to fold everything unless both cards are jacks or better. Each player is initially given two cards facedown. The dealer slowly unveils five other cards on the table, with a round of betting after the third, fourth, and fifth card.

Half an hour into the game, I play my first hand and win with a queen and a king. The three-card flop and the one-card river shed two queens ("flop," "turn," and "river" are the names given to the five cards the dealer turns faceup on the table for players to share). I play three hands in two hours, losing only one. I am still hovering around thirty dollars, having lost and gained nothing.

My last hand is a pair of aces. A pair of aces!

Don't move.

Don't blink.

Don't smile.

"Patience. This game rewards patience and aggressive betting," I think. I lay four bucks on the table after the three-card flop. I lay four more after the one-card turn.

"I can't afford to do this," I think.

The lady across the table raises me another four. The fifth and final card, the river, is unveiled. I call and raise. I'm broke. I'm praying for a miracle.

She calls, and then we lay down our cards.

She bluffed. She bluffed and lost! She should have known not to bluff an idiot. I was not playing smart, only desperate.

I've got $120. That's twenty-four cans of expanding foam. I drag my chips to my little corner, flip one to the dealer, and slither off to cash in.

Meanwhile, Denny has been watching and waiting. He's got a bankroll of eight hundred dollars that he didn't have a little while ago. We find Tom in the bar and hustle off to Mexican food on Denny's dime.

Lake Pepin is enormous. "Where do you want to go in?" Denny says.

"The map says there's a boat launch ahead," I reply. "That should be a good spot."

The boat launch sends boaters into a stream two hundred feet from the lake. The stream passes through a tunnel under Highway 61 before entering Lake Pepin. I can see giant waves crashing into the tunnel, sending ripples far upstream.

"I don't think you want to go in here," Tom says, without taking his eyes off the short, choppy waves. They would easily pour over the pontoons of my raft and into my lap. The three-foot waves would undoubtedly push me upriver against my will.

"That looks kinda dangerous," Denny adds. I don't need much convincing.

Finally, in the town of Wabasha, on the south end of Lake Pepin—the last of Minnesota's ten thousand lakes that I'll see on this trip—I reintroduce the new and improved, foam-filled *Bottle Rocket* to the Mississippi River. A north wind latches onto the raft and nearly rips the rope out of my hand. The raft is bobbing like a cork. The foam raises the raft an amazing six inches out of the water. I quickly load gear while giving Tom and Denny relentless thanks. With the wind at my back, a little bit of current, and a large dose of stubborn persistence, I just might make it. Tom and Denny watch the *Bottle Rocket* blast away.

"I hope he doesn't drown," Denny says.

Tom, watching the wind pull the *Bottle Rocket* faster than it's ever gone before, replies, "I think he can swim pretty good."

9

RIVER RAT

"Yahhhhhh!"

Optimism renewed, I'm cruising down the river at almost three knots. It feels like fifty. With the wind at my back, I fly by sandbars, parked barges, and red and green buoys.

The river is numbered. Wabasha, Minnesota, is mile 760.5. Only 1,710 miles to go. There are white, diamond-shaped signs marking the miles, like a highway: 750.0, 743.5, 741.0. It's impossible to get lost.

Flat-topped, green "cans" on the right and pointed, red "nuns" on the left, the barrel-shaped buoys anchored to the river bottom alert boats and barges to the location of the river channel. Towboats, pushing up to fifteen enormous barges, silently slip by my raft, slow and unstoppable, gliding between the buoys to avoid snags and shoal water. There's virtually no wake created from their passing. Powerboats, with their deep V-shaped hulls, are the ones that rock the *Bottle Rocket*.

There are thirty-seven dams on the Mississippi River. The

lower twenty-nine have locks, which act like a watery escalator to carry boats and barges up and down the river. As I approach the upriver side of the lock, I look for the pull cord along the wall attached to a bell. This alerts the lockmaster to the presence of small boats. As soon as the lock fills to the same level as the upriver side, the massive, yellow gates begin to open.

I slowly row toward the center wall and grab a rope tossed to me by the lockmaster. The upriver yellow doors slam closed behind me. The river level in the lock drops to the level of the downriver side. The walls appear to rise around me.

"What the hell is that?" the lockmaster says. "I've seen lots of things come down this river." Apparently, eight to ten people attempt this trip every year. Most of them are in canoes, but occasionally a raft floats by.

"One guy had his raft fall apart as he left my lock," he explains. "Barrels just sort of went out from under him." He studies my raft with keen interest. "Looks like yours might make it." I'm delighted with his vote of confidence.

The water drains from the lock like a giant bathtub, downriver gates slowly open, and I'm on my way.

By 6:00 p.m., I drag my raft up a sandbar at mile 736 UM. There's a giant forty-foot dune of dredged sand. In the 1930s, the Army Corps of Engineers created a channel at a depth of nine feet from Minneapolis to St. Louis, which they continue to maintain. The braided stream that once meandered across the river valley is now a single, deep, narrow channel, except behind the dams where lakes form.

There is abundant driftwood for a fire. I warm a can of soup and a can of peas until the labels burn off, and then wash them down with a can of fruit cocktail. Raccoons lick the cans clean when I forget to toss them into the embers. Across the river, cormorants are circling and slowly roost in the trees. A beaver slaps its tail in the water in front of me, causing ripples that distort the reflection of stars.

"When you have a chance, get a sail and longer oars," Denny had suggested a week ago. With a hundred thousand people living in La Crosse, Wisconsin, there ought to be tarps and wooden poles somewhere. I pull into the Municipal Harbor next to a one-room marine supply shop.

"Sure, you can dock here if you want to," Brock says, standing on the deck below the shop and above my raft. He's about to take off for his daily jaunt around the harbor and then down the river for an hour or two of walleye fishing. He's short and skinny with shoulder-length hair. He's a mechanic in town, but spends most of his life on the water. He gives me a helping hand off my raft and directs me to town.

Everyone's preparing for Oktoberfest in a few days. Some talkative Midwesterner on a bus explains, "We've also got Cornfest, Butterfest, Cheesefest, Applefest, and June Dairy Days. It's just an excuse to suck down more brats and beer." I find the Salvation Army thrift shop on the edge of town. For four bucks I add a fleece vest and a Wisconsin Badgers sweatshirt to my river wardrobe. I discover that the hardware store is on the other end of town. It's a long walk back to the marina, where a small crowd is trying to make sense of my raft.

"Where ya goin' on that?" a thin, old fellow asks.

"As far south as weather permits," I reply, adding, "I need a sail if I'm gonna get outta here before it ices over."

"You need a sail?" cracks a low voice from under a dirty baseball cap. Steve is a short marine mechanic who lives in a houseboat stuck in dry dock. He's a river rat if I ever saw one, with grease stains across his flannel shirt, rubber boots, and fewer teeth than the nine sausagelike fingers he's got left. "I saw a sail this morning in the garbage," his words gargle from his throat. My ears perk up.

"You mean a real sail?" I ask, making sure I heard him right. We walk over to a large green dumpster that reeks of fiberglass resin and dead fish. Lying on the ground is a blue-and-white sail with two 12-foot-long, two-inch-diameter poles. It is a gift from heaven or a devil's prank.

Brock gives me a lift into town, first stopping at a roadside chicken barbeque for a three-dollar dinner. I get one too, with coleslaw and corn on the cob to go along. At the hardware store I buy rope and duct tape. Everything else I need is on my raft or lying next to the dumpster.

I cut a five-foot square from the center of the sail. The aluminum poles become my new, lightweight oars. I transfer the blades from the old oars to the new ones. The old oars become the mast, and a broom handle becomes the crossbeam for the top of the sail. A little tape and rope make this beauty shine.

"Ya oughta be fishin'," Brock says, giving me a fishing pole and a brown-and-yellow walleye lure. "Just drag it behind your boat. Jerk it a little bit now and then. They'll grab it for sure." He's delighted to pass river secrets on to a burgeoning river rat.

Every river rat's got stories. Brock has a library of his own. "Before you get to Dam 8, you'll pass through a stump field called Reno Flats."

Stump fields are common in the flooded sections of the river, where the forest floodplain has been devoured by the pool of water that formed behind the dam. Stump fields are boat killers. Earlier in the week, I floated through a small stump field and discovered the broken half of a large boat propeller embedded in a one-foot-diameter log. It would have made a good souvenir.

"Back in the 1930s, a hundred and fifty duck hunters got caught in Reno Flats when winter came real fast," Brock says. Apparently, the temperature went from sixty degrees to twenty in just a few hours. "A bunch of them died 'cause they got stuck in the ice. They had to cut their legs off to get 'em out." Brock is serious. Sensing my disbelief, he adds, "My grandfather has a picture of all the stumped survivors sitting on a bench!"

~

"Yahhhhhhhhhhhhh!"

With a stiff north wind, I sail my raft three, maybe four knots. My new lightweight aluminum oars give the raft an added push. Combine the sail and oars with the super-buoyant foam-enhanced pontoons, and I average fifteen miles a day. Maybe I'll get to New Orleans by the new year?

I've got walleye lures up the wazoo. Eighteen of them, with abundant fluorescent colors and designs, hooks cut off, dangle from the outside edge of my raft like Christmas ornaments. I find them stuck to logs and washed up on the riverbank. A plastic mallard decoy, duct-taped to the mast, leads the way, like the figurehead on a Spanish galleon.

The river sometimes straightens for miles, then bends gracefully as it follows the contours of the river valley. The tiny town of Dakota, Minnesota, appears on the west bank. I can see a glowing soda machine standing in sharp contrast to the row of whiteboard houses. I judge that the effort required to secure my boat to a tree and scramble up the bank is worth it for the chance to stretch my legs and enjoy a cold pop.

The soda machine turns out to be one of many vintage machines decorating the front entrance to an antique shop owned by C. J. Papenfuss. The old man turned his family deli into a junk shop decades ago. Through the glass window of a pastry rotunda, I discover a pair of boat navigation lights among a few salt and pepper shakers and glass doorknobs.

"Two bucks," Papenfuss yells.

C. J. Papenfuss has watched the river all of his life. He saw the river before the big locks and dams. "My father helped build Lock and Dam Number Nine," he says. "They were gonna make him foreman until he fell and broke his arm. Almost fell in the wet concrete."

He shares stories of the family deli, the old family farm and the cows he still keeps on it, and his fondness for the Mississippi. I'm eager to get back on the river to take advantage of the intermittent tailwind. Before I depart, he scrounges around his shop for D-cell batteries for my new navigation lights. They look like chrome flashlights, one with a green-and-red lens, and the other with a white lens. Maybe I'll have a go at night rafting.

I search for a sandbar as the sun dips below the canopy of trees along the west bank. A powerboat rapidly approaches and comes to an abrupt halt, sending waves over my pontoons. "Wanna drink?" the swaggering skipper says. "We got whiskey!"

On weekends, the river becomes a favorite spot for canoeists, swimmers, campers, fishermen, water-skiers, and dozens of party boats motoring about. There are two drunk couples on board, unloading a barrage of questions about my trip. They hand me a highball. "Hey, can we give you a tow?" They're going to Clancy's in Lansing, Iowa, for dinner. They've got a buffet.

"Sure," I say. They toss me a rope, which I loosely wrap around the base of my mast. For the first time, I experience six to seven knots. The front of the pontoons rises above the wake, and the paddle wheel spins like mad. It's soon dark, drizzling, and cold, but I'm enjoying the few quick miles.

In a moment of drunken stupor, the skipper forgets I'm there and guns the engines. The paddle wheel and front half of the raft take a nosedive underwater.

"Hey, hey, HEY!" I'm about to abandon ship. The rope has tightened itself around the mast, which is now about to crack. I'm going to jump. "HEY!" I'm crawling up the back of my seat. The raft is starting to turn on its side.

The skipper finally looks back. "Sorry!" he yells.

We're almost to Lansing. A bar with glowing neon beer signs has a dock on the river where we tie our boats. In Clancy's Diner down the street, we drink a few more rounds and then settle down for the buffet. It's a pork extravaganza. There's ham roast, pork patty, pork chops, pork loin, sweet and sour pork, pigs in blankets, and something that looks like SPAM.

I make a pig of myself with several full plates. I'm also a filthy pig, with a week's worth of dried sweat lending a putrid fragrance to my clothing. My grotesque consumption is a spectacle, which appears to sober my benefactors.

When the night ends, I find refuge under the riverside bar, next to a barbeque pit, slipping softly into slumber with swine-o-plenty swirling in my stomach. I feel bloated and tired. I have been on the river for five weeks and have lost twenty pounds. I've put two new notches in my belt.

SEPTEMBER 29, 2003—WISCONSIN RIVER CONFLUENCE— MILE 631 UM

September in Iowa brings brilliant fall colors to the slope of the steep bluffs. The Wisconsin River lazily adds a little more push to the current of the Mississippi. The confluence comes to a point on a beige, sandy beach covered with slender, white willow branches stripped of their bark by beavers. Young spiders, dangling on long strands of silk, parachute across the river. Turtles have left their tracks in the sand where they climb the bank to lay their eggs on high ground. Raccoons have gotten to a few, evidenced by the dry, shriveled eggshells near the excavated nests.

I tie the raft to a tree washed ashore and drag my gear into the shelter of the forest edge. A woodpecker noisily searches for insects in the canopy. I stand on the beach and watch a lighted barge illuminate the bank with powerful floodlights that scan the river for buoys and mile markers. The moon allows me to see the shadow of beavers swimming near shore.

"It is a perfect evening," I think. I was able to push twenty miles out of my oars and sail. I walk along the sandbar scavenging for fishing lures, with a smile across my face.

An aluminum can bobs next to a log in the water. It's an unopened can of Busch Light, chilled by the river, delivered to my doorstep.

"Yeah!" I say aloud, wiping a layer of scum from the top of the can. I give a toast to the river, to the towboats, beavers, raccoons, and drunk captains. I toast my perfect evening with a cold brew.

I rise before the sun on most days, pack my gear, and shove off in time to watch the first wisps of mist swirl up from the surface of the river, like little tornadoes. This morning is different.

"Get back over here!" a fisherman yells to his cocker spaniel, which has leapt off his aluminum flatboat and is now running up and down the sandbar. He ties his boat next to my raft.

"Whatcha catchin'?" I ask with polite curiosity. He's wearing a camouflage jumpsuit under bright yellow bib overalls. We talk a bit about my raft, and then he roots around under a giant stump and pulls up a rope. He hauls in a ten-foot-long hoop net that was apparently submerged just below my raft. There are three catfish inside. Two are too small and luckily find their way back into the river.

"They gotta be a foot long or better," he explains. The third catfish, a two-footer, flops inside a basket with other catfish collected from other traps earlier. He's got a dozen more to check before the morning ends.

"These are the small ones," he says matter-of-factly, baiting me for conversation.

"What's a big one look like?" I ask. His dog drags a dead turtle into the water.

"Well, sometimes you catch the two-hundred-pounders, but they aren't the biggest fish out here." He's enjoying the opportunity to shed his expertise. While he talks, he baits his trap with chunks of some unknown meat. "You got paddlefish out here that are worth a good bit of money. I once hauled in a ten-footer." He stretches the net to make sure there are no snags and no holes. "You've got to throw the sturgeon back though. You can't sell them anymore."

His dog splashes into the water and climbs into the boat with a helping hand from above. He's off to the next trap up the Wisconsin River. He'll be done by noon and on his way to the market just after lunch. He'll be back in a couple days, weather permitting, to check the same traps, in the same way, in the same place he put them years ago.

"Hi, are you visiting here long?" Mike asks, as he slides into the seat across from me in Joe's Pizza Place. An hour ago, I slipped through Lock 10 in near darkness. The air is cool and crisp. I set up my tent on the bank of the river below the town of Guttenberg, Iowa.

Mike's a skinny, blond, seventeen-year-old high school senior with nothing better to do than hang out with friends at Joe's. He's cordial and sincerely interested in hearing about my journey.

Mike is in the process of growing up on the Mississippi. "Sometimes after the winter thaw, you can see two dozen deer up there on the bluff," he says fondly, looking out the window to the dark forest on the hillside. He's absorbed by the culture of fishing and hunting, skillfully rambling off the names, sounds, and behaviors of the animals he knows.

"Hey, Dad. I met this guy floating a raft down the river. He's from New Orleans," Mike says into his cell phone. Tonight I will be a grateful guest in his home. I will wash clothes, eat soup, shower, and sleep in a warm bed.

"I gotta show you something I found," he says. From under the bed in his room, he drags out the skulls and antlers of two male deer, locked together. He found the scattered skeletons half buried in a streambed by the river. The ten-point and fourteen-point bucks had made an irrevocable mistake when their antlers became entangled. Their fight for dominance ended in exhaustion, then death.

They're Mike's greatest material possession. He even refused a $25,000 offer for them. They're part of the story of his life on the Mississippi. He'll likely never let them go.

OCTOBER 1, 2003—WAUPETON, IOWA—MILE 600 UM

"First frost tonight . . . with a low of twenty-two degrees," blurts the crank radio sitting in my lap. A couple of unlucky fishermen sneak up to the side of my raft with a couple of soft drinks in hand.

"Ya know it's supposed to freeze tonight," one of them says with a smirk.

"I've heard. I've got a decent sleeping bag." I'm lying. I bought a synthetic bag from Wal-Mart years ago for fifteen bucks. It's not worth a penny more, with its uneven insulation, and it's barely long enough to cover my shoulders.

The north wind blows seventeen miles into my sails, but brings with it a chill that promises to steal warmth from the night. I did not expect winter to happen so soon. My strategy of deliberate ignorance only pays off as long as luck or the goodwill of strangers prevails. It's 3:00 p.m. and it's already getting cold.

Below the bluffs, on either side of the river, are train tracks, Burlington Northern Santa Fe Railway on the west bank and I & M Rail Link on the east. The navigation channel has hugged the west bank for most of the day, with no break in the bluff. To my delight, a train bridge crossing a small stream entering the river allows me to peer upstream to a group of trailers and a boat launch.

The town is Waupeton, Iowa, a seasonal village that springs to life for fishing tournaments. Otherwise, the two dozen trailers are empty. You wouldn't know it existed unless you knew where to find the one dirt road that scales the four-hundred-foot cliff, or you had a fishing boat. A single two-story home and a barn are perched next to the railroad tracks. Smoke is pouring from the chimney.

"Pardon me, ma'am, would you by chance have a barn or a basement that I could sleep in tonight, to get away from the cold?" I politely ask Ruth, a sweet lady of seventy-six who slowly opens the door.

"Sure. C'mon in," she says, signaling me to follow her inside. There are nearly a hundred stuffed bears piled in the spaces between furniture. The television is blaring. We chat for a while about the river and about her drunk son, whom I must have missed outside. A cat brushes against my leg, then another. Ruth grabs a key from a nail on the wall. "You can sleep in the bar."

Downstairs, behind boxes and a stack of firewood, there's a door leading to Anthony's Resort, a one-room bar with a fisherman's décor. A pile of barstools and Christmas decorations fills one corner. Broken neon beer signs, a dartboard, tired newspaper clippings, and a dusty trophy fish adorn the wood-paneled walls.

Five years ago, Ruth was diagnosed with esophageal cancer. She shut down the bar and her life in anticipation of dying. She survived, but kept the barroom door locked.

I retrieve my bags from the raft, while Ruth disappears upstairs. When I return to the bar, Ruth appears with a hefty chunk of carrot cake on a JFK memorial plate. "Here you go, sweetie," she says, with a comforting, maternal smile.

"I think the furnace still works," she mumbles. "I'll get Kenny to take a look at it."

Kenny hides in the ancient bar whenever his boss, Ruth's son, is on a drunken rage. Kenny, thin and in his midfifties, has been a handyman for ten years, ever since he lost his job as a master plumber.

"I like being here on the river," he tells me. His monotone mumble, muffled through his thick gray beard, takes a moment to make out.

He's got his entire life history on a folded piece of paper he keeps in his wallet. He's been a gravedigger, a raccoon and squirrel trapper when the season's right, and for a few extra bucks he collects wild ginseng. He proudly shows me a picture of the biggest ginseng root he ever found. "Looks like a pair of fat-lady legs," he says. He carefully slides the photo into the folded plastic sleeve in his wallet, where family photos usually belong.

Every once in a while, he gets a call to eradicate bats, one of his other eclectic talents. "You gotta block up every hole in the wall in the attic, and don't stir up all the guano," Kenny explains.

He even once rafted a hundred miles down the Mississippi River on steel barrels, until the oars broke and the beer keg went empty. His best days were as a clam diver, collecting large mussel shells from the river bottom to be cut into pea-sized spheres and then slipped into live scallops in Japan, to make pearls.

We devour a six-pack with elbows perched on the dusty bar. Kenny rustles through a drawer and emerges with a "Where the Hell is Waupeton" bumper sticker. He also hands me a "Waupeton Whoppers Club" card, which was only issued to the winner of a fishing tournament, and earns the recipient a free drink every night for the rest of the fishing season.

Just before midnight, Kenny shuffles off to his own trailer. He figures the boss is passed out by now. The wall heater is glowing red. I lay my sleeping bag below the shower of warmth. Outside, through the large front window, I can see the *Bottle Rocket* lying on the concrete ramp of the boat launch. A thin veneer of frost is beginning to form.

"Only fifteen hundred miles to go!" one captain yells from the bridge of his towboat. The towboats are massive, but handled gracefully by their crew. "Good luck!" the captain yells, sending me a thumbs-up. The crew looks on with curiosity. Half of the time, I can see the silhouette of their arms raised to their eyes, holding binoculars, like a teacup with two handles. I always wave, and they always wave back.

The river is large enough for two towboats to easily pass each other, with room enough for my raft to slide between them, although I hope to never be in that position. The closest I come to towboats is to rapidly slip behind them, as they pass, and ride the rollercoaster of waves and turbulence churned up by their massive propellers.

The lock workers on the Upper Mississippi River seem to know who I am. "We heard about your raft," says one lockmaster.

The boats and barges make room for me on the river, but in the locks, might makes right. "You've got to get out of the way of that boat behind you," yells a lock worker running along the outside wall of the lock. I look back and throw myself into a fit of instant anxiety as I discover what he's talking about. Unbeknownst to me, the *Mississippi Queen,* a faux paddlewheeler launched in 1976 as a floating hotel, is two hundred yards away and gaining.

I have a personal rule to look over my shoulder every ten minutes to see what's coming down the river. Between barge checks, the *Mississippi Queen,* faster and quieter than a barge, sped around the bend and is bearing down on my raft. She must be enjoying the spectacle of my struggle to clear the lock gates. At least she entertains me with "Dixieland" and "Oh Suzanna" whistling loudly through her pipe organ.

The river is changing. Each stream, river, and city sewer that enters her makes her different. There are fewer bald eagles. Small river towns, commercial and recreational river traffic, replace the solitude I cherished in the headwaters. Although I cannot deny that what the river loses in natural wonder it gains in cultural heritage.

In the headwaters, I knew a wild, untamed river. Slowly I began to feel that I was part of the river, part of a system, and not an entity of my own. Mortal, yet infinite in the current of life. Despite the hardships, the way the river embraced me was extremely peaceful and cathartic. That feeling is stronger now. The river is my friend some of the time, but more often it is my indifferent teacher. In time the river will ask me to become its steward.

The novelty of the river has worn to a way of being. The river trip is no longer a fantastic adventure; it's just what I do now. I've got my own tales of the river, glorious wildlife, sunken ships and gambling chips, bottle boats that wouldn't float, and a song or two that I've invented.

Everything is about to change.

"Here's our river rat!" Trish exclaims, escorting me through the offices of the National Mississippi River Museum and Aquarium. I've landed in Ice Harbor in Dubuque, Iowa, after making prior arrangements to hang out there for a few days.

The three-month-old museum will display my raft to visitors for a weekend, while I talk with them about my journey. I plan to rest for the few days that I'm here. That does not happen.

After dinner, wine, music, and a whirlpool bath, I'm whisked away to an evening get-together. Trish is the ultimate host and local social butterfly. I meet more Dubuquers in one weekend than the number of people I've met on the river thus far.

The next evening begins with a dinner party and ends with dancing at the Coliseum in East Dubuque.

The next evening begins with a birthday party for someone in the museum and ends with karaoke. No one is impressed with my off-key attempt to sing "Proud Mary."

Weekend visitors throng to the new museum, which emphasizes riverboats, river wildlife, river rats, and, of course, Mark Twain. Visitors peer over the rail with inquisitive looks and eagerness to ask questions about my journey.

"Where did you start?"

"Where are you going?"

"Is it cold?"

"Do you get lonely?"

"How long will it take you to get home?"

"Does that boat really float?"

"What do you eat?"

"Where do you use the bathroom?"

I haven't slept much these days. I drag my boat onto the dock of the museum and proceed to take it apart in order to redesign it for two travelers. I have so much work to do to the raft and so little time left. Jenna arrives tomorrow.

Everything is about to drastically change.

During the last two weeks, I've been calling collect to Los Angeles from pay phones, negotiating with Jenna about the logistics of her joining me on the trip. I met Jenna in 1993 and for six years we were engaged. We moved to Los Angeles from New Orleans so that she could become an actress. Three years ago I left her. She's now a successful freelance journalist. She hates me, but thought that a story about traveling the Mississippi River on a raft with a cheating ex-fiancé would make a great book.

She will be here tomorrow. I'll move my seat to the back of the pontoons. The paddle-wheel assembly will go as far forward as possible, and Jenna will sit in the middle on a new seat.

I hope it works.

I hope it still floats.

I hope she doesn't kill me.

She walks to the front steps of the museum. "I thought I said only to bring two bags?" I say to Jenna, who's dragging five. That's probably the wrong thing to say, but I've got concerns about buoyancy, logistics, safety, time, and weather.

I know what the river demands. Jenna is still as stubborn as I remember. She convinces me that a portable toilet seat is crucial to her survival.

In a futile attempt to reign with some command over my domain, I offer a fact of the raft. "Jenna, don't forget who the captain is." Apparently, that was also the wrong thing to say.

Our time apart seems like seconds.

Every river rat has a story about the one that got away, the storm that almost killed 'em, or the one he truly loves—could be a girl, a boat, or the Mississippi River itself. Jenna and I will leave Ice Harbor from the dock of the museum tomorrow in the early afternoon. I hope to make a few miles, just enough so that she can get a taste of the Mississippi. Maybe she'll quit after a few days?

On the night before Jenna and I depart, Trish treats us to a lavish home-cooked farewell dinner. Others from the museum arrive to join the feast and give their fond wishes. In the morning, Trish and I stand in her kitchen, holding opposite ends of a wishbone she salvaged from one of the Cornish hens.

"Make a wish!" she says as we gently pull. Secretly, she wishes Jenna and me Godspeed and a safe journey. Secretly, I wish that we make it down the river alive. The wishbone snaps in two places, sending the center of the wishbone flying into the air. We each wished for the same thing, and we both lost.

"Oh dear," she says.

"Oh shit," I reply.

10

SAND AND WATER

Amorphous clouds of red-winged blackbirds swarm above us, appearing abruptly as they pour out of the thick morning mist. The flock resembles a giant serpent coming out from camouflage, suddenly taking shape, evoking instant fascination. Their deafening chirp is heard before the swarm appears.

The thick white mist forms droplets on my clothes. I cannot see the bank of the river. My navigation charts guide me around islands and channel buoys. Jenna and I listen intently for the sound of barge engines and breaking bow waves.

"Stop paddling!" Jenna yells.

"What? What's going on?" I'm frantically looking for a barge rounding the bend ahead of us, or anticipating a collision with a tree trunk or hidden buoy. "What? What?" I yell.

"Save it," she says. A ladybug fell into the river and glided under her seat. Now it's under mine.

"You wanted me to stop rowing for the sake of a stupid beetle?" I say calmly. "It's fish food now," I mumble as I continue rowing. We argue incessantly about my disregard for nature's cruelty. We argue about what time we should get up in the morning and when we should stop for the night. We argue about the things couples usually argue about, but we do so in the context of nomadic river life. But when arguing doesn't prove persuasive, she keeps a rolled-up magazine by her side to enforce her point with incessant tapping on the brim of my weathered cowboy hat.

My solo trip down the river is permanently altered and unrecognizable. The raft is overflowing with bags, boxes, and colorful bungee cords, similar to the disorganized display of irregularly shaped boxes and bows under a Christmas tree. There's a toilet seat strapped to the side of the paddle wheel. I might as well paint the whole raft pink.

Jenna's vintage 1950s glasses, with new prescription lenses, rest on her nose like a school principal's. She wears a blue skullcap and a pair of white rabbit-skin earmuffs. Everything about her is colorfully inconsistent: yellow fleece jacket, black boots, safety-orange pants, white scarf, and a red lifejacket.

When she argues, she dresses her language with colorful adjectives in a style of banter that could put any marine to shame. The conversation moves like the river, meandering from casual conversation to old argument, and then to blame, with a current of precise rhetoric that usually leaves me bewildered and unresponsive. I wish her mouth could move the paddle wheel. My only recourse is what I do with the raft.

"What's that?" she asks.

"I don't know," which is a lie, because I can clearly see that there is a bloated white-tailed deer floating belly-up directly in front of us.

"Ew!" she screams. "Get away from it!"

"I can't help it," I say, which is another lie, adding, "The current is too strong." I feel like a cat sitting calmly with one foot on a mouse's tail.

~

Hwwwwaaaaaaa. Wwwwaaaaa. Wwwaaa. Waa.

"Is that a duck?" Jenna asks, seeming confused, having been rustled from sleep by the poultry alarm. "Is it duck season yet?"

"I don't hear any gunshots," I reply, as I unzip the tent door. Yesterday, we observed duck hunters climbing into their straw-covered blinds, and learned that the opening of duck season was only hours away.

Blam, blam, blam. Seconds later there's another volley—blam, blam, blam!

"I guess it is," I respond to her question and the gunshots. Outside of the tent, we see duckboats parked across the pool at Dam 13. A duckboat camouflaged with straw and branches, looking more like a giant hula-skirt, or a haystack, scoots across the water in front of our little sandy island.

"I wanna go," Jenna sobs, for the sake of the thousands of ducks and geese that will soon find their way into Midwestern freezers.

It takes an average of an hour and a half for the two of us to leave the sandbar, as opposed to the minutes that measured my expedience when traveling solo. I want to make the morning miles while the wind is calm and the air is cool. I don't need a sponge bath, or a morning movement on the portable pot, or a cup of coffee before I grab the oars. I'm ready to go, now.

"C'mon, get on the goddamn raft!" That doesn't go over very well.

"I have to pee, and YOU'RE JUST GONNA HAVE TO WAIT!" Jenna snaps back. I realize that I've forgotten about the defiant little beast that resides in her.

"We've got to get to New Orleans by Christmas. If I say get up, then get up. That's just the way it is," I try to explain.

I may as well be herding cats. Jenna is on her own time schedule. I am still on mine. Why can't she pee on the raft between the pontoons, or rinse her toothbrush in the river? What's wrong with week-old underwear?

I fail to realize that she's only been camping once in the last ten years. She's never gone more than a couple of days without a shower, and a world without caffeine and nicotine is going to take some getting used to. I also fail to realize that I've arrived at my expectations after six weeks of minimalist survival and a very steep learning curve. I'm also a filthy pig.

"Besides, I'm the captain of this raft. It's my river trip, and you're just along for the ride." Okay, even I know that what I've just said will not pass as negotiation.

She stops shaking the sand out of her sleeping bag. She takes a deep breath, lowers her forehead and burns a stare into my eyes. "I'll let you know when I'm ready," she says slowly and definitively.

What I begin to realize is that resistance is futile.

"Barge check!" Jenna yells, turning to look behind me, and far beyond the raft. The river is clear. She then stares directly at me and says, "Gimmie a snack cake."

Behind my seat I've made a platform with chewed beaver sticks and tied a large milk crate to it. That's where I store a cache of individually wrapped cakes, brownies, and cookies within arm's reach. I grab three and hand her one with a smile. That's just enough fuel to get us to the last sandbar of the day, where we'll pitch camp and crawl into our sleeping bags.

The following morning, "Hey, where's the raft?" Jenna inquires after poking her head out of the frost-covered tent.

At least once each night I make sure the ropes are tight and the raft is on high ground. I seem to remember tying the raft to a giant log yesterday afternoon. There were no trees within reach of the rope. I seem to remember checking the raft before I fell asleep. Then I remember that I only draped the rope across the log, threw the drybags over my shoulder, and walked away. I never tied the rope and never came back to check.

I spring to my feet in a panic. From the tent, perched high on the bank behind a thick brush, I cannot see the raft. I slip my boots over bare feet and run down the sandy slope, but not before taking a nosedive and tumbling to the shore.

I see the rope stretched across the water, the end of it still draped across the log. I see the raft floating almost twenty feet from the river's edge. It was washed into the river overnight.

I give thanks to the river for the luck I have so undeservingly been awarded. I have once again emerged unwittingly on the correct side of fate. I tug on the rope and realize that the last two feet of it, lazily coiled like a sleeping snake, have frozen themselves to the log.

The beautiful towns of Princeton and Muscatine in Iowa, and Albany, New Boston, Keithsburg, and Oquawka in Illinois, once earned their vibrancy from the river, and now seem to survive on the nostalgia of better days. Some still live off the railroad; others harbor a factory or two that hasn't yet gone south for cheap labor. And others are near dead, having been weakened by the 1993 flood, a Wal-Mart or a casino.

Jenna and I paddle, row, and sail eighteen miles into a dark, cloudy night above Keithsburg, Illinois. The bright light of a barge dock illuminates the bank. Jenna hops off and holds the rope while I secure the oars and hop ashore. Together we drag the raft out of the water and proceed to unload all of the bags, including all of the individually wrapped snack cakes, for fear of raccoons looting the raft.

The sheriff in town discovers us on the levee and offers us a ride to the bar a block away. Jenna and I order burgers and share a pile of fries.

"The whole town got flooded out ten years ago. A quarter of the town never came back," explains Janice, bar owner and mayor. Half of the town is abandoned. There are grassy lots where houses used to be. The train stopped running after a couple of kids burned down the bridge with fireworks. The printing museum sits empty, with ancient presses, the size of small cars, rusting in an alley.

Exhausted after dinner, we stumble over the levee, back to our raft, and slowly erect our tent on a flat, sandy terrace. In the morning I discover that we've set up camp on an ancient landfill. Broken bits of ceramics, purple glass, and globs of rusted metal dot the shoreline. Hundreds of clamshells litter the beach, with perfect, circular holes cut out of them.

I find a button, then another. Before plastics emerged on the market, buttons cut from clamshells held together millions of shirts and blouses around the world. Button making reached its heyday by the mid-twentieth century, then died. I fill my pockets with weathered buttons before Jenna wakes. Fifty white pelicans sit motionless on a sandbar in the middle of the river, waiting for the rising sun to warm their hollow bones. The river is flat and the air smells like earth.

We make our daily miles past dozens of small river towns, stopping every once in a while to scout for rations and stretch our legs. In one such town, I meet Andy, a white-haired gentleman with the only keys to a one-room museum in town. He waxes fond about the days of button making along the river.

"There would be stacks of clams taller than this house, with twenty or thirty men and women churning out thousands of buttons a day," Andy says. There's an antique button machine in the corner, which looks more like an overgrown sewing machine. "Go ahead. Make a button," he says to me. I flip on a switch and the ancient contraption whirls into action. I hold the clam and crank the drill bit into the pearled shell. The rough-cut disk pops out of the hollow drill bit. I make a few more.

Every town seems to have a little museum and an Andy to go along with it. The towns themselves are museums, struggling to hold on to their culture, while shops close and buildings fall to ruin. They defend their heritage with futile care while the present engulfs a collapsing way of life.

OCTOBER 20, 2003—OQUAWKA, ILLINOIS—MILE 415 UM

It's fifty-cent draft in the local bar in Oquawka, Illinois, population 1,500 before the flood. "I'm losing my best buddy," Captain Ray says, keeping tears from cresting over his watery eyelids. In five days his seventeen-year-old son, Zack, will leave for Marine Corps boot camp.

"He could've joined the Coast Guard. At least then he would have been closer to having a river pilot license." Ray has spent his life and raised his family on the Mississippi River. He's terrified his son will go to Iraq. "You make good money as a river pilot," Ray says, pausing for a few seconds, then exclaiming, "He had to go and join the Marine Corps. The worst one!"

We're invited to Captain Ray's front porch for fried chicken and sodas. Zack is sitting there waiting. He wants to borrow the car. Captain Ray wants his son to change his mind and stay home. The tension is obvious.

"What's your MOS gonna be?" I ask.

"I'm gonna be a gunner," Zack replies. He's skinny, with dark sunglasses and a Chicago Cubs tee-shirt.

"You know, you could find a job that you can use in the outside world," I say. "There's not much use for machine gunners in civilian life." My words are meaningless, going through his ears lightning-fast. The warrior myth has got him good. Maybe he was lured by decorations, driven by emotion, hooked by a slick recruiter baiting high school hallways with posters and brochures. Maybe it's the façade of job training. Maybe it's the free health care and a steady paycheck. He's stubborn and decided. Whatever it is, they've got him.

Four days later in Keokuk, Iowa, we brave a storm on a patch of grass next to the Keokuk Yacht Club, on the west bank in southern Iowa. My earplugs and gluttony-induced sleep keep me from noticing Jenna's 2:00 a.m. struggle to hold up the tent as wind flattens it over her face. Earlier, I had enjoyed beer and enchiladas at the Mexican Night buffet in the club dining room.

Standing next to me at the bar was a skipper and his young son, complaining about how their ninety-foot yacht must bear the harsh salt water of the Gulf of Mexico as they make their way from Minneapolis to Key West to escape the cold Northern winter. These were the richest of the "snowbirds" I'd seen.

Their boat, docked near my raft, dominated the harbor. Through the etched glass windows, I could see carved teak and mahogany walls and furniture, a wine rack, and a woman in a custodial uniform clearing dishware from a table.

The skipper's son appeared to be of similar age to Zack, the son of Captain Ray from Oquawka. Skipper's son likely doesn't need a bribe of school tuition, job training, three meals a day, or free health care.

Skipper's son likely will not serve for the sake of patriotic duty. There's too much to lose and too little to gain. Skipper's son will join the many clubs that other skippers' sons belong to, where they learn to nurture fortunes and barter influence.

Skipper's son will go south when it gets cold, while Captain's son will go into the fire for the empty promise of a better life.

OCTOBER 28, 2003—HANNIBAL, MISSOURI—MILE 309 UM

The steep bluff before Hannibal, Missouri, is aflame with gold and burgundy leaves that shower the river surface. A train bridge ahead rises vertically for a barge and then drops in line for a train to rumble across, just as we pass underneath.

We dock in Hannibal, check e-mail in the library, and wander down Mark Twain Street to the pizza buffet, where I shove food down my gullet with vigor.

"Where are we gonna camp?" Jenna asks. Across the Mississippi River there are sandbars and hidden islands. We make it across in time to catch a point bar a quarter mile downstream. I purge my gut in gross heaves on the other side of the sandbar. I return to Jenna with a few pieces of waterlogged wood. There's no use for a fire anyway. It's beginning to drizzle. The tent is warm. Jenna is happy here. Hannibal glows behind the tree line.

The next morning begins with a short float to Lock and Dam 22, eight miles south of Hannibal. We pass several motionless barges and discover they're waiting for the Corps of Engineers to replace the giant yellow lock gates. They're also building a twelve-foot chain-link fence around the outside of the lock station to restrict visitors. One of the men standing on a barge yells, "They're not gonna be done till tonight. No one's going through the lock today."

Jenna has the bladder of an elf, so we run aground in a wooded cove below the lock and scamper down train tracks to the main gate.

"I really gotta pee," she explains to the lockmaster.

"I'm sorry, but since 9/11 no one is allowed near the lock."

Every lock up and down the Mississippi is restricting public access with fences, but apparently you can still bring any boat through, including a raft made with 232 two-liter plastic bottles.

After a moment behind a tree, Jenna and I discuss our options, and decide to go over the dam. We row and pedal the *Bottle Rocket* to the Illinois side, where the river is almost level with the crest of the dam. There's twenty feet of flat pavement on top of the dam, and a forty-five-degree slope to the water fifteen feet below on the downriver side.

"Grab some straight logs to put under the pontoons," I explain to Jenna. A perplexed fisherman who hasn't caught much all day finds our dilemma amusing. He helps us to roll the raft across the dam and send it barreling down the other side, splashing into the water as if this were its maiden voyage.

We've got a routine figured out. When dusk lures us to a sandbar, Jenna leaps to land with a rope in hand. I hop off and tie up the *Bottle Rocket* with two ropes, while Jenna hauls gear ashore. I search for the flattest expanse of soft sand for the tent, and drag my boot across the sand to carve a flat square. In the space where I anticipate placing my sleeping bag, I sculpt a concave pit for my aching back. Jenna unrolls the tent, and together we set it in place. We scavenge for firewood. With a handful of straw, twigs, and kindling, I adhere to my motto, "One match—one fire."

From the plastic milk crate behind my seat, Jenna gathers the night's meal of canned soup, veggies, fruit cocktail, and sometimes a couple of potatoes she buries in the sand beneath the fire. We watch our pile of driftwood burn, count shooting stars, and talk less about the world and more about the river.

When we crawl in the tent, Jenna settles with a book and a flashlight while I root around for a comfortable position in my concave pit on the floor, earplugs snug in my head and 1,000 mg of ibuprofen swirling in my stomach.

Another fifteen miles down the Mississippi.

In my lap, I've got a map of a ten-mile section of the river, torn from the Corps of Engineers navigation chart. With a wide river, a tight bend usually indicates a decent sandbar on the inside of the meander. Sandbars are plentiful from Minneapolis to Baton Rouge, but there are many twenty-to-thirty-mile stretches with only rock-strewn levees between them.

There's a perfect sandbar ahead, with a low sloping beach and piles of driftwood washed up against the tree line. I paddle while Jenna readies herself with rope in hand.

Strangely, the raft grazes the sandy bottom almost thirty feet from the bank. It's still too deep for Jenna to walk the raft to shore. Her boots are four inches shorter than mine.

"Just sit tight. I'll drag it closer," I say, hopping off the raft and wrapping the rope around my wrist. The raft is grounded after a few feet.

"It's too heavy. I gotta take the bags off," I explain, my voice laden with irritation.

"I can just walk myself," Jenna says, recognizing that I was implying that she should get off the raft. She isn't wrong, but I only wanted to voice a complaint, to whine a bit, not have her act on it.

"No, it's too deep." I know she'll get her feet wet. "Let me carry you." Now it's just funny.

In the twenty feet between the raft and the beach, there is a five-foot-deep channel dug out by a shoreline current hidden by the silt-laden water. The underwater edge of the channel is a cliff. I step into the hole with Jenna in my arms. I plunge into chest-deep water and try desperately to keep her out of it. My water-filled boots impede progress.

Jenna flails her arms like an unwilling skydiver. I slowly lift us out of the water to the safety of dry land.

Her intuitive selflessness emerges naturally. She's far more concerned about my wet clothes than hers. Using her maternal voice, Jenna says, "Are you okay? Let's get you out of those wet clothes." I finish unloading the raft and secure one rope to a single willow tree and the other rope to the corner of our tent. Shuffling around like a stubborn child, I don't want to change clothes until we get camp set up.

I slosh around the sandbar, dragging whole trees to the shoreline for the massive fire I will use to dry clothes. Jenna has the tent erected and her wet clothes hanging on the limbs of trees. She's dumped her drybag on the floor of the tent and has discovered that wet sand is stuck to everything.

"There's sand on my peppermints," she says with disgust. I tell a story about the United Service Organization (USO) in Kuwait that supplied us with bags of Jolly Rancher candy. We learned to suck on them and spit out the encrusted bits of sand before actually enjoying the flavor. My suggestion is met with a grimace at first, then a pause to reflect on the logic of the idea, followed by her consumption of the mint.

She learns the adhesive power of wet sand. I can see it still stuck to the side of her face from her dip in the river. I build the fire as high as possible, with Stonehenge-like vertical sticks propped in a circle around the fire, each sporting a wet sock, boot, or corner of a piece of clothing. In a few of hours everything is dry and smoke-flavored.

I notice a change in Jenna. She genuinely appreciates being warm, dry, and fed. She's made most other things trivial. She's the best river rat I know, second to none.

The wind howls down the river valley, channeled by the steep bluffs that flank the river. Each gust sends a cascade of leaves into the water, forming a swirling kaleidoscope of red and gold. The sail pulls the *Bottle Rocket* around one bend, then pushes her backward with a fierce headwind. Drop sail, raise sail, row, pedal the paddle wheel, ride the current. Progress is painfully slow.

"Are you ready to call it a day?" I ask. I know she's tired of fighting the wind. We make a break for the nearest sandbar.

Our gear is piled high and the tent is staked in the sand, but not erected, for fear of the poles breaking. Gusts hurl sand against our sunburned cheeks. Miniature sand dunes form around our bags and in the wrinkles of our deflated tent.

"Maybe the wind will die down in a little while," I say, hoping that the setting sun will take the torrent with it. We walk across the sandbar collecting driftwood. There's a half-buried skeleton of an Asian carp, several other dead fish, and scattered deer bones littering the beach.

The sandbar is wide and flat, the largest we've camped on thus far. I can look across it, with the river's edge and the tree line barely in my peripheral vision. I walk slowly, in my own world for a moment.

I see only sand.

I feel only wind.

The stench of dead animals fills my nostrils.

"Hey, Jenna." She catches up to me and walks by my side. "This is just like it was."

MAY 1991—THE LAST DAYS ON HILL 99

It's 11:00 a.m. and already 110 degrees. The horizon surrounding Hill 99 is an impenetrable cloud of wavering dust, colored green through my tinted goggles. "Who's left?" I wonder. Half of STA Platoon sit on cots with sleeves rolled down, goggles on, and their heads in their hands.

Thousands of flies huddle motionless on the windless side of all things above the sand, including ourselves.

"Who's in sick bay?" I yell to Banks.

"Tomas... and somebody else," he yells back, taking time to answer and quickly disengaging from the conversation. At least three guys are in the sick bay tent with IVs in their arms, having succumbed to dysentery or heat-induced dehydration.

I can count a dozen dead goats, sheep, and chickens around our tents, unearthed by the endless windstorms.

Officially we are here to show a military presence, but no one knows we exist.

They call us the Lost Battalion.

FEBRUARY 1991—THE FIRST DAYS ON HILL 99

We made a home of our hill the moment we arrived.

Saenz stumbled upon a concrete factory somewhere nearby. By the end of the day, he had liberated forty sacks of concrete for the purpose of building a basketball court. He's gray with dust, which does well to keep the flies off his head. "You're gonna build a what?" Langston shook his head and walked away.

One week later I asked, "You still gonna use the rest of your concrete?" It had been sitting for two weeks. Several bags had gone into making dumbbells of various weights. Saenz had scavenged pulleys from the Iraqi jeep in order to create *Flintstones*-style weightlifting equipment.

It took Saenz a few days to answer my question. "Yeah, I guess you can have it," he said, then asked, "Whatcha gonna do with it?"

I replied as casually as possible, "Build a Jacuzzi." Over the next few days, he watched as Sellers, Crawley, and I transformed an empty foxhole into a ten-foot-diameter pool with a wrap-around bench.

With a little coaxing we convinced the water truck to save some juice for us after filling the swimming-pool-sized water bladders the battalion used for sixty-second showers. The platoon took turns floating in the Jacuzzi, until the water clouded beyond our concept of sanitation. Within hours we discovered the intense itch caused by lime, a common ingredient in cement. Our skin became dry and white. Crawley, being practically albino anyway, looked like the walking dead. We never used it again.

Somewhere in Kuwait there's a poor-man's Jacuzzi engraved with "US MARINES."

The Bedouin family pitched their white tent beneath enormous power lines on a patch of concave desert where ankle-high brush flourished. Hundreds of goats and sheep grazed throughout the day under the watchful eye of a dozen foul-smelling camels.

Women, clad in flowing black robes, ran into the privacy of their tent as the men emerged and met us no less than a hundred yards away. We gave them SPAM.

The USO had kindly provided every serviceperson with a bag of pencils, paper, razors, toothpaste, a bag of Jolly Rancher candy, and SPAM. STA Platoon had already created a pyramid of SPAM cans in camp. We could not rid ourselves of it. We burned it, shot it, played baseball with it, but more accumulated. The Bedouins accepted it with smiles.

Corporal Sanchez, a chef in downtown New Orleans when he's not a grunt, had a plan that included the unsuspecting Bedouins, or at least one sheep. In the middle of the night, with K-bar in hand, he liberated a sheep from our neighbors.

To complement his Lamb-o-SPAM, he revealed a liter of

vodka he'd received in the mail, ingeniously smuggled to him from the States in a mouthwash bottle. A sack of rice from the cooks and generous amounts of Tabasco sauce further complemented the feast.

It was a meal fit for kings, devoured by pawns, drunk on hidden liquor and the success of their deviant and richly novel endeavor. The only trail of evidence to betray the plan was the splatter of rice and vomit that was spewed outside the chef's tent the next morning.

"Does anybody have any food to give away?" I asked a group of marines from another company, taking shelter in an enormous sandbagged pit on the other side of the hill. I was pelted with cans of SPAM and half-eaten MREs, which will be delivered to the bishop of Kuwait. Captain Broussard, the battalion chaplain, had organized a food drive for the entire regiment. I volunteered so I could leave the hill.

The highway was black with soot, and so were street signs, parked cars, buildings, and the surface of the desert all the way to the three-story flames jetting out from ruptured oil wells. We toured the international airport, which was surrounded by craters and demolished hangars.

We rode through downtown Kuwait City. Only military vehicles occupied the highways and major roads. Flames had gutted every government building. The beachfront was covered with metal obstacles that had been intended to repel an amphibious assault. A cruise ship near shore bore the brunt of tank target practice.

The bishop of Kuwait hurriedly thanked us, while his minions assisted us in unloading our donation. There was a basket of useless Kuwaiti and Iraqi currency. "Go ahead, take a handful for souvenirs," the bishop said.

We raced home to outrun the black sky, returning to Hill 99 in time to prepare for the midday darkness. The wind shifted and the pungent smell of petroleum was beginning to flood the air. Black clouds from the burning oil wells were headed our way. A seemingly infinite chain of electric towers leading to our hill began to disappear from sight, one by one, as the dark wall advanced and engulfed them. By 1:00 p.m., noxious night was upon us.

It was instantly cold. I rolled my sleeves down. Without a flashlight I was absolutely blind. Dozens of flickering light beams wandered around the hill as others made their way to shelter. For hours we waited for this surreal world to pass. When it did, we took note of the black smudges around our mouths and noses and the inklike mucus that filled handkerchiefs. Our clothing, hair, and skin were peppered with the crude we fought to preserve.

Staff Sergeant Honeydew, our platoon commander, earned the Navy Cross in Vietnam for giving of himself well beyond the call of duty by saving the remainder of his platoon while under heavy fire.

"I'd like to do this one more time," he said to me, referring to the unfair swiftness of the ground offensive, as if the hundred-hour war had robbed him of something. He was a marine's marine, with a hard-on for the fight. He was our Chesty Puller, with bullet scars and faded tattoos. He collected pipes, which I discovered when I told him about the hookah pipe I'd left in a foxhole I'd ratfucked weeks ago.

"Damn. Can we go back and get it?" he asked.

He gathered STA Platoon around him for a marine-to-marine chat, Vietnam story time. "Two decades ago I was in your boots, a combat veteran, with all the fears and hopes that...." Saenz was sitting next to me in the back of the huddle. We were engaged in a staring contest. His body odor was burning my eyes, but I figured I could take him. In one rapid motion, like a chameleon catching a fly, he grasped a handful of sand and shoved it in his mouth, then spat it out like a fountain.

"You're fucking nuts, you know that?" I said under my breath. It pained me to keep from laughing. I was hiding an ear-to-ear grin, in light of the emotional outpouring from our platoon commander. For the next twenty minutes Saenz picked his teeth and spat individual grains of sand between his legs.

Honeydew's monologue occupied almost a full hour of the day, which left roughly twelve more to grind away. We, the marines of Third Battalion, Twenty-third Marines, were not well suited for idle storage, like a shovel left to rust in the garden.

We played "Dodge the Three Hurling Frisbees," a game in which the platoon stands in a thirty-foot-diameter circle with one poor sucker in the middle getting pelted with high-velocity Frisbees hurled at close range. If the sucker catches your throw, then it's your turn in the middle, the "hole." Everyone in the platoon had his turn.

We liked it when Crawley was in the hole because the welts showed up well on his white legs. When he tried to leave, someone yelled, "Where the fuck do you think you're goin'?" No one let him leave.

When Privates First Class Crawley, Edwards, and Wurst simultaneously received the rank of lance corporal, the platoon formed two columns, a gauntlet that the newly promoted had to walk through, enduring the pummeling fists, thrown like baseballs into their arms and shoulders, with an occasional ricochet to the chin.

We hated like the Marine Corps wanted us to hate, but there was no one to receive our rage and brutality but each other.

Somehow, the Marine Corps had decided that our battalion deserved the General Harry Schmidt Award for being the best reserve unit in the Corps, according to *The Brown Side Out,* an in-house paper published for marines in Operation Desert Storm. "Who the hell is Schmidt?" someone asked.

"Does this mean they're gonna send us home?" someone else asked.

We knew that we were useless there. We found random ways

to pass the time with desperate attempts to extract novelty from an otherwise monotonous life. Lance Corporal Benson had the Book of Mormon in his hands and a pacifier in his mouth. Corporal Loop was building a sand castle. Private First Class Office was rapping into a tape recorder. Sergeant Sirker was teaching tai chi to Corporal Madden. I had a bag of marbles I'd found under an upside-down tank at the Highway of Death. Saenz, Banks, and I were in the middle of a game. The rest of the platoon was somewhere else doing something strange, random, novel, pointless, and momentarily entertaining. Sometimes they just wandered in bored stupor. The minutes crept by slowly.

Like characters on a stage, we surrendered ourselves to the foolish roles created for us. Frustrated hope, desperate longing, and discontent over misinformation all became worthless pursuits. We submitted to the puppet master. In a yellowed paperback novel with dog-eared corners, likely read a hundred times before me, I read a poem and copied it to my journal on the morning of April 6, 1991.

> Tiger got to hunt,
> Bird got to fly;
> Man got to sit and wonder, "Why, why, why?"
> Tiger got to sleep,
> Bird got to land;
> Man got to tell himself he understand.
> —Kurt Vonnegut Jr., *Cat's Cradle*

We listened to Armed Forces Radio most of the day, hearing occasional updates on the hostage situation in Iraq, where American civilians and a few downed pilots were still captive. Their immediate release was one of the terms of cease-fire agreed to between Iraq and General Schwarzkopf on March 3, 1991.

"What about us?" one marine added, after a broadcast. The

reservists had walked away from jobs, wives, families, school, and now months after the end of the war, we were still here as an unknown military presence.

"Okay, we did our job. What's the point now?" another marine in the platoon said.

The radio crackled, "Chickennnnnnnnn Mannnnnnn!!! He's everywhere! He's everywhere!" He's 107 on the dial. It was our daily dose of humor, a revision of *Good Morning Vietnam*. They dedicated another song to us, The Lost Battalion.

Days later, "Today, more hostages were released and flown directly to Germany, where family members anxiously..."

Wurst interrupted the radio, "Free the reservist hostages!" We laughed at this sentiment, refuted by no one.

On April 28, an article appeared in the *Washington Post* by William Booth, titled "Forgotten Troops Hold Hill 99." Other marines in the battalion had contacted five senators and representatives. The secret was out about the dysentery, heat exhaustion, and dead goats.

MAY 1991—THE LAST DAYS ON HILL 99

It's 11:00 a.m. and already 110 degrees.

The walls of the tent hover horizontally with a fierce wind that occasionally bursts with the force of a hurricane, ballooning the roof of the tent and lifting the supporting poles off the ground. There's no point in moving except to eat or shit. There's nothing left to say to each other, nothing to think about or look at.

"You're alive, so just shut the fuck up and deal with it," I say to myself.

I drink three to four gallons of water each day, and watch it drain out of my body like a sieve. Enormous white rings of salt radiate from under my arms, around my neck and waist, and behind my knees. Forty marines out of 650 in the battalion are in the sick-bay tent with IVs in their arms.

I weigh a ton when I walk. Mud puddles in the wrinkles of my neck and wrists. I wish I could burrow underground and endlessly sleep in cool, dark, quiet comfort. I chew a pork patty from an MRE, careful not to let my teeth touch so I don't grind sand. Across the hill I can see a free seat on the shitter box, which is the size of a large ice chest with two holes on top. There's only one marine there now. At least his ass will keep the flies from pouring out when I squat on the other side.

Neat piles of disarticulated goat skeletons, held loosely together with patches of black and brown fur, dot the path from here to there. There's a dead sheep and at least a chicken or two if you choose to go the scenic route around the fire pit. The platoon consensus is that Hill 99 is a slaughterhouse landfill.

No one knows we exist except the family of Bedouins and their four hundred goats and sheep that occupy a patch of flat lowland a klick away. I can still see a couple of Iraqi tanks and armored personnel carriers the TOW teams lit up months ago. I still see plumes of burning oil.

I hate this place.

I despise this putrid desert with unfathomable intensity. I harbor deep resentment, betrayed by every grain of sand in it.

11

ILLUSIONS OF HOME

It was the automatic instinct to live. He ceased swimming, but the moment he felt the water rising above his mouth the hands struck out sharply with a lifting movement. The will to live, was his thought, and the thought was accompanied by a sneer. Well, he had will, —ay, will strong enough that with one last exertion it could destroy itself and cease to be.
Jack London, Martin Eden

MAY 8, 1991—LAST DAY IN KUWAIT

It is midday. A distorted mirage of five-ton trucks extends for miles into Kuwait. The convoy, with lights on, snakes across the baked sand. "Oh shit. Banks! Come check this out!" I yell to him as he turns around and realizes, at that same moment, that our tour is over.

Through my eyes the image invades my brain, triggers emotional cues, and pulls muscles on my face I haven't used in a while. Banks looks like I feel. We give each other an embrace and a shake of the shoulders.

"Break down your shit and stand by," Staff Sergeant Paden yells to everyone.

"We're going home?"

"We're going home!" he yells again. The entire platoon is on their feet. Everyone stands around questioning reality, seemingly confused, looking at the oncoming convoy as if it's an alien ship landing before us. Paden repeats his command with an aggravated tone to a platoon in disbelief. The rumor mill has left such a long trail of disappointment that it has lost its power of persuasion.

It takes several minutes and confirmation from marines of other platoons to convince us that this is our ticket home. It takes less time for us to gather our gear. Everyone suspends his disbelief for the certainty that this time the approaching empty trucks are truly for us.

Fuck the tent. Fuck the T-rations of lasagna I was about to stick in a fire pit for lunch. To hell with everything that isn't issued. No, screw that too. My animosity toward everything here is certain. Let me leave this desert now and walk into my hometown on American soil. Let me smell the grass and lie in the shade of pecan trees. Let me walk down Veterans Boulevard to the St. Charles Parish line, go over the fence and into the swamp, and waste away the day catching water moccasins and red-eared sliders.

Let me pretend for a moment that none of this is real, that the world is a hopeful place and I have only dreamed this. My seabags are packed, and in a matter of seconds my mind will leave this world behind. Everyone scrambles to pack what's worth packing and burn or bury the rest. In the end, Hill 99 is abandoned, an instant ghost town. We're gone before anyone can change their minds.

We rumble through rural Kuwait, past the oil fires, through Khafji, in Saudi Arabia, where eleven marines died in the first battle of the Gulf War, seven by friendly fire. We find ourselves returning to Camp 15, stepping into new barracks with air-conditioned rooms, private hot showers, hot meals, and the greatest place to spend our few remaining American dollars—Baskin-Robbins Ice Cream.

Corporal Benson approaches me after one of the lectures by U.S. Customs agents about the ills of smuggling weapons and illegal equipment with our gear. Iraqi weapons and ordnance hidden in your pack will buy you a vacation in jail. We hear stories of grenades sent in the mail, the sender returning home in handcuffs.

"I've got this Iraqi night-vision scope I've got to get rid of," Benson says. It's a British-made, Iraqi-issue, night-vision scope, better than anything the Marine Corps has, secured in a padded, waterproof case. I can see the disappointment in his face. He's lugged it this far, but fears the promised jail time he'll earn if busted. We decide to bury the treasure in a four-foot hole outside the walls of the barracks and make a map with X to mark the spot.

We share Camp 15 with British marines, distinguished by the pattern of camouflage on their uniforms and their green berets. A British intelligence unit occupies barracks across from us.

"Hey, what do you guys make of this?" I say, handing a British marine a heavy piece of Iraqi communications equipment I brought back from Kuwait. I pretend to express pride in my find, as if I'm certain what it is and what it's worth to them, which encourages envy in their eyes. We barter for an hour, which finally ends in a trade for the desert uniform off his back, including his green beret and a few extra patches.

I've managed to mail one seabag home, the other two are dragged around Camp 15 to the customs station where we endure an onslaught of further lectures about smuggling weapons. The final inspection takes an hour. No one finds the two scorpions and camel spider tucked away in plastic canisters in my shaving kit.

I am still King Rat.

A winding trail of two hundred marines across the tarmac at Aljabal Naval Air Station waits to board a Continental jetliner, decorated with a giant yellow ribbon painted around the door. Amid a deafening roar, we touch down in Cherry Point, North Carolina, and for five days we deprogram before the final flight to New Orleans.

NOVEMBER 6, 2003—CONFLUENCE OF MISSISSIPPI AND
MISSOURI RIVERS—MILE 185 UM

The shriek of a cicada stands out in the audible landscape as something familiar, but foreign to my river experience thus far. Heard, not seen, they suck the veins of plants and live nearly all of their lives underground in thirteen- or seventeen-year cycles. In my youth, in the deep south of Louisiana, the deafening whine of cicadas filled the air at dusk, breaking thick summer silence, alerting children in the neighborhood that the day was over and dinner was likely on the table. Jenna smiles when I tap her on the shoulder. She already knows what I want to say. We're on our way home.

The Missouri River joins the Mississippi in a boiling reunion of water that hasn't mingled in eons. The fast-moving, silt-laden Missouri, colored like milk in coffee, slides by the slow, dark, greenish-brown giant of the Mississippi. Eddies and a bubbling froth form at their meeting. I match terrain features on the navigation charts with the world that unfolds before me. What the charts do not communicate is the nearly tripled rate of speed immediately beyond the confluence. In less than half of a mile, I must make my way to the east bank so that I can enter the 8.4-mile channel leading to the last lock and dam. It's a critical point of no return. If I miss the channel, I will crash over Chain of Rocks, the last and largest swath of rapids on the Mississippi, known to devour boats and lives.

The river pulls me faster than the sail ever could, first pulling me away from the safety of the channel entrance, as if it's resentful of my trespassing. With terrifying defiance, turbulent whirlpools repel my raft, then abruptly, thankfully, suck me into the still water of the channel entrance. The raft is motionless.

Jenna and I move slowly in the channel for hours into chilled darkness. It's hard rowing. There is no current, except for the moment when the lock miles ahead opens the gates for a barge. We feel the short lunge forward, then stillness again. We decide to camp on the bank, on the rocks, in the cold. Moisture on the tent from the previous night freezes before it's erected. We wear everything we own. My body demands energy. I consume cold cans of creamed corn and peaches. Cold follows hunger. I am convinced that a stomach filled with food is a stomach filled with fuel to heat my body, otherwise the cold pierces me with ease. A shivering Jenna looks on with disgust.

In the morning, we exit the last lock and enter a raging river covered with masses of floating suds churned by the Chain of Rocks rapids we bypassed. I am awestruck by the speed of the river, the color, the violent turbulence behind the footings of bridges, the increased competition with barges and ships, and the novelty of a river that is free-flowing for the next 1,100 miles.

I've got Jenna's marine radio in hand so that I can communicate with barge captains, if necessary, or just listen to them ramble on with each other.

"Yeah, I saw that bottle raft coming out of the lock earlier," I hear one captain say to another. "I don't think they're gonna make it down the river."

"I can hear you!" I respond into the radio, followed by silence.

In a few moments I catch a glimpse of the stainless steel St. Louis Gateway Arch, almost camouflaged against menacing silvery, swirling clouds. Just the top of the Arch is visible above the Eads Bridge, the world's first steel bridge, built by James Buchanan Eads in 1874. Industry flanks us on both banks, along with parked barges, towboats, floating casinos, and several bridges carrying the sounds of morning traffic.

We land on the paved riverbank under the Arch. James Powell, an educator from the St. Louis Science Center, steps out of a large truck and walks down to the water's edge.

"Hi, Marcus," James says. He will transport my raft to the Science Center for a weekend of show-and-tell. Thousands of visitors will choose to spend their weekend entertaining themselves with push-button exhibits, touchscreens, and IMAX presentations, spending money on gift-shop gadgets and substantially overpriced cafeteria food. If they make it to the second floor, they will see the *Bottle Rocket* dripping on a carpeted walkway overlooking a growling robotic *Tyrannosaurus rex*.

"Yes, it's made of bottles. Each one will keep approximately five pounds neutrally buoyant," I say to a couple of visitors. The Science Center has provided me with empty bottles, weights, and a tub of water to demonstrate this concept. I gladly work the weekend in exchange for a warm place to sleep and a good meal in downtown St. Louis on their dime. I answer the same questions here as I did in Dubuque.

"Where did you start?"

"Where are you going?"

"Is it cold?"

"Do you get lonely?"

"How long will it take you to get home?"

"Does that boat really float?"

"What do you eat?"

"Where do you use the bathroom?"

Jenna and I stay an extra day so that my raft may also visit a couple of public schools, first Kirkwood Elementary and then Blewett Middle School. In the heart of inner-city St. Louis, I walk with students through the school hall, past oversized portraits of African American leaders in science, medicine, and civil rights.

"I met that guy a few months ago," I say to one student, while pointing to a picture of Jesse Jackson.

"I thought he was dead," he responds. We walk through the door to the *Bottle Rocket,* sitting oddly on the playground blacktop, much like a fish out of water. The children are inquisitive about the boat design.

"How'd you put this together?"

"How much can each bottle float?"

"Can you stop it in the water if you have to?"

I enjoy the thoughtful questions. The school bell rings. The day ends. The raft returns to the river.

The comfort provided by our hosts at the Science Center is a sharp contrast to life on the river in Missouri in November. South of St. Louis it begins to rain, falling first as ice, and then melting upon contact with skin. The trickle down the back of my neck sends a chill through my bones that promises to steal warmth. Jenna is miserable.

The day warms to a crisp forty degrees. The gentle slope on the Illinois side is covered with leafless trees, broken by the occasional riverside home in a clearing. Winter is here. The risk of not finishing the trip begins to creep into my thoughts, as it did above the Twin Cities. If I get sick it's all over. A sense of urgency now taints every thought, driving my persistence to make as many miles as possible each day.

"Must make zee miles!" I yell to Jenna in my best German accent.

I notice a red flag flapping wildly in the middle of a clearing that extends to the water's edge, a state flag perhaps. It is difficult to recognize in the brisk wind, but a moment of still air allows for quick recognition of a blue X with white stars. It's a Confederate flag, which I haven't seen on the river until now.

Like the biogeographical boundary I crossed when cicadas sang their Southern chorus, I've now meandered across a sociocultural boundary. I make no excuses for the transgressions of my Southern culture, yet I embrace what is good. The evidence of the South makes itself known in subtle ways—a glimpse of a brown pelican, a cypress tree, or the tone of conversation from onlookers fishing on the bank.

"Whar ya'll headin' to?" an old fisherman asks, and later responds, "Noo Awlins?! Ya'll know it's cold, huh?"

Like a carrot on the end of a stick, each subtle confrontation with the unveiling South lures me further downstream. I think of the river delta and the rich biodiversity thriving in the swamp, marshland, pine forests, and coastal wetlands. My Southern culture conforms to this land like a blanket. The seasons of the Deep South are: hurricane season, hunting season, fishing season, and Mardi Gras. I pass the hours thinking of the spice of well-prepared seafood, family day at a crawfish boil, or the lazy days spent watching the ripples around a bobbing cork. Jenna and I agree to grab po-boy sandwiches at R&O's restaurant as soon as we get to New Orleans, and maybe a half-dozen beignets at Morning Call Café.

Entering familiar territory is comforting, as if I'm already home, but a thousand miles of cold, winding river still separate me from New Orleans.

MAY 17, 1991

From the New Orleans International Airport we were bussed to the Drill Center on the lakefront. As we rolled into the parking lot we were greeted by hundreds of friends and relatives waving flags and banners. This is the way it should have been twenty years ago. We have been the luckiest of war veterans. The war was short and patriotism was high. This would be a great way to end our country's long history of war, but I'm sure that the US will find another one. As for me, my military career is over.

Melida, my college sweetheart, stood next to my mother with a sign, WELCOME HOME. Melida and I had revived our relationship in the days before I deployed to the Persian Gulf. Nearly six months ago, my mother had stood by her side in tears as her only sons stood in formation in front of the Drill Center.

The marines were in formation again, waiting anxiously as Captain Dustin gave his last remarks, while the world of civilian life, parents, children, wives, future wives, and future ex-wives, waited patiently behind us. We stood straight, but with darting eyes and strained faces, unable to control ear-to-ear smiles.

"Company dismissed!" followed by a roar, then an excited

frenzy as friends and family rushed in. I held Melida tightly and embraced my fragile mother. I turned to say goodbye to the men of STA Platoon.

"You take it easy," I said to Saenz, our eyes watering. Somehow I knew I would never see him again.

"We made it home, didn't we," I said to Banks. We had talked about this moment a million times and now we both understood that it was time to go. I turned around and walked away.

"I would have given my life for any of you," I thought to myself. I walked back to my mother, Melida, and a dozen friends from home. I left a family in arms and returned to the arms of family.

Melida and I decided to get married, with the prodding of her mother, "What are you waiting for?" Melida is beautiful. I grew to love her through letters and longed for her immensely. The eight thousand dollars I earned while away quickly dwindled on a honeymoon through Italy. The last of my cash was spent on a used car, back home.

I resumed classes at the University of New Orleans as if nothing had happened, but with a strange, newfound determination to finish. Prior to the Gulf War I had consumed four years of a typical college life with only half a degree to show for it. Now I pursued academia with vigor. For three semesters I practically lived in the library, and had my own key to the geology lab, where I frequently studied till after midnight.

Academia became a fine distraction, self-medication to prevent introspection. It would simply be easier to think about everything while thinking of nothing. In eighteen months I became a high school science teacher.

What I knew about the Gulf War left only bitterness. What I knew was that no one fought for democracy. No one fought for human rights. And no one fought for the safety of America. What I knew was that my country had drawn a line in the sand and now had a firm foothold in it, with Saudi Arabia and Kuwait as allies and investors. Saddam Hussein, our bastard son, was still in power, and Kuwait, a country of only eight hundred thousand citizens, had been returned to its former monarchy. All this for the bargain price of only a few hundred soldiers and marines killed in action.

Months after returning to New Orleans, McKeehan and I, both civilians now, bought a dozen pizzas for STA Platoon one Sunday afternoon. McKeehan was back at work with the ATF, his hair getting longer by the day. We talked about how the whole thing had been pointless. We had had our war and came home heroes for doing little, at least when compared to our perception of other vets from other wars. Our Kuwait Liberation Medals were now in the first days of collecting dust.

We agreed that it was mildly nauseating to return to the Drill Center. We walked through the gates and into the shade of a group of oak trees, STA Platoon's favorite spot to kill time. Instead of desert fatigues, the platoon was wearing woodland green uniforms like the ones we wore before the war. McKeehan was greeted by the platoon with eager smiles. It was amazing to watch the men gravitate toward him as if welcoming home a lost brother.

A year and a half later, on February 28, 1993, McKeehan was one of four ATF agents killed in Waco, Texas, when his team was ambushed during a raid on illegally armed civilians with automatic weapons and explosives. He took one round to his chest, slicing through his bulletproof vest and piercing his heart. He survived the Gulf War, only to be gunned down by an American with a machine gun. Corporal Madden would play taps at his funeral.

SUMMER 1991—NEW ORLEANS

Sitting on the concrete steps that lead into the waters of Lake Pontchartrain, the same place I sat a year ago, on the night

Rusty, my college roommate, was killed, I feel the seeds of pessimism begin to sow themselves deeply. The image of the Grim Reaper appears in my mind in a vivid game around a square table. I sit across from him while he stabs at me.

"The world is fucked," I say to myself. It is our destiny to conquer and consume, explore and exploit, like every other living thing, like mold on bread. There is no choice. This illusion of free will is self-deception.

Every time I see road kill on the highway, I think of the dead men in the desert, rotting in burned vehicles: the man praying to the sky before falling back on his heels, stomach opened by shrapnel, or the man who lay prone on his back, arms across his chest, his moustache peeling off his face and waving in the breeze, or the sleeping dead man giving up his dog tags to the bastard King Rat.

I want those bloodied faces of dying soldiers to look away. I loathe myself for the thought of complaining. It is not for marines to do.

"I didn't kill anybody," I think.

"No one in my platoon got hurt."

"What the fuck am I whining about?"

"You're alive so just shut up and deal with it," I angrily mumble to myself, sitting alone on the bathroom floor with the lights off. Secretly, I want someone to explain it all with something more intelligent than sound bites and political rhetoric, but a deep sense of futility hangs there like wet heat on a sweltering August afternoon. Was I a sucker? Was I their mercenary for the bribe of a college scholarship—a little "Yes, Sir" bitch, doing what I was told? I thought I was a warrior. I was only a good marine, obedient to the government, expendable for national interests, answering to everyone but myself. I was not a warrior at all.

The despair that weighs heavy on my mind is the difference between the motivations that led my government to go to war and the justice that ought to be. Why were there American weapons in Iraq used against American soldiers? Why did we continue to sell weapons to Saddam Hussein even after he had gassed five thousand Kurdish people? If Saddam is so horrible, why did we leave him in power to kill tens of thousands of Shiites weeks after the end of the cease-fire? We just fucking stopped the war and let that genocide happen. We didn't go all the way. How could my government have been so successful at cloaking a drive for political influence in the Middle East with an insincere, self-righteous fight for democracy, justice, and self-defense? Was it all a lie? Why doesn't anyone ask why? We wrap ourselves in flags and yellow ribbons as instructed, screaming, "Freedom! Freedom!" as ordered. We take the subliminal pill of war tolerance as we enjoy our nightly opportunity to ride smart bombs to precise targets. Are we so gullible? Are we so lustful for entertainment?

I feel predictable, like a puppet making awkward movements across a stage. But the Gulf War gave me a glimpse behind the curtain. With patriotism betrayed, trust erodes to cynicism, hope yields to pessimism, and freedom dies. My deductions are putrid and hopeless. Apathy is justified. To what end do I exist? I have no purpose except that which is decided for me. I despise the war, the deception, the unchallenged notions of greed and power, and my participation in all of it. I don't even know if I can trust what I know.

The Grim Reaper sits across from me and kills me slowly. In darkness he seats me at the table with the Iraqi dead and dying, so that I can never forget their faces. They take turns sitting next to me just to remind me. It goes on for hours sometimes.

Melida and I live in an apartment near the hospital where she works. Eighteen months of marriage end after another night of fighting. Lying in bed, I say, "One of us ought to get out." She painfully agrees. I'm never there anyway. I'm not even there when I'm sitting next to her. The next day, I disappear in the few hours that she is away at work. We divorce.

I disappear from everyone.

I seek answers. I need to control my destiny. I bury myself in hidden corners of quiet libraries, far from everyone. Everywhere I look I find confirmation of my belief that freedom is a farce.

FEBRUARY 23, 1993

On Mardi Gras Day, I walk through the French Quarter among the revelry of sweaty, drunken tourists in decadent costumes, and carnival chaos with the wafting aroma of vomit and urine rising above the roar of music, laughter, and screaming. Suddenly, two marines in dress blues walk by, creating an awkward juxtaposition of culture and costume.

The marines walk through the crowd with a radius of empty space around them where no one seems to trespass. They walk in front of me slowly. They pass. Standing in their wake is Corporal Banks.

"Banks?" I say in disbelief.

We smile, shake hands, share a quick hug, and hastily update each other on the last two years. We walk through the French Quarter together. We walk around the corner to my new apartment on the corner of Orleans and Dauphine, behind the St. Louis Cathedral, one block north of Bourbon Street.

He's sorry that I'm getting divorced. I'm happy that he's married and has a child on the way. I'm happy that he's beginning his own business. It's really good to see him. For an hour we walk together until he has to go away to meet his wife on Canal Street. We promise to get in touch again.

I want to see the other guys from my platoon. I wonder where they are and how they feel about the Gulf War, but I have other distractions that lead me away from reminiscing and send me plowing through the sweaty crowds clogging Bourbon Street. I'm on my way to Pat O'Brien's bar, to see my favorite waitress, Jenna.

～

"Will you stay with me?" reads the sign pinned to the inside of my jacket, which I flash to Jenna, who is holding a tray of Hurricanes. We steal away to my tiny apartment a few blocks away. Beyond the wrought-iron fence, into the courtyard, around the giant magnolia tree, to the third floor, we enter my one-room hideaway with a rickety wooden balcony overlooking the slate-tiled roofs of the French Quarter. Large white blossoms from the magnolia tree explode into the room.

On Sunday mornings we walk through quiet streets to get fresh bread at La Madeleine, then to the Farmers Market by the river to pick the sweetest basket of ripe strawberries that smell like sugar. I sit basking in the delight of such sweetness overflowing, bursting, a euphoria for the senses. The fruit drips, warm drops sliding over soft flesh. Down my cheeks and neck it pours, like sweat on a cool glass of water. It's a fine romance.

She enters my soul and lifts me out of all this despair. She illuminates the world where I see only darkness.

Jenna is an actress/waitress determined to make it in Los Angeles. In two years we find ourselves arriving in Pasadena, California, with our used furniture stuffed in the back of a moving truck. I find work in the Museum of Natural History, and she finds her calling as a journalist. I return to school part-time, hoping to finish my last degree in five years or less.

But the darkness follows. I don't want to be here. I don't want to be anywhere. To what end do I exist? Everything good and evil is a human invention, like freedom. Purpose and love are illusions. Do we choose whom we love? We paint love as a splendid expression of our deepest purpose, unifying two people into a powerful whole, but this idealism is corrupt with sex, control, dependence, security, and money.

I despise my callous conclusions and fall into pessimism.

I love other women selfishly.

SPRING 1999—LOS ANGELES

I was predictable. I was my nation's puppet with a gun. I hate and love like I eat and sleep. I live a life that feels like slow death.

I escape from Jenna in the early hours after midnight, walking to the bus stop on Sunset Boulevard at Micheltorena Street or Whitley Avenue. No one rides the bus at those hours except for janitors, security guards, prostitutes, and the occasional homeless person that the bus driver doesn't bother to hassle. I ride to the Pacific Coast and sit next to the shore. I sit with my despair that physically feels as if my chest is caving in, over and over again. Sometimes I wade into the cold surf. Sometimes I sleep.

One night, a piece of glass buried in the sand sliced through my foot. The red sand stuck between my toes. The pain curiously felt like life struggling to save itself. It didn't feel like suffering. I tried not to let it hurt. In fact, I scoffed at it. I only felt scorn for my preprogrammed desire for self-preservation. It was an assault against free will. I cringed at my difficulty in summoning the ability to control this most primitive response to pain. I wanted to kill it. In choosing death over life, I would have life over death! But the degree to which I wished to end this life was equal to my cowardice about acting toward that end.

I came and went from Jenna over and over again, each time spiraling deeper into darkness. Then I was gone. I left Jenna crying on the steps of the home we no longer shared. I had destroyed whatever she had desperately held together for five years. I dragged her to hell with me and then walked away.

I left to wander.

12

WISDOM BEFORE ME

O my brothers, so far there have been only illusions about stars
and the future, not knowledge: and therefore there have been
only illusions so far, not knowledge, about good and evil.
Friedrich Nietzsche, Thus Spake Zarathustra

A problem leads to a question and motivates the pursuit of an
answer. I traveled in Central and South America, Africa, and
Southeast Asia, I opened my eyes, and I listened.

JUNE 8, 2000—VIETNAM

"Xe-om?" the Vietnamese teen on the Honda motorcycle yells,
daring me to hop on. It literally means "hugging" but might as
well mean "hold on for your life!" I've just arrived in Ho Chi
Minh City, formerly Saigon, at 11:00 p.m., with nowhere to go
and hundreds of young men barking from behind an airport
fence.

"Take me to a cheap motel," I yell above the roar.

It's a typical budget hotel in a third-world country, where
five bucks gets you first-class service in primitive accommodations, and if you stay long enough you'll likely get to know the
manager's family, who live in squalor behind a curtain and never
want to leave.

A rooster startles me out of jetlag delirium. The same teen on the motorcycle is waiting for me. I don't think he ever left.

"*Xe-om?*" he says again.

"Yeah, sure. How about we go to the market," I say.

For a buck you can hop on the back of a motorcycle—they outnumber cars 100:1—and go anywhere. The other alternative, besides walking, which is equally risky, is to hire a cyclo. The three-wheeled cyclo pedals tourists around the city for a dollar an hour, in a large bucket seat mounted a foot off the ground in front of the bike. The cyclos, bicycles, and motorcycles blend together to create a fast-paced menagerie of wheels and horns swirling in a frenzy on crowded streets with no stop signs. Few of the major intersections have traffic lights. It's analogous to intersecting columns of ants, where individuals or small groups swarm en masse and push their way across.

In the Ben Thanh Market hundreds of vendors selling cheap electronics blend with farmers selling all things edible. Live eels, chickens, ducks, and fish are dismembered before your eyes to guarantee freshness.

"What is there about my appearance that makes you think I would want to buy a raw pig's ear?" I say to the old lady squatting with a machete in one hand and waving the ear in the other. To get their attention, the vendors taunt foreigners with "Hay-low. Way-U-from?" Sometimes I think they say it just to get a reaction, like whistling to a dog. After eating a bowl of *pho* (noodle) soup and watching a chicken meet its maker, I visit the Museum of War Crimes.

Captured American armor surrounds the small two-story building, which chronicles a century of struggle from Chinese invasions, French imperialism, Japanese occupation, and French rule again, followed by a twenty-five-year American war. The story of human suffering hangs heavy on the shoulders of America, the subjective history of Vietnamese independence written clearly by the victors.

A collage of photographs adorns the walls in the room dedicated to atrocities performed by Americans. One photograph is of a Vietcong soldier being dragged behind an American armored personnel carrier. The photo was taken by Kyoichi Sawada of United Press International, in the Tan Binh province, Vietnam, in 1966. The caption next to the photograph reads, "Arrested, a man is pulled by an armored-car to death."

The photograph appears later in the museum, in a traveling exhibition titled Requiem, The Vietnam Collection: By the Photographers Who Died in Vietnam. The international exhibition will only be here for a few weeks longer. In this context, the caption under the same photo reads, "The body of a Vietcong soldier is dragged behind an armored vehicle at Tan Binh en route to a burial site after fierce fighting."

I wander through the town, absorbing information to fill gaps in the hundreds of stories I've heard from the old Vietnam veterans I knew in the Marine Corps and in my old neighborhood. On Pham Ngu Lao Street I wander by decrepit outdoor cafes with old white men gorging on what looks like hamburgers and fries. I reject offers to buy heroin and prostitutes. By 8:00 p.m. I board an overnight train for Nha Trang.

I expected to be despised, rejected, and chastised for being an American in Vietnam, but in less than forty-eight hours I find myself singing Paul McCartney's "Yesterday" and something by the Carpenters in Vietnamese at a karaoke bar. I am the tallest human being in the discotheque, among a sea of straight, black hair, belonging to thin bodies jumping around to a tune by Madonna.

Nha Trang sits on the east coast of southern Vietnam, a former R&R post for American officers. Hoang, stricken with polio since the early 1970s, sits in the doorway of the hotel. With crutches, he drags his legs behind him to the restaurant across the road. We unravel rice and meat wrapped in banana leaves.

He is a treasure of oral history and gladly describes the houses where the GIs lived, and the prostitutes that paraded through the American district.

"Life was bad with the communists," Hoang explains. Rice and fuel was rationed. Everyone tried to escape. He sold his mother's necklace for a chance to hide in the hull of a fishing ship bound for California, but instead he found himself in prison for three months. Today, Hoang gathers tourists for Mama Hahn.

"Now the Americans are coming back," he says joyfully. Mama Hahn operates a fleet of party boats, each with a floating bar for tourists, Australians mostly, who flock here by the thousands. The sunburned Westerners float in life preservers, while Hahn's minions serve unlimited helpings of cheap wine and fat joints. "Life is better now," Hoang adds. "We make parties again."

Highway 1 takes me north to the former demilitarized zone (DMZ) at the seventeenth parallel. Water buffalo march across flooded fields, with people in straw hats bent over tending their crops, perhaps as they did half a century ago, before 58,196 Americans and over two million Vietnamese nourished the soil with their blood. War seldom appears to improve the lives of those people tied to the land.

The citadel in Hué City is pockmarked from heavy fighting between NVA and U.S. Marines three decades ago. In my pocket I've got a couple of old photographs of marines lying dead in the street in front of the nineteenth-century, red brick citadel. A three-wheeled cyclo spins me around the city. Cicadas whine in the trees as they do in New Orleans.

The air is warm and heavy. My tee-shirt sticks to my back. Hundreds of people quietly stroll at dusk. A vendor sells plastic bags filled with chilled coconut water. In the middle of the street, I stand alone trying to match a photograph of a dead marine to the surroundings before me. I place my hand on the ground in the place where the man died. I think about his war and what brought him here. On the day I was born, August 8, 1967, eighteen Americans died in the war in Vietnam:

James Donald Davenport, 23, Army
Earl Kent Eichbauer, 25, Army
Anthony L. Franks, 18, Marine Corps
John Richard Freiling Jr., 19, Army
Bobby Ray Gardner, 21, Army
Charles A. Jones, 18, Army
Robert Ivan Klootwyk, 18, Army
Robert Thomas Lohman, 19, Army
Sotorios Milto Margaritis, 20, Marine Corps
John Lee Moreland, 20, Marine Corps
Willie Michael Rhodes, 18, Army
Leonard Wade Roberson, 20, Marine Corps
Herbert Cleveland Samples, 19, Army
Robert James Scott, 27, Army
Clarence E. Tackett, 21, Army
John Brady Walters, 20, Navy
James Joseph Weest, 20, Marine Corps
James B Wiltse Jr., 18, Army

What is the lasting effect of their war? Do memories fade and disappear with distance and time, like ripples that form from a pebble tossed into a pond? Did the death of common Americans mean anything to common Vietnamese?

In front of the citadel sit the rusted remains of American tanks and howitzers, with children scrambling over faded white stars. I walk across the barrel of a defunct American tank, as I walked across the barrel of a defunct Iraqi tank a decade ago.

Five kids follow behind me and straddle the barrel. I jump down and lift the barrel like a seesaw. They laugh hysterically, unaware of the history of their playground, their cultural memory separated from it by two generations.

The elderly on park benches smile. Even the coconut water vendor laughs. All animosity seems washed away with mutual amnesty, as if nothing had ever transpired.

"Hold Khe Sanh at all costs!" President Johnson demanded of the marines surrounded by the Vietcong in months of nonstop shelling leading up to the Tet offensive, in late January 1968. One hundred thousand tons of explosives were dropped from B-52 bombers or shot from offshore battleships onto a five-square-mile area around the base. Napalm and defoliants, like Agent Orange, cleared what forest remained. George C. Herring, author of *America's Longest War: 1950–1975,* suggests that more explosives were used in Vietnam than in all theaters of war in WWII.

Four hours west of Highway 1, I step off the bus into red mud at Khe Sanh. The red soil that made up the landing strip is now a winding path leading to a small village. A one-room brick museum stands in the center of a field flanked by the rusted shell of an abandoned tank and what looks like an aircraft engine. Glass cabinets line the walls of the museum, their contents commemorating the NVA victory over the Americans. A pile of dysfunctional American weapons sits in the middle of the room. I pick up an M16A1 rifle, missing the bolt, and try to imagine the marine or soldier who lost it. Was he one of the 248 who died here during the siege?

"Hay-low. Way-U-from?" the young boy says from outside the doorway. He holds a wooden tray covered with artifacts he's found in this battlefield. Other children rush over with their treasures spread on dinner plates and plastic bucket lids. I pick through rusted NVA insignia, American-made and Russian-made rifle shell casings, a corroded Marine Corps emblem, and American dog tags. The dog tags are fakes, with first names only and five-digit Social Security numbers. I buy the Marine Corps emblem for fifty cents.

The land surrounding Khe Sanh is devastated. The cloud forest that covered the hills fifty years ago has been reduced to low shrubs and grasses. White phosphorus, leaking from abandoned ordnance, smolders on warm days. In an effort to thwart topsoil erosion, enormous groves of eucalyptus have been planted in the valleys.

The road back to Highway 1 winds past the Rockpile, an old mountaintop observation post overlooking the DMZ. I stop in Quang Tri to see a pockmarked church, the only building left standing in a large village that evaporated after fierce fighting and bombing. I climb through the Vinh Moc tunnel complex, where seventeen babies were born when the tiny village went underground for four years.

On the way to Da Nang, Vinh, and Hanoi, the land is littered with swimming-pool-sized bomb craters. Fields of corn grow around them, while whole trees grow out from within. It's easy to conclude that the damage to the land will last longer than the memory of the dead and the life span of the survivors.

There is an endless sea of people along the road to Hanoi, stooped over in rice paddies, riding heavy Chinese bicycles, or congregating around *pho* soup stalls. We cross the Red River that surrounds Hanoi, bathes its people, washes their clothes, and carries the waste of 35 million citizens and the poisons of a burgeoning economy out to sea. After another two hours of buses, taxis, and a *xe-om* ride, I arrive at the doorstep of a cozy, warm, dry hotel located within a short mile of the old "Hanoi Hilton," a prison most recently used to house U.S. servicemen shot down over North Vietnam a quarter-century ago.

The prison, now a museum, weaves a story of French occupation and persecution of political prisoners. A guillotine stands at the end of death row. Mannequins sit in shackles to give the visitor a sense of the despair that loomed about. Only half of the prison remains, including the main entrance, death row, interrogation rooms, and solitary confinement. The other half was razed to make room, ironically, for a five-star hotel.

In the center of the city, on the edge of the Hoan Kiem Lake, whose name means "Returned Sword," dozens of citizens perform tai chi as their early morning ritual. Restaurants abound and vendors sell their wares on busy, narrow streets. The architecture and city plan reflect decades of French colonial occupation. The evening is alive with karaoke bars. Government billboards read, "Vietnam: Destination for the New Millennium." In many respects Hanoi is a jewel waiting for an opportunity to shine on the rest of the world.

"Hay-low?" a little voice says. "You want a postcard?" he asks. He is persistent until I buy one. "You want a book?" he asks. He is persistent until I buy one. "You want a map?" he asks.

"No," I say. "That's enough." For twenty minutes the thin boy dressed in dirty clothes and homemade sandals trails behind me, persistently begging, dodging a barrage of neglect. "No. No. No. Leave me alone."

"Go away!" I say loudly, which stops him in his tracks. We stare at each other for an uncomfortably long time, long enough for me to change thoughts. Maybe he harasses everyone until they buy something, maybe he wants me to give him money, or perhaps he's just hungry.

"Do you want to get something to eat?" I ask. He looks surprised.

His name is Chau. His father is dead. His mother ran off with a Chinese man. He left his little brother behind in a village west of here when his grandfather sent him to make money in Hanoi instead of working the field. He is one of two hundred children who shine shoes or sell postcards in exchange for a piece of floor to sleep on in an empty warehouse. He was a shoeshine boy first, but he's moving up in his world until he learns English well enough to get a job in a restaurant.

He devours three large plates of sautéed pork with green beans, rice, and chicken, and some red meat with bamboo shoots. We walk through Hanoi at night, talking about his optimism for his future, his brother, and his country. He only wants to survive, and he will fight for the freedom to plant rice in his family plot again, and he will collaborate with whichever government leaves him alone to do it.

Before I leave for my motel, I grab Chau's hand and put ten dollars in it. He starts to sob. I don't know how long it takes him to save that much, after buying his maps and postcards, feeding himself, and paying off his landlord. I feel uncomfortable, embarrassed that my student budget can buy affluence in another country. I reach into my backpack and hand him a blank postcard addressed to me with a new stamp already affixed to it.

"When you get settled somewhere, write to me," I say to him.

"I learn English. I write," Chau says.

Whatever threat Vietnam ever posed to the world is lost in history. Helicopters whirled above the jungle canopy, farms were reduced to craters, and defoliants killed whatever forest napalm didn't burn, while millions of people still planted crops, tended livestock, and harvested their fields.

They operated under the same program to survive, regardless of the environment. Through war, genocide, extreme poverty, and famine, above all else, regardless of freedom, they will bear anything to survive. The battle cry of freedom has long been silenced, replaced by the wailing masses struggling to make it for the day, trudging blindly across the face of a tiny planet on the verge of overconsumption.

NOVEMBER 15, 2003—CAPE GIRARDEAU, MISSOURI—MILE 51.5 UM

"Just pay attention!" I yell.

"Shut up and focus!"

"...or get off my boat!"

A barge is a steel box measuring 35 feet wide and 195 feet

long, with a carrying capacity of 1,500 tons of coal, corn, pig iron, oil, scrap cars, logs, wheat, and whatever else the world buys from Middle America. Barges are lashed together with two-inch-diameter cables that stretch and moan as the river attempts to twist them apart, and sometimes, to the fear of deckhands, they snap, hurling themselves like a horizontal guillotine against unsuspecting bodies.

Traveling upstream in the middle of the river, bearing down on our raft, is a massive aggregation of thirty barges in a single tow. Whitecaps form beneath the bow, which is four barges across. It's the largest tow I've seen yet. The river is swift, requiring that I negotiate my position at least a quarter mile in advance.

Knowledge, not faith, must guide the future.

There is another barge behind the behemoth ahead, and another one at our stern. I make a dash for the riverbank beneath the Cape Girardeau bridge. Above the roar of the river, and the roar of Jenna, I gulp a healthy dose of terror.

We argue about past transgressions. We argue about whether I'm still a whore. We argue about money and about how my withholding affection destroyed our relationship. We argue about my insufficient acknowledgment of her investment to come on this trip, and my lack of appreciation for her commitment. I argue to save my soul from her damnation, and our souls from being consumed by the river.

"I am the captain. Whatever I say in situations like that is not negotiable. I am in charge. If you don't like it, get off my boat!" I yell.

We argue about details excavated from the past, based on obscure facts of fiction that cannot be proven or denied. We barter information and bury the truth in a mound of triviality that blurs the real objectives at hand. I wanted control and independence, and Jenna wanted accountability and connection.

I run ashore with the waves of a towboat flying portside the raft, launching us on the rocky bank strewn with broken side-walks and driveways with rusted prongs of rebar jutting out of them. I tie the raft to a half-buried railroad tie. She unloads everything, including her toilet seat and the snack cakes from the milk crate behind my seat.

"You evil bastard!" she says with a snarl above her tears. She's certain that it's over. It begins to drizzle. I follow her over the levee and across a church lawn to a pay phone, where she sits and cries next to a pile of everything she owns in Missouri.

"I'm sorry. Please come back on the boat," I beg. "Look, I can't leave you here ... C'mon, I know you want to finish this trip ... Okay, I will not be an asshole anymore," I plead with her to come back. "You are important to the success of this project."

The important truth is that Jenna has come on this trip to support me, but I am blind to this. I am so focused on this adventure that I begin to believe my own story. I create a new world based on facts I exaggerate and inconvenient ones I neglect. But quickly I discover there's more wisdom beneath the surface of Jenna and the river than I ever knew.

It takes two hours of coaxing for Jenna to return to the raft. We make six miles to the next sandbar, where we fall asleep holding hands.

13

WAVES OF DECEPTION

> Statesmen will invent cheap lies, putting blame upon the nation
> that is attacked, and every man will be glad of those conscience-
> soothing falsities, and will diligently study them, and refuse to
> examine any refutations of them, and thus he will by and by
> convince himself that the war is just, and will thank God for the
> better sleep he enjoys after this process of grotesque self-deception.
> *Mark Twain, "The Chronicle of Young Satan"*

NOVEMBER 16, 2003—CAIRO, ILLINOIS—MILE 0.8 UM

Cairo, Illinois, is around the corner, where the Ohio River and
Mississippi River converge, but strangely, the Mississippi has
slowed to a crawl for the last ten miles before Fort Defiance
State Park, the southernmost tip of Illinois. Night falls as Jenna
and I struggle around the confluence. I can see the illuminated
mile marker sign on the point. It reads, "0.8." The Upper Mississippi ends here.

A reverse current along the bank of the Ohio River jets us a
hundred yards upriver, where my map indicates there's a boat
landing, but a towboat and fleet of small wooden boats block
the way.

"Excuse me. Where's the boat ramp?" I yell to the silhouette
of a large man standing on the upper deck. Captain Bill of the
J. S. Lewis, a vintage 1930s towboat, is a sturdy man who could
convincingly tell stories of wrestling bears in the wild North.

"You can't park here on account of this here barge blocking the way," he replies.

Jenna and I remain stationary for a few minutes, tired and wet. I'm cursing under my breath, "Goddamn bullshit. What the hell do I do now?" Suddenly, a thin man steps on the lower deck nearest to our bobbing raft. He's dressed in the attire of a nineteenth-century frontier explorer, including knee-high boots, heavy cotton shirt, and pants with a buttoned back seat, much like a diaper.

"Hello. I'm Captain Meriwether Lewis. Welcome aboard." Meriwether Lewis, the famed partner of William Clark, is leading his team of historical reenactors on a three-and-a-half-month voyage from Pittsburgh, Pennsylvania, down the Ohio River, and up the Mississippi to the Missouri River confluence. They are recreating the expedition of Lewis and Clark across the West that began exactly two centuries ago. They travel in replicas of the keelboat and pirogues used in the original expedition.

I fling a rope to Captain Lewis. We tie the raft to the towboat under the suspicious eyes of Captain Bill, looking down from the deck above.

"You're here on a good night. We're celebrating our arrival to the confluence," Captain Lewis says. He helps Jenna and me drag our bags onto the giant keelboat. "You guys can sleep on our boat if you like." I smile from ear to ear. There is no way I'm passing up an opportunity like this. "Well, come on in. We're all about to have dinner," Captain Lewis says, adding, "I'll introduce you around."

Jenna and I climb aboard the *J. S. Lewis* and up the stairs to the galley, where a dozen frontiersmen cheer and sing to the strumming and thumping of the Booneslick Strings. They sing old English sailor songs and belt out guttural laughs like haggard pirates. In quiet corners they talk about their handmade clothes and the latest vintage rifle they bought from some obscure catalog.

The crew of the *J. S. Lewis,* in jeans and tee-shirts, mingle among the frontiersmen, completely numb to the novelty that Jenna and I are being inundated with. Captain Lewis grabs a fife and joins the band.

Smitty, the short and skinny, toothless, seventy-one-year-old engineer in overalls, takes Jenna's hand for a two-step across the deck. He's practically lost all hearing after forty-one years in the engine rooms of riverboats. He spins her around while I laugh till my ribs ache.

Peyton (Bud) Clark, acting as the other half of Lewis and Clark, is actually a descendent of William Clark. Under a wide-brimmed black hat, he sports large wire-rim glasses and thick gray sideburns. He sits next to me with a full dinner plate. "Venison again?" he yells jokingly above the raucous bunch still singing and dancing.

I chuckle, thinking that a little more than an hour ago, I was wet, miserable, riding the bank of the Ohio River in darkness, longing for the simple comfort of my damp sleeping bag.

Captain Lewis pulls me aside. "Can we go outside for a moment? I've got to talk with you."

Captain Lewis, also known as Scott Mandrell to friends and family, is a textbook American ideal, a staff sergeant in the National Guard and Gulf War veteran, who met his wife while serving as an aide to Ronald Reagan and George Bush Sr. He speaks fluent French, is a proud father, teaches middle school in Alton, Illinois, enjoys socializing with army generals, and jokingly considers himself the better-looking of his historic duo.

"There's some dissention in the ranks about you sleeping on our keelboat. Some of the men don't think we should allow strangers on board like that. You know, since you guys are not members of the historical society. You understand, right?" Scott explains.

"Hey, you're the captain. It's your decision," I respond. I've strangely got that alpha-male, bristling-hair-on-the-back-of-my-neck kind of feeling.

Thankfully, Captain Bill offers to let Jenna and me stay on the *J. S. Lewis*. Scott helps move our bags off the keelboat and into the towboat. It's a far better deal after all, since the bunks have mattresses, there's a warm shower down the hall, and by midnight a severe storm will soak the inside benches of the keelboat, where we had planned to sleep.

Scott and I return to the party, but take refuge in the kitchen, where he dabbles a shot of fine scotch into two Styrofoam cups. He begins a long-winded lecture about the history of the enormous dragon painted on the bluff above the river in Alton, Illinois.

"Could you see it from the river?" he asks. The dragonlike creature, called the Piasa Bird, looks like an amalgamation of an eagle, a deer, and a lion. It was painted on the bluff by Native Americans of the Mississippi River Valley long before modern tribes arrived. An early French explorer, Louis Joliet, made the first written record of the image in the 1670s. In the late 1800s it was destroyed to make room for a road, then redrawn on the bluff after public outcry.

"Sure, I saw it." I enjoy the scotch.

We talk about the bicentennial commemoration of the Lewis and Clark expedition and its importance to American history, and obvious importance to Scott.

"We're making our own history," he says assuredly, an unnecessary justification.

The last gulp of liquor warms my chest. We gather ourselves and join the crew celebrating in the galley for the last few moments of the night, one last dance between Jenna and Smitty, another song from Scott, and a tearful toast from Captain Bill to the men of the Discovery Expedition.

Jenna takes the bottom bunk. It rains like mad, as if the river has turned upside down. We sleep late into the morning, unwilling to let go of our warm situation. We emerge when the downpour ceases.

The Ohio River is a raging torrent. Hundreds of logs swirl and disappear in spinning pools that burst from the deluge. Many weeks of heavy rains in the Northeast have trickled down streets and streams, into rivers and sewers, all draining and converging on this point, joining the other half of the great Mississippi watershed. Billions of gallons race by in seconds. I learn that the reason for the deceleration of the Mississippi River before the confluence was the damming effect of higher water on the Ohio River.

The reenactors are tending to their camp on the point of the confluence, which was hidden from Jenna and me last night when we turned the bend and crept up the Ohio River in darkness. White canvas tents encircle a campfire ablaze under a cauldron of beans. Two men sit joyfully admiring a vintage rifle with inlaid brass designs on the stock. "These men really take this reenacting stuff seriously," I think. Seaman, the camp dog, a large black Newfoundland, also a replica of the canine companion from the original 1803 expedition, fetches a stick I toss into the confluence.

Captain Bill gives Jenna and me a tour of the bridge and briefly explains the function of the dozen polished brass knobs and levers. He offers us another night of comfort on his towboat. Outside, there is a class of high school students visiting the camp. I notice a large white canopy and a couple of humvees a hundred yards away. The National Guard has set up a recruiting booth.

Night comes quickly, but this evening is more subdued, more businesslike. Everyone is tending to tomorrow's departure of the Discovery Expedition, as they continue their journey around the confluence and up the Mississippi River.

Charles Arbogast, a photographer from the Associated Press, arrives to interview Scott and instruct him on how he wants the boat positioned in the river tomorrow for the perfect photo. He begins his interview, but first he jokingly yells above the crowd of men gathered in the galley, "Remember, this is all on the record!" In other words, anything said in the room is fair game to be quoted and printed.

Scott seems a bit uncomfortable with the interview. Charles says, "I want your response to sound like this..." then he elaborates on how Scott should speak, awkwardly feeding him the story he wants to write.

When the interview ends, Charles announces, "I'm gonna show my slides of Afghanistan in a little while." He was on assignment in Afghanistan last year when a wedding party was mistakenly bombed, killing twenty-five people. He was the first journalist on the scene with a camera.

Scott and I resume our conversation from the previous night about the particulars of the historic expedition he is emulating. We talk about the rivers we respectively know well, and when the conversation turns back to history, I ask a question I rehearsed earlier in the day.

"Thomas Jefferson's belief in Manifest Destiny was the driving force supporting the Lewis and Clark expedition. Do you think the United States has a Manifest Destiny today?" I say my words with calm, clear, and precise punctuations, so that no mistake can be made as to the direction I hope to point the conversation.

"Can someone turn out the lights?" Charles yells across the room. There are a dozen reenactors huddled behind him, waiting for the slide show to begin. Our conversation ends abruptly. We join the huddle gazing at the computer screen, with a closeup shot of a young Afghani boy with empty eyes.

Before the lights go dim, Scott leans close to answer my question. With guarded confidence he slowly whispers, "Well... yes."

July 1, 2002, was a great day for Malik, in Kakrak, Afghanistan, where a festive gathering of relatives and future in-laws was celebrating his wedding and a hopeful future. AC-130 gunships trained in on the mistaken target, unaware of their festive intentions, and strafed them with explosive rounds from their cannons, killing Malik's father and two dozen others.

"That's an ear lying in the garden," Charles says, referring to a square patch of human scalp, the size of a waffle, with blood-soaked hair matted with bits of grass and sand, and a complete earlobe in the center.

There are pictures of neat rows of shoes, the ones that people from the wedding party took off in the foyer and never returned to. There are photos of the courtyard where explosions shredded bodies, and photos of a backyard cemetery filled with the newly dead family members.

In one photo, Malik is stooped over a pile of stones. "He's got the red shirt and black turban, traditional for the Taliban," Charles explains. "He's mourning one of his relatives. But what's going on here is that he's buried so many of them in the last few days, that he's not sure who's in that grave." Charles speaks with the callous disconnection of a combat photographer. "It took him a while to figure out where his dad was."

In the next photo, Malik's face is in his hands as he kneels before the grave he has remembered to be his father's. "When his face went into his hands I zoomed in and nailed the shot!" Charles exclaims proudly.

The last slide is of the same young Afghani boy in the first slide, with the empty eyes conveying innocence betrayed. Charles explains the rampant prostitution of children that led this boy to look into his camera lens with fear and disillusionment, perhaps thinking Charles might intend more assault.

"I'd like to adopt him and show him Christianity," Charles says, while closing his laptop to end the show.

"Did he really just say that?" I think. I can't tell if the crowd is shaking their heads in empathy for the suffering child, for the massacre of Malik's family, or in response to Charles's statement of religious superiority.

"Perhaps we should consider Islam to be a haven for pedophiles," I sarcastically mumble.

The crowd quickly dwindles. I wander to my top bunk on the *J. S. Lewis*. Jenna is fast asleep below. I lie awake for hours thinking of the river, the Iraq War, my conversation with Captain Meriwether Lewis, the future of my country, and the selfish manipulation of truth.

JANUARY 21, 2003—TWO MONTHS BEFORE THE IRAQ WAR

"I don't know what depleted uranium is?" was my response to a question from a man in the back row of the auditorium. His question was preceded by a sympathetic monologue about the radioactive waste left behind when American tanks kill Iraqi tanks.

"Hey, I climbed all over those tanks," I thought.

I was sharing a panel with three other veterans, from WWII, Korea, and Vietnam, to talk about our experiences in war. The Green Party in Orange County, California, had found my name in an online petition I'd signed a few weeks earlier, along with a thousand other veterans, to voice opposition to the government's rush to war against Iraq.

"Can you come down and tell us about the Gulf War?" they asked over the phone. I brought a few war souvenirs. I showed slides. I told stories, and I listened to their stories with openminded skepticism.

I didn't know anything about depleted uranium, School of the Americas, or Project for a New American Century. I didn't know that September 11, 2001, was preceded by September 16, 1920, the first terrorist attack on New York's financial center, when a horse-drawn carriage detonated in front of Morgan Bank, killing thirty Americans and injuring hundreds more caught in a war against greed. I didn't know that the British were the first to use poison gas to kill Kurdish people in the 1920s, when the Kurds refused to accept the national boundaries drawn in the sand for them. I didn't know that Rumsfeld and Saddam were old chums negotiating business deals. Harry S. Truman once said, "The only thing new is the history that you don't know," and I didn't know a damn thing.

Depleted uranium is the radioactive waste left over from the uranium enrichment process. It's heavier than lead, perfect for warheads. It is expensive to dispose of, so it's given away cheaply to the defense industry to use in armor plating, tank rounds, and other munitions. The Veterans Administration considers it to be a possible contributor to Gulf War syndrome. The United Nations labels depleted uranium a weapon of mass destruction (WMD).

In the beginning of 2003, the U.S. was focused deceptively on Iraqi weapons of mass destruction, as if we were immune to scrutiny for holding bills of sale for WMDs sold to totalitarian regimes, as if billions of small arms sold around the world are somehow incapable of causing mass destruction.

All weapons are destructive of the masses. The only variable is time. Two atomic bombs dropped on Hiroshima and Nagasaki on August 6 and 9, 1945, killed over a hundred thousand people instantly and injured just as many. The M16 and AK-47 rifles killed fifty-eight thousand Americans and more than two million Vietnamese in twenty-five years of conflict in Southeast Asia. Agent Orange and Gulf War syndrome continue to kill veterans, like a slow-motion nuclear explosion. The only difference is time.

What makes some weapons more ruthless than others is the distance and disconnect from the act of killing. Weapons of mass destruction circumvent the incremental regret that comes with killing your enemy one by one. Robert E. Lee at Fredericksburg said, "It is well that war is so terrible. We should grow too fond of it." The sights, sounds, and smells endured by the foot soldier are replaced by flashes on computer screens, representing the rockets lobbed thousands of miles, reducing war to the push of a button instead of the pull of a trigger.

When Dwight D. Eisenhower gave his farewell address to the

nation on January 17, 1961, he warned the nation, saying, "In the councils of government, we must guard against the acquisition of unwarranted influence, whether sought or unsought, by the military-industrial complex. The potential for the disastrous rise of misplaced power exists and will persist."

Well, I knew this. I had proof.

I knew that war is a racket, and that British and American corporations profited from arms deals with Iraq. After a dozen years of my war souvenirs collecting dust, I flipped through the British defense equipment catalog I had found in an Iraqi bunker in Kuwait. On page 52, there's a submarine I could buy; page 22, a warship; page 101, anti-aircraft guns; page 240, anti-radar equipment; page 243, machine guns and sniper rifles; page 502, a helicopter; and on page 195, my choice of tanks. There's even the address and phone number of the companies, printed below the captions. There are howitzers, mortars, night-vision and thermal sights, artillery cannons, radios, bridges, barbed wire, parachutes, laser sites for pistols, tactical guided missiles, and everything else a dictator might need to arm himself against the world. It's all for sale with discounts for bulk purchases.

"Buy our bombs and we'll buy you a war," they say. They'll buy TV time to sell fear and empathy, and think of catchy slogans to dehumanize your chosen villain.

We the wealthy, in order to form a more profitable union, enforce our justice, ensure domestic servility, profit from the common defense, promote the generals and their men, and secure the blessings of prosperity for ourselves and for all our trustees, do disdain this established constitution of the United States of America.

These nation-destroying and nation-building corporations are amoral bastards, wholly un-American; intelligent in their ability to manipulate markets and lobby the fat cows they suckle, they pledge allegiance to no one. They are traitors at large, exploiting workers and depleting resources for short-term gain. They cloak their greed with altruistic-looking stunts; they destroy competition with indirect access to military force, through political pigs on their dole; and in the end they'll sell the rope to hang themselves, leaving a broadening wake of destruction until the last penny is stolen.

Eisenhower's farewell address concluded, "Only an alert and knowledgeable citizenry can compel the proper meshing of the huge industrial and military machinery of defense with our peaceful methods and goals, so that security and liberty may prosper together."

There was much for me to see through the crack in the wall the Gulf War had opened. Light poured in, and the crack became a door from which there was no turning back. The freedom I embrace requires a choice, which is validated by knowledge and demands truth. But there was no truth in this rush to war in Iraq, only illusions about good and evil.

The propaganda war on the home front was on in full earnest, leading up to the Iraq War. The neoconservatives who advise and administer the president's policy either thought that American citizens were too ignorant to understand the complexity of their foreign policy, or that we were too steeped in American idealism to be able to fathom their ruthless and corrupt motivations.

Incessant rants from pundits and politicians became reality for lemmings, pitching pseudo-altruistic crap to pull predictable heartstrings. "The poor crippled children sucking on sarin gas at the hands of pure evil, with eyes for your kids next." That's all it took, as if U.S. foreign policy had ever taken a cue from Amnesty International or Human Rights Watch. So they mouthed their pretty words and patriotic mantras, with smiling faces and Old Glory lapel pins, and like salivating dogs at the sight of a bone, we responded. "Sit, boy! Roll over! Pull that trigger for freedom, boy!"

I learned that the current administration had its plan spelled out years ago by the neoconservatives from Project for a New American Century. Dick Cheney, Donald Rumsfeld, and Paul Wolfowitz contributed to a 1992 document titled "Defense Planning Guidance," which states, "Our first objective is to prevent the re-emergence of a new rival.... Regions include Western Europe, East Asia, the territory of the former Soviet Union, and Southwest Asia.... We must maintain the mechanisms for deterring potential competitors from ever aspiring to a larger regional or global role."

Globalization, neocon style, is a Trojan horse that rationalizes preemptive war, free trade, and the exploitation of people and resources. It is not sustainable.

There it is. Young Americans with love of country in their hearts are sent to spill their blood, not for freedom, democracy, or protection of the homeland, but for the profit and political survival of a powerful few.

There's your Manifest Destiny.

NOVEMBER 19, 2003—ENTERING THE LOWER MISSISSIPPI AT CAIRO, ILLINOIS—MILE 953.5 LM

Scott and I never resume our conversation about Manifest Destiny. The next morning the men of the Discovery Expedition continue their journey up the Mississippi River to the Missouri River confluence. The *Bottle Rocket* continues its journey down the Mississippi River beyond the Ohio River confluence.

We part in opposite directions, both geographically and perhaps ideologically, yet we found common ground as fellow Gulf War veterans and contemporary river rats.

Jenna and I float past their wooden boats poised to depart momentarily. The mile marker reads "0.8." In less than one mile, the count restarts at 953.5, the beginning of the Lower Mississippi.

Scott, the dignified embodiment of Captain Meriwether Lewis, stands with his men on the edge of the water, waving joyfully.

"Three cheers for the *Bottle Rocket!*" he yells.

"Hip, hip, hooray! Hip, hip, hooray! Hip, hip, hooray!"

They begin to sing another of their old sailor songs, one that is fitting to our destination, titled "Cape Cod Girls." They replace "Australia" with "Louisiana."

> So heave 'em up my bully, bully boys.
> Haul away, haul away.
> Heave 'em up and don't you make a noise.
> We're bound away for Louisiana.

I yell to them, "Travel well, my friends!"

Jenna begins to chuckle. "Travel well, my friends?" she mumbles with a smirk. While waving goodbye, she asks again, "Did you say, 'Travel well, my friends'?" before breaking into hysterical laughter. "Blah ha ha. You idiot."

"Just shut up," I say. We're both waving and arguing.

The milky brown water swirls wildly. The line of convergence of the two great rivers is nearly a quarter-mile long. The river narrows quickly at the lower end of the confluence. The *Bottle Rocket* enters the Lower Mississippi with a noticeable thrust.

The river is rising. We share the river with whole trees that race by. A loud boom echoes behind us. A billow of smoke rises from the keelboat a half mile away, as it turns up the Mississippi River. They send another volley from their cannon to signal their departure from the Ohio River, a milestone in their journey.

But I can't look back for long. The river is strangely unfamiliar. Once again, I find myself in need of knowledge where I once felt sufficient. The current spins the *Bottle Rocket* at will. It's so much faster, and unpredictable. I get the feeling that the future is going to be a rough ride.

14

TURBULENT AMERICA

> No people in the world ever did achieve their freedom by goody-
> goody talk and moral suasion: it being immutable law that all
> revolutions that will succeed must *begin* in blood, whatever may
> answer afterward. If history teaches us anything, it teaches that.
> *Mark Twain,* A Connecticut Yankee in King Arthur's Court

NOVEMBER 19, 2003—FIRST DAY SOUTH OF CAIRO, ILLINOIS— MILE 926 LM

"Faster, faster! You gotta paddle faster!" I yell to Jenna in a desperate tone that comes from the emergence of a common enemy,
the Lower Mississippi. Giant whirlpools spin the *Bottle Rocket*
and pull the corners of the pontoons underwater with loud
sucking sounds that end with a snap when the deep funnels
collapse.

Enormous elongated dikes constrict the river, but they're
flooded over. The river slows before the submerged rubble barricade and appears flat like a parking lot. Approaching the dike,
short, choppy rapids dance on the surface of the water. Then
comes the slump, a ten-to-twelve-inch drop over the dike into violent whirlpools.

The Corps of Engineers built the dikes in the 1930s out of
rock and useless concrete scrap, in order to force the river channel to meander in a predictable direction. They intrude into the

river perpendicular to the bank. At the point where the dike breaks the surface and emerges from the river, hundreds of trees and logs are snagged, along with defunct green and red buoys.

Sometimes the *Bottle Rocket* slips into an eddy that momentarily carries us upriver with a countercurrent moving faster than the downriver deluge in the middle of the channel. If luck escapes us, we will be dragged into the middle of the eddy where the dead water sits, stale and idle, spinning slowly. It requires great effort to leave those dead zones.

Just beyond the edge of the dike, the river churns madly with tall waves that pour over the pontoons of the raft, giant fifty-foot-diameter plumes of water that mushroom from the river bottom and quickly push us away in random directions. All of this must be dealt with while keeping a watchful eye for passing barges.

"Check out that one!" Jenna yells. A renegade red buoy screams by our raft, bearing deep scars from having traveled under a barge or two, providing a powerful visual lesson of what would happen to the *Bottle Rocket* should it meet a similar fate. Buoys are usually anchored to the river bottom with a long chain and a concrete block the size of a refrigerator. Passing next to an anchored buoy gives a good reference for speed. We are flying through Missouri.

We make twenty-seven quick miles and find a precarious campsite along a flooded willow forest in quiet darkness. A cliff of sand protrudes above the water. I haul the raft half out of the river onto a beach between two-inch-diameter saplings and tie the two ropes to separate trees. There is barely enough dry wood for a fire.

I've developed a habit of building the campfire as close to the river's edge as possible so that extinguishing it only requires a splash from a few feet away. I've set the fire near the edge of the sand cliff. As the flames lick the sky, I tread carefully around the embers to get a better seat. Suddenly, without a fraction of a second to speak or even to look at Jenna, the cliff disappears beneath me, and instantly I fall backwards into the river five feet below. Entangled in the roots of submerged trees, I can feel the current tugging at the leg of my pants.

"Give me your hand!" a terrified Jenna yells.

"I'm okay," I say, laughing my words to her, perhaps in an attempt to comfort myself. I am amazed by my disappearing act. I simply vanished from sight. The river had undercut the bank, unbeknownst to me. We move the campfire and prop all of my clothes on sticks. I'm thankful that it's only fifty degrees tonight, that I have dry clothes to sleep in, and that Jenna is there to laugh with me after lending a comforting hand. I accept the lesson from the river to pay attention to how it is changing. I assume nothing. "This is your last warning," the river says.

The *Bottle Rocket* is floating where it was dragged on land the night before. The Mississippi has risen at least a foot in twelve hours. I push the raft through a logjam to get into the current. There is so much debris on the river. The current licks the bottom of the raft's pontoons, and soon we are hurtling through a gauntlet of waves, logs, and ugly clumps of beige foam.

"Just kick it away!" I yell to Jenna. She's got her foot on a two-foot-diameter tree, sixty feet in length, that's peacefully bobbing next to us through Tennessee. The roots climb vertically into the sky above the raft. The trunk gently bumps against the aluminum frame of our left pontoon.

"What about the buoys?" I think. I imagine the tree slamming into an anchored buoy. Maybe the tree temporarily stops in the river, dragging the chained buoy along its trunk and against my raft. Maybe the current pushes the raft under the tree, or we flip over and get caught between the buoy, the tree, and other floating debris.

From my perspective everything appears to gently float together in relative calm. What an illusion! It is the folly of victims to make shallow assumptions. With a subtle sense of urgency, I help Jenna to push the raft away from the tree.

On the map, the river looks like a piece of folded ribbon, meandering in giant loops. On one page the river leaves Kentucky, enters Tennessee, then returns to Kentucky. Oxbow lakes and sloughs show the history of this river's ever-changing direction.

"Hey, there's that tree again," I say to Jenna. It's hung up on a submerged dike that prevents the river from entering a slough. The current is rushing over the rocks and drags the *Bottle Rocket* over the dike against my will.

"Might as well camp here," Jenna suggests. I drag the raft high on the bank and tie it securely to thick willows. Jenna unloads bags and gets the tent started. I'm collecting firewood after a short visit behind a tree. Cans of veggie soup and clam chowder warm on glowing coals. Soon the bright band of the Milky Way stretches from horizon to horizon, accompanied by strange blue clouds and orange stripes radiating from the northern horizon. "Are these the Northern Lights...in Tennessee?" Jenna asks. I heat a can of corn and chase it with a whole can of fruit cocktail. I give Jenna the cherries. My boots, propped upside down on sticks, steam next to the fire.

The morning is crisp. We break camp with unspoken efficiency and load the *Bottle Rocket* in record time. Again the raft is floating where it was lugged up the bank the night before. The campfire has been swept away. The river's still rising and will continue to do so for another week.

The channel is swift and hides barges sneaking upriver around tight bends. I prefer to hug the bank, since my raft is slow to respond to my commands, and barges don't seem to stop for trees, buoys, or a fool on a raft.

I push and pull twenty miles out of the oars. I've learned to ride the dikes like a rodeo cowboy, catching the current on the outside and riding the edge of whirlpools that jettison us beyond the most violent turbulence. My arms and shoulders ache from the endless ride, never recovering from the day before.

~

Each night we find vast sandbars with leafless willows to tie the raft to. We pitch our tent high on the bank, and collect firewood for giant fires to dry our clothes and warm our tired souls. We skillfully navigate through at least twenty miles each day. On one evening we dance to jazz wailing from the crank radio. The river flows through me like music in my ears, and I begin to think again that I know the river. I think I've tamed the current, but then there's Caruthersville, Missouri.

The wind roars after midnight, keeping Jenna awake, but I enjoy the solace of my earplugs. I wake to the tent bent over my face. The wind is fierce. In the morning, the sand stings my face and hands as I pull the bungee cords to secure the drybags to the raft.

Jenna looks at me attentively. "You sure you want to go now?" The radio alerts us to certain storms today.

"Must make zee miles," I say, offering her my tired mantra.

It's ten miles to mile 848 LM, three miles above Caruthersville, where the Mississippi River makes an unprecedented, sharp 90-degree left turn. Up ahead I can see white froth on the tips of giant waves. Several large, short dikes push the mass of water away from the bank and around the bend. I haven't seen waves that big yet.

"Jenna," I say sternly, to get her attention, "You'd better hold on."

The current grasps the pontoons of the *Bottle Rocket* and attempts to spin us. I can barely keep us straight. Waves splash over the pontoons and one lands in my lap. My boots are heavy with water.

An upriver barge thankfully edges away from us, moving toward the opposite bank. But the gesture is not for us. I look back to discover that the barge has changed course only to make room for a downriver barge that's rapidly bearing down on our raft.

"Paddle! Paddle!" I yell to Jenna above the roar of wind.

We enter tremendous turbulence in the river bend at the same time as the downriver barge, which swings its stern unknowingly in our direction to avoid being washed against the bank.

The river is merciless as it thrashes around us. Jenna pedals to save her life. I push the oars with all my might to get us away from the propeller blast and the enormous waves rushing beneath us. The only escape route is toward shore, but my effort is ineffective against the current.

SNAP! Just then, one of the oars lunges forward.

"Something's wrong!" I yell to Jenna. The raft spins and rapidly whips around the submerged edge of a dike. It races around the dead water and gets caught in a reverse current that slams it against the downriver side of the dike. I leap off and hold the raft against a rock. Jenna tosses a rope and I tie us off.

We're safe. We're both quiet. But soon we realize that we're not going anywhere for a while.

A section of a willow branch makes a temporary splint for the metal brace that snapped beneath the oar ring. In awkward motions, I can row along the shallow edge of the bank, but the reverse current is too strong and thrusts the raft back into the flooded willows. A headwind howls with twenty-five-mile-per-hour gusts. A light rain begins to fall.

"We're gonna get soaked," I mumble to Jenna. She's quiet, which signals to me that the cold is settling into her bones. I can see a clearing on the levee a couple hundred yards downriver, but getting there would require entering the channel again, which seems nearly impossible at this point.

A camouflage flatboat appears from out of the willows, with four men and a dog perched in stoic repose, like a calendar photo pinned up in a bait and tackle shop. Everything is camouflage, including beer insulators. They're close enough for a yell.

"Hey! Can we get a tow to Caruthersville?" I quickly exclaim, suppressing my normal instinct to refuse help and deal with discomfort on my own. I don't allow my ego to create a false sense of self-sufficiency against common sense. This time I need help. Jenna and I are cold and exhausted.

"Sure! I've had my share of tows on this river," Mike yells from the space between his hat and scarf. Mike's been fishing on the river for twenty-two of his thirty-four years. Today he's got his friend Jeff and two teenage sons out for a day of island-hopping to scout for deer. With a fifty-foot rope tied between us, we tow slowly at first, and then accelerate as fast as my sense of security will allow. Jenna and I stay on our raft. In a few minutes I motion to Mike to go a little faster when I look behind me and discover a gray wall of water pouring from the sky. I cannot see the willows where we just were.

Mike stuffs a cigarette between his lips and loudly mumbles a lecture about fish, over the roar of his outboard engine. I tell him about the river cats another fellow caught under my raft in Iowa. "That's nothin'! You should see the ones that come outta the river here," Mike boasts.

He gives us a tow to a giant pile of concrete blocks under a grain elevator. I tie the *Bottle Rocket* in the shadow of another river casino. There's a hotel on the end of Main Street. The wall of water quickly catches up to us.

"Thanks a million," I yell to Mike and the men, as they quickly turn around to race home.

"No problem. Y'all take care." Jenna and I have the same thought. We quickly drag the raft as high as possible, and tie it down with three ropes. Piling all of our gear on our backs, we waddle over the casino lawn, across Main Street, through the parking lot, and into the generic comfort of the Country Hearth Inn.

In the morning, leaving Jenna to rest a bit more, I visit the raft and unbolt the frost-covered oar ring. My hands quickly numb against the cold steel. There's a large red truck parked on the levee, sputtering steam from the tailpipe. An appropriately large fellow steps out with mirror glasses, a white cowboy hat, and a ten-gallon belly hanging over his chrome belt buckle.

"What the hell is that?" Wade says.

"It's a bottle raft," I say in my most nonthreatening, "I'm a nice guy, I need a lift into town" kind of voice. Wade is a WWII army veteran; restaurant owner; car, bike, and gun collector; and farmer, with a toothpick stuck to his bottom lip. He takes me to Pylate's Machine Shop to get my broken parts welded. The morning is strangely familiar to the day I broke down in Little Falls, Minnesota, and found myself riding shotgun with Kevin Schroder in his truck, headed to a weld shop with an oar-ring in my hand.

Wade likes the audience and insists I grab Jenna for a tour of Caruthersville. "Yeah, you stick a Wal-Mart on one end and a casino on the other, you'll damn well kill a town," he says to Jenna and me as we drive down Main Street. Most storefronts are closed. "That casino restaurant killed my steak house," he explains. "First, people ate there cause it's cheap. They gamble on the boat, and then come back to my restaurant writing bad checks 'cause they're broke."

Jenna's got a supply list already drafted. We go to Wal-Mart anyway, because the other shops in town are out of business. Eventually Wade brings us to his farm, in the middle of cornstalks. In a large metal barn he unveils his antiques.

"That Cadillac Limo once carried JFK in a parade," he boasts, with a collector's zeal. A dozen other cars hide quietly under dusty covers. He lets me have a rubber floor mat from a stack of fifty so that I can build Jenna a splashguard under the pedals of the *Bottle Rocket.*

Soon the raft is ready, but a cold and rainy afternoon easily overcomes my ambition to get back on the river. Jenna and I indulge ourselves with one more day in the hotel, another hot shower, warm blankets, and a continental breakfast.

NOVEMBER 27, 2003—THANKSGIVING DAY IN ARKANSAS— MILE 785 LM

"We can stop in Osceola if you want. It's only fifteen miles more," I suggest to Jenna in the tone of a question, adding, "Looks like it's close enough to walk to." We savor the possibility of a feast on Thanksgiving Day in some small diner that's open for the lonely and elderly in town. But soon we find that there's no place to land.

Blam! Blam! Blam!

"Did you hear that?" I ask Jenna, which earns me an exasperated look for asking the obvious, followed by a look that communicates sincere concern for the shotgun blasts, then a look of terrified surprise as I ground the raft on the bank directly below the edge of the wooded thicket where the shots came from.

"What are you doing?" she sternly whispers.

"I just wanna ask directions." I look at her as if she's asked the stupid question this time. I hop off and follow a rabbit trail to a clearing where a young couple and another young teen are shooting bottles off a log. The man directs his wife to get back in the truck. The startled young men look menacing with their trucker caps and shotguns.

"I don't mean to bother you folks, but we're rafting down the river and can't seem to find the landing," I say with a smile, from twenty feet away.

"Just around the corner," is all he says, followed by a long pause. I take this opportunity to explain the nature of my trip and the design of my raft.

"If you look over the bank you'll see us float by." I can tell that they're still startled and confused by my abrupt appearance from the river. Jenna and I continue on. While I explain the details of the encounter to her, I see the three of them peering over the tall grass to get a peek at us.

"Jenna, wave to 'em," I say as we float by. They wave back,

in slow motion, while staring with their mouths open. When we make it to the Sans Souci boat ramp a quarter-mile downriver, the three of them are already there.

"Y'all floatin' on that?" the younger fellow asks. We talk for a while and soon realize that Osceola is a few miles farther inland than we thought. The visitors depart as darkness descends. Jenna and I decide to stay put and camp in the middle of a park next to the landing.

Hours later, glaring headlights illuminate the side of our tent. The visitors have returned, carrying two plates piled with turkey, ham, stuffing, cranberry sauce, mashed potatoes, green beans, and cornbread. A third plate appears with enough slices of pecan and pumpkin to make half a pie, along with a couple big chunks of yellow cake.

The day after Thanksgiving is windy and cloudless, a sharp contrast to the midnight thunderstorm that left an ocean between Jenna and me. Soon after we'd inhaled our Thanksgiving feast, the first big drops began to fall. Within two hours we were huddled against the dry side of the flattened tent, using dirty clothes to dam the river at our feet, and fighting intensely over the last two inches of disputed dry territory between us.

An old fellow in an old Ford pickup parks above the boat ramp facing the sun and sits for at least half an hour. Jenna and I hang our gear in the trees, and it dries quickly in the breeze. The old fellow walks over to us.

"Is that your outfit?" he asks. Soon he and I are off to Osceola to grab breakfast to go. The road winds through wilted cornfields wintered over and flooded with last night's rain. Chained gates of long-abandoned factories line the streets into town.

"Most of these places closed down and moved south," he explains. "They used to make mattresses over there." He gives me the downtown tour of boarded storefront windows along Main

Street and provides running commentary on what used to be. He joyfully stops in front of the beautiful courthouse with a mosque-like copper dome. We enter the drive-thru at McDonald's outside of town. His wife works at Wal-Mart another mile down the road.

Jenna's eating her Egg McMuffin when CeCe and Andy from the Memphis Children's Museum arrive with an empty trailer. In less than twenty-four hours, the *Bottle Rocket* will be perched on blocks in the center of the museum like a fish out of water, dripping on the carpet, while hordes of inquisitive kids climb over it, playfully imagining pirates and submarines.

Tony Peck, the documentary filmmaker from Los Angeles who filmed my departure from Lake Itasca, Minnesota, three months ago, has made arrangements for Jenna and me to have a weekend stay in Memphis to talk with museum visitors about the trip and enjoy a couple days of being warm and dry.

Memphis is delightful, and our hosts surprise us with an empty house to ourselves, with unlimited hot showers and a washing machine to take the smoke out of our clothes. We take a quick tour of the city, including Graceland. I'm on a mission to find a tapestry of young Elvis, like the one that eight drunken marines from STA Platoon bought here fifteen years ago and later carried into Kuwait City. With no similar tapestry in sight, I settle for a tee-shirt of fat Elvis in rhinestones. Andy's family invites us to enjoy a home-cooked dinner that leaves us gorged on great food, wine, and conversation.

Downtown Memphis is quiet on Sunday morning. We are the first ones in the front door of the National Civil Rights Museum when they open.

The façade of the museum is the Lorraine Motel, including the balcony where Martin Luther King Jr. was assassinated. A path leading a couple hundred yards away takes visitors to another motel, where James Earl Ray knelt in a bathtub with a

.30-06 Remington rifle balanced on the windowsill. The modern museum inside the motel guides visitors to a large window where sunlight shines through.

You're on the second-floor balcony of the motel.

Look down.

There's a small, square patch of concrete where Martin Luther King Jr. bled to death after the bullet tore through his jaw and ricocheted into his chest, and his soul lifted away.

It is impossible to stand here and feel nothing.

MARCH 15, 2003—FIFTY THOUSAND AMERICANS MARCH IN LOS ANGELES, SIX MILLION WORLDWIDE.

"How many more Martin Luther Kings are we making?" I ask Preston, referring to protest signs for tomorrow's demonstration.

"I want to finish the boxes of Malcolm X and King before we quit," he replies. By morning there will be nearly a thousand signs piled into the back of my van, after a sleepless night of stapling the posters of the civil rights leaders back to back with a four-foot-long, two-inch-wide wooden handle between them. The wood is only a quarter-inch thick, which is the limit the LA Police will allow, for fear of a peaceful protest turning into an armed riot. We're expecting thousands of citizens in the street for tomorrow's march.

Endless miles of passionate souls, unified by moral zeal, carry their signs in a chaotic circus of civil action. While the U.S. military buildup along the border of Iraq surpasses a hundred thousand troops, fifty thousand Americans march in Los Angeles, joining an estimated half million people in cities and small towns across the country, and six million more around the world. Outgunned, but not outnumbered, we protest the rush to war.

The antiwar movement is a diverse lot from all corners of Los Angeles. The Vietnam-era organizers rally the radical youth with bandanas over their faces, while the immigrants who know suffering from their own countries verify the stories we hear about the covert American history most Americans don't know. Palestinians, Cubans, Koreans, Venezuelans, Colombians, Guatemalans, and Haitians beat their own drum against the same foe.

The black man and the Latino man, the striking custodians and hotel workers unite with the pacifists and anarchists. U.S. veterans come forward with their own stories of war and indoctrination, and the bullshit of it all. The intellectuals escape from their home libraries and coffee shops, leading others through long conversations peppered with obscure facts and figures about foreign policy and philosophy that are barely digestible in the span of a few shared steps in the middle of the street.

The police stand in rows, dressed in full riot gear, watching, waiting, and listening to little microphones in their ears, for instructions from someone else. Some of them have video cameras. They speak in robotic monotones when in groups, but let down the charade when separated and surrounded. We've got our cop watchers from the National Lawyers Guild in fluorescent green caps, carrying video cameras of their own. The local TV news is here with spotlights and hairspray. Their helicopters above juggle for space with police helicopters that hover and whine like mosquitoes. Behind everyone are the short, silent immigrants with dark skin and bright orange vests, waiting to move trashcans and barricades when it's all over.

Across the street, barricaded by cops and yellow police tape, are the anti-antiwar protestors, outnumbered a thousand to one, capitalizing on red, white, blue, and Bibles, confusing compassion with compliance, and unable to separate support for troops from support for war.

The protest organizers try to keep it all together, preaching, "We must find a common approach, a common solution to a common problem." The hippies with Hula-Hoops and bongos drag behind, smoking weed in the dense crowds.

But most of the faces belong to average Americans stepping

into the street for the first time to protest. They are also here to learn, to build confidence in their deductions, and to associate with the common conscience. They are prepared to take the next step, but they want direction. They take special notice of free speech and bring their children for this great civics lesson.

"Get 'em off the street!" Preston yells to all the other organizers. Of the fifty thousand who marched a few hours ago, a thousand are still here. The cops on horseback charge the crowd and bludgeon a man who gets between two horses. The roar is deafening. They separate a group of a hundred protestors from the rest of us and arrest them all. Between the rows of cops, I can see them on their stomachs hogtied with thick plastic wristbands. The rest of us are surrounded.

We learn quickly not to separate.

My blood is boiling. I savor the familiar aggression.

"They can't arrest us all," Jim Lafferty from the National Lawyers Guild yells to me. Hundreds of youths are huddled together in front of a thick row of police in riot gear. Adrenaline surges through me and nothing hurts.

There's a fire in the street and I see a pile of signs light up. Another group of youths dressed in red and black are lighting the corner of an American flag on fire. My blood boils stronger, as if it might pour out of my eyes.

Internal switches hardwired in my brain begin to flip as I lunge toward the group. I grab the flag and extinguish the flames with my left hand. The melted nylon sears my palm and forms instant blisters, and I say with calm, certain, focused anger, *"Don't do that!"*

"ARE YOU A FUCKING COP?" the kid yells in my face.

"DO YOU HAVE ANY IDEA WHAT PEOPLE HAVE DONE FOR THIS FLAG!?" I blast at them like the drill instructors who created the gut reaction I now employ.

"DO YOU KNOW WHAT THIS FLAG HAS DONE TO MY PEOPLE?!" he screams.

I'm not letting go of the flag.

"This accomplishes nothing. You're pissing off the wrong people," I yell back, not realizing that this statement could also be his point.

"Do you know what this government did to my people in El Salvador?" he says. I know he's too young to have suffered personally from the not-so-well-known covert U.S. intervention of the '70s and '80s, and his English is too perfect for an immigrant, but I'm sure the fireside family stories would surprise most of our countrymen.

Everyone is yelling in all directions. I only hear this angry young man. I am silent, intent on giving his passion the benefit of my attention.

"Do you know?" His sorrow comes to the surface. "Do you know what they do?"

If I took the time to learn about his suffering, would I be able to turn my back on him? Could I enjoy the benefit of my nation's wealth, knowing that it weighs on the backs of so many so far away? What has our government done to him, his family, and his country?

His frustration blends anger and sorrow, but his anger is greater.

His rage is different from my rage. No. It's the same rage, but the injustice is different. His anger reflects his betrayal, the lies, and the suffering of his own people.

I let go of the flag and run to another group of protestors screaming at the cops for dragging a protestor out of the crowd. I watched the police engulf the man, like ants swarming on a caterpillar, their black uniforms completely obscuring sight of the man.

"Get on the sidewalk!" the organizers yell to the crowd. "Stick together!"

The cops in the street yell to get back on the sidewalk. The cops on the sidewalk yell to go down the subway. The cops in the subway yell to get in the street.

"Stick together," we yell.

The police continue their attempt to divide us, but we congregate and continue to protest. They finally recognize the stalemate and open one corner of their perimeter to the street. We learn. They learn.

MARCH 20, 2003—FIRST DAY OF THE IRAQ WAR

The first missile erupts in a Baghdad palace in a spectacular inferno. The troops will never see it, but it is fed to the American public in digestible doses intended to show our precision and our dominance over a feeble enemy sufficiently dehumanized with stories of torture, murder, and rape rooms.

The images from the ground invasion sting with familiarity. It's strangely reminiscent of the excitement Saenz and I recognized in our smiles to each other when we were lying half-buried in the sand, waiting for an Iraqi assault, as random volleys of artillery rained down near our position. I'm white-knuckled and hypnotized in front of the TV. I want to be there. I'm missing the action.

American forces rush in from Kuwait, and soon the first body bags are filling with dead marines and soldiers.

Everything changes.

"I can't be here," I think. "Fuck this antiwar circus."

I want to be there in that desert. I want the discomfort of sand between my teeth and sweat burning my eyes. The fraternal bond is unbelievably powerful.

I want to reenlist. I remember that Sergeant Sellers, five years after the Gulf War ended, placed an MRE in the back of my truck, which he happened to see parked somewhere in New Orleans. He left a note saying, "If you want to come back to the Corps give me a call." He had stayed in the Marine Corps and became the company gunny. There was no way I would go back then, but I would not hesitate one second to be there now.

"Marines are dying and I'm carrying a goddamn antiwar

sign," I think while alone, watching Americans suffer, watching Iraqis suffer. I watch the media paint a rosy picture of success and convoluted compassion, as my deceptive government spins lies with no consequence, no risk, and none of their own sons or daughters bleeding in the sand.

I leave the antiwar movement. For two weeks I sit alone and do nothing but watch a televised war unfold. Thoughts I buried from the Gulf War surge through my head. All the details of life in the sand are coming back in a flood of memories: the stench of rotting bodies at the Highway of Death, the war trophies I collected from corpses, and the hatred and dehumanization I tried with futility to resist. I remember and relive the sense of betrayal at finding American weapons in Iraqi hands. I know that good Americans are dying for a political and economic war sold to us as self-defense and a humanitarian mission.

I walk into a Marine recruitment office. "You're too old, but each year of prior service will subtract a year from your current age," the recruiter explains. I grab a handful of brochures off the rack on my way out the door. One booklet reminds me of why I joined the Marine Corps days after my seventeenth birthday, nineteen years ago. In large letters across two pages, it reads, "Unhappiness does not arise from the way things are. But rather, from a difference in the way things are and the way we believe they should be."

Soon everything changes again.

I know this war is bullshit. Do I join the moral fight, or turn my back on justice? It would require much less effort, much less thought and action, to do nothing. I could just sit back and mumble my complaints to whoever would listen.

But what I know requires that I act, otherwise my inaction makes me complicit. This war is wrong. I know this with certainty. I can't watch Americans and Iraqis die for lies. I cannot be a domesticated revolutionary, like the social in-activists who bitch in the background while doing nothing, despite the long-term consequences of this immoral war. If I do not fight, then who will?

I had joined the Marine Corps for the GI Bill, for the prestige, but mostly because I wanted to do the right thing. The same love of justice that sent me into the Marine Corps recruiter's office so many years ago propels me back onto the street to protest.

I return to the antiwar movement.

There is no other choice.

"I hope it doesn't rain," the rally organizers plead to each other. But though the day begins with a thunderous roar and a downpour, the people are coming. They begin to trickle in from side streets, with raincoats, umbrellas, and plastic bags with armholes punched out. They pour into the intersection of Olympic and Broadway to march through downtown Los Angeles, their loud protest echoing through the urban canyon of modern skyscrapers and defunct hotels and factories lined with cheap camera shops and fast-food stands. We're an hour away from the noon step-off, and already there are twenty thousand Americans amassed.

Waves of angry citizens flow through the urban maze of buildings and barricades into side streets and onto sidewalks, meandering around streetlights and parked cars, then rejoining in an organized dissent that uplifts the revolutionary heart of my countrymen.

When we get to the rally site, civil leaders and activists take the stage to rouse the rain-swept crowd. Jesse Jackson blasts, "How can we accuse Saddam Hussein of having weapons of mass destruction when we hold the receipts for them?"

"Can you help Ron Kovic up the steps?" Preston asks. I turn to see a gentle man in a wheelchair, with a neatly trimmed white beard and glasses. His outstretched hand grabs mine.

"I am so glad to be a part of this protest. I hope you'll be proud of what I say up there," Kovic says, as four of us carry him and his chair up the wet steps to the microphone on stage. He radiates humility and compassion, and roars justice.

After a passionate speech in a cold drizzle, Kovic asks me, "Can someone give me a ride back to my car?" I quickly borrow a car and escort Kovic to the passenger side, but not before a shaggy Vietnam vet in tears and a tattered green military jacket confronts him with an emotional barrage of joy and thanks.

In January 1968, while on his second tour as a marine infantryman in Vietnam, two rounds of enemy fire hit Ron Kovic, one entering his ankle and the other shattering his spine. In and out of consciousness, he recalled the chaplain giving him his last rites. His tour in Vietnam segued to a tour of VA hospitals, and then the antiwar movement, culminating in Kovic and other veterans shouting down President Richard Nixon during the Republican National Convention in 1972.

In a quiet apartment in Santa Monica, California, Kovic bought a manual typewriter and poured his life onto paper, writing *Born on the Fourth of July.* "I wrote the book in one month, three weeks, and two days," he tells me, adding, "I did it all in lowercase and typed till dawn on some nights."

I realize more than ever the greatness of this man. For nearly an hour, as we drive around downtown Los Angeles, we talk about life in the Marine Corps, his life in a wheelchair, the antiwar movement past and present, and the heroes who led us here.

"I grew up with Tommy guns and John Wayne movies," Kovic says.

I think for a moment and reply, "I grew up with Rambo knives and you."

JUNE 15, 2003

The summer arrives and I still think daily about the Gulf War, the men I served with, and the thousands of troops fighting in Iraq today. I think about the conversation Lance Corporal

Tomas and I had in the sandbag bunker, twelve years ago, about rafting the Mississippi River.

On a napkin in a small diner around the corner from my apartment in Los Angeles, I sketch out the design of a pontoon raft filled with plastic bottles. By the end of the first week in July, I've begun cutting steel to build the *Bottle Rocket*.

15

VETERANS IN OUR MIST

So much for the dead—they have paid their part of the war profits.
So much for the mentally and physically wounded—they are paying
now their share of the war profits. But the others paid, too—they
paid with heartbreaks when they tore themselves away from their
firesides and their families to don the uniform of Uncle Sam—on
which a profit had been made. They paid another part in the training
camps where they were regimented and drilled while others took their
jobs and their places in the lives of their communities. They paid for it
in the trenches where they shot and were shot; where they were hungry
for days at a time; where they slept in the mud and the cold and in the
rain—with the moans and shrieks of the dying for a horrible lullaby.
Major General Smedley Butler, USMC, War Is a Racket

DECEMBER 3, 2003—HELENA, ARKANSAS—MILE 662 LM
It's cold. Jenna is testing her new nylon-mesh rain gear, which
I advised against, arguing that "water-resistant" isn't synony-
mous with "waterproof." A ceiling of thick clouds hangs low
over leafless willows barricading the bank from surrounding
lowlands. She is cozy in her bundle of layered thrift-ware, talkative and paddling contently. Then a light drizzle falls.

"You should've bought a poncho," I mumble.

Soon she's quiet. I told her not to wear those stupid pants.
We've got a perfect fluorescent orange plastic poncho in the
back milk crate. It begins to rain harder. For a half hour it rains,
sending a chilling trickle down my neck and up my sleeves. I
know she's wet.

Soon she stops paddling. "How much longer is she gonna sit

213

there?" I think. She's sitting in a puddle on her plastic seat, quiet and certainly miserable, but absolutely stubborn. The devil on my shoulder excitedly waits to see the drama unfold. For another half hour she sits quietly, then, while bouncing out of her seat in a fit of saddened frustration, she exclaims loudly, "I'm so miserable!"

"Do you want to stop in the next town?" I ask quietly, with a hint of "I told you so" and a devious chuckle in my voice. I look at the two soaked pages of the map I tore out this morning. "Helena is just around the bend."

We make thirteen miles, which is okay, since yesterday we floated a record thirty-six from Memphis. Helena, Arkansas, sits behind a slough and over a levee. The Magnolia Inn, a former USO club during WWII, sits perched atop a hill overlooking the empty river town. Jenna springs for a night in a warm bed, with a warm shower, warm food, and a chance to watch our clothes steam over the room radiator.

"We gotta leave early tomorrow, okay?" I ask, as the only condition for such extravagance. There are 394 miles between Helena and New Orleans as a crow flies, 550 as a catfish swims. I am anxious to get back on the river.

The next hundred miles is accomplished in three days, with the same routine: wake-pack-row-eat-row-unpack-sleep. The river is a bloated monster, climbing above the sapling willows on the edge of sunken sandbars. The *Bottle Rocket* slumbers on dry land and awakens on water. We're moving fast.

"Hey, Jenna, Greenville, Mississippi, is coming up soon," I exclaim, knowing that she'll respond enthusiastically. She's been reading the history of the 1927 flood that nearly washed Greenville away. Those who didn't move away rebuilt the town and improved the levees. It's thirteen miles downriver, but it's landlocked, thanks to the natural meanders of the river and the encouragement of the Corps of Engineers.

"There's no way I'm gonna paddle up that slough for three

miles to Greenville," I say to Jenna, who insists that we're stopping there. Under swirling clouds I drag the raft up a treeless bank south of town and tie it to the biggest rocks I can find. There's a small city park above us, dotted with pecan trees, a wrecked towboat, and a pay phone. I put two pecans in one hand and use one to crush the other, as my stepfather once showed me.

We eat pecans while we wait for a cab. It's a good appetizer to the collard greens, mashed potatoes, yams, liver and onions, navy beans, and peach cobbler we find at Bishop's place. It's heavenly food that lifts you out of your seat and warms your soul, a smile chasing every bite. We indulge in familiar culture, while riding out a thunderstorm that surely would have raised nervous eyebrows seventy-five years ago.

We're almost there. I can feel it, see, smell, and taste it. I dream of a soft-shell crab po-boy from R&O's restaurant in Bucktown. The novelty of the river is now overshadowed by the chill of winter and the incessant threat of silent barges. Sometimes I think I only tolerate the river, like the desert in Kuwait, as a loathed state of being, standing between the present and home.

DECEMBER 12, 2003—VICKSBURG, MISSISSIPPI—MILE 437 LM

"Must make zee miles!" I loudly exclaim. We make another hundred miles in three days, forty-two on December 11, thanks to few barges, allowing us to ride the fast current in the middle of the river.

We can see the Vicksburg Bridge rising above the tree line, miles before we arrive, but the town riverfront is a mile up another river, the Yazoo River. The town of Vicksburg, once on the Mississippi, became landlocked on April 26, 1876, when the river cut through DeSoto Point. The river changed course, turning a wide loop into an oxbow lake. The lost access to the Mississippi River ended rail and river commerce to the town. Then on January 7, 1903, the Corps of Engineers opened the flood-gates on the rerouted Yazoo River, letting new life flow into Vicksburg through the same channel where the Mississippi River had been.

Jenna and I overshoot the confluence of the Yazoo River by a couple hundred yards, which costs us an hour dragging the raft upstream along the bank. In quiet, windless darkness we paddle against a slow current up the Yazoo. We pass eerie, dark barges sitting high above the water. A logging company is unloading one, unknowingly swinging its grappling arm over our heads as it transfers one-ton logs to a massive conveyor belt inching up and over the levee.

We pass a small refinery with a web of pipes stretching over us, and above the river. Towboats glide by, lighted like colorful floating birthday cakes. We paddle around a barge casino, de-signed to look like a steamboat, and find a concrete boat ramp and dock. We tie our raft next to the Mississippi Tours expedi-tion boat. Exhausted, we drag our bags to the casino motel. I in-sist on a room facing the river so I can watch my raft.

The next morning, "Hey, the raft's on land!" I say to Jenna. The raft, untouched by anyone, is high on the bank. The river is receding.

"Y'all floating on that thing?" Jimmy asks with a chuckle. He owns the tour boat and the dock I tied the raft to. Jenna ex-plains the trip, while I attempt to drag the heavy *Bottle Rocket* to the edge of the water.

"How about Italian?" Jimmy invitingly says to us. Over lunch he explains the history of Vicksburg, the history of the river, and the history of his life, including his wife, Ann.

Soon, the four of us are touring Vicksburg, once known as "The Gibraltar of the Confederacy." We drive by dozens of his-toric homes that tell the history of the Battle for Vicksburg in 1863, which began with a stubborn reply from Colonel James L. Autry to the Union army's request that they surrender. "Mississippians don't know and refuse to learn how to surrender to an enemy."

Weeks of constant bombardment from the Union army drove Vicksburg citizens into caves, until on July 4, after forty-seven days of siege, General John Pemberton of the Confederate army surrendered, with the condition that the thirty thousand remaining Confederate troops be paroled rather than imprisoned.

On top of the hill we drive through the Vicksburg National Cemetery. Seventeen thousand weathered headstones of Civil War casualties adorn rolling hills. Eleven thousand are unknown soldiers.

"There are a few Confederate ones buried here, but they're not supposed to be," Ann explains. We visit the remnants of the ironclad gunboat the *U.S.S. Cairo,* which was sunk in the Yazoo River on December 12, 1862, by electrically activated underwater mines. Divers found the gunboat in 1956, and finally displayed it in the National Military Park in 1977.

The tour ends when we join the congregation at a local church to hear the St. Joseph's Orchestra play holiday tunes. When the night ends, Jenna and I unroll our sleeping bags in the warehouse of their studio, where Ann paints portraits and Jimmy sells plastic dishware.

In the morning we pack our bags and get a lift back to the dock from a fellow whose only request is a few dollars for a forty-ounce beer picked up along the way. We drag our gear over the levee and discover that the *Bottle Rocket* is at least fifteen feet from the river's edge. The flooded river continues to recede.

Jenna layers herself with cold-weather gear, while I drag the raft to the water. We'll strap in the bags last. I lift the raft from the middle. It weighs a ton. Half of the bottles are covered with foam, so I can't see whether they're filled with water or not. Perhaps the foam is acting like a sponge. I can only lift the back end and drag the raft a few feet before I rest. Lift—drag—drop.

"Snap!" An audible pop emanates from my hip, then excruciating pain.

"Jenna. Something bad just happened." Instantly, she drops everything she is doing to help me crawl to the dock and lie down.

"Just give me a few minutes and I'll be okay." But when I try to stand, a lightning bolt of pain stabs the muscles in my back and legs. I crumple to the ground. For an hour I lie there.

"The trip is over," I say to Jenna. There's no way I can get back on the raft. The drunk fellow waits for us. For another beer he drives us to a cheap motel near the casino. For three nights Jenna and I sit and calculate our next step. On the third day the pain subsides and I can limp to the casino salad bar. On the fourth day I figure I can sit on the raft while Jenna pedals the paddle wheel. We decide to return to the raft.

DECEMBER 19, 2003—NATCHEZ, MISSISSIPPI—MILE 380 LM

It's impossible to sit comfortably in my seat. I move the paddles only to steer, otherwise we ride the current, still averaging twenty-five miles a day. The tense muscles in my legs, hip, and lower back are hard as stone. Every mile marker gives me a chance to count the miles traveled since the morning, miles to the next big sandbar on the map, and miles left to New Orleans.

The *Delta Queen* appears ahead, docked against the bluff below the town of Natchez.

"Let's find a cheap motel," I suggest to Jenna. We're soon on the doorstep of Jane's Motel, managed by Miss Jane, a cancer survivor with an impressive display of over three hundred angel dolls. Down the street, Jenna and I enjoy burritos and guacamole. When we return, Jane's husband, Austin, meets us in the parking lot. He's a slender man in his fifties, with a checkered blue-and-black flannel long-sleeve shirt and a dirty baseball cap with a curved bill molded to the shape of a beer can.

"I heard about you guys," he says, adding, "Y'all are from New Orleans, huh?"

"Yeah, we're almost there," I exclaim, with agonizing enthusiasm.

"Welcome home," he says with sincere Southern pride.

Austin is a Vietnam vet. We talk on the porch of the motel for an hour. I explain my trip down the Mississippi and the conversation with Lance Corporal Tomas in the Kuwait desert thirteen years ago that started this whole thing. I've told him that I'm from southern Louisiana—that I've seen the river change from a cool trickle through a Minnesota marsh to a raging torrent past big cities and small fading river towns, but I'm on my way home to New Orleans. His welcome home is a kind gesture of shared affinity for a way of life that thrives in the backwoods of the Mississippi Delta.

We're also both marines. He fought in Khe Sanh. I share with him what Khe Sanh looks like today. He describes the last days of fighting on that hill in 1968.

"I was the last marine to leave that hill," he says. "I remember the day we left. The helicopter was taking off and I stomped my boot in that red mud." He explains that he did it as a final assault on a worthless hill that took the lives of hundreds of his brothers.

"Welcome home," I say.

DECEMBER 26, 2003—ST. FRANCISVILLE, LOUISIANA—MILE 266 LM

Leaving Natchez, Jenna and I stick to the east bank of the river. At mile 315 the Army Corps of Engineers manages the Atchafalaya Basin River Control System, a series of floodgates on the west bank, which allows the Mississippi to discharge some of its surge into the Atchafalaya River. A blinking light and a horn blast every ten seconds indicate that the gates are open. All ships should stay clear of the strong currents that suck a million gallons a minute into the outflow channel. We camp across from the opened floodgates and enjoy a pre-Christmas dinner of canned yams and stuffing, and a nibble of dark chocolate for dessert. The siren blasts all night long.

Arriving in St. Francisville, Louisiana, on the morning of Christmas Eve, we take a break. Jenna visits family for a few days, while my brother takes the front seat of the *Bottle Rocket*.

Dave and I depart from St. Francisville on the heels of the *Delta Queen,* whistling a hundred yards in front of us. It quickly paddles away, leaving us in the middle of the current, a tiny speck in a widening river.

I enjoy seeing the Mississippi through my brother's eyes, as he savors the novelty of a new perspective on a river he has known all his life. I tell him stories of river rats, wildlife, locks and dams, wild currents, rainstorms, and everything else to get him up to speed to this point. We round a bend a few miles above Baton Rouge and camp on a secluded sandbar covered with beaver sticks and washed-up willow trees. We build the biggest fire that two brothers can.

"Remember the time I dropped a brick on that bullet and shot you in the leg?" I say. "I had to get Mom's tweezers to dig the pieces of casing out of your knee."

"Remember the time I sat on your head and farted while you were watching TV?" he says with a chuckle.

"Ha ha. Remember the time I spit in your cereal?" I reply.

"Remember the time we used to steal bubble gum and candy bars and sell them in high school?" I say.

"I didn't do that. That was you. You're the one that got arrested."

A couple empty cans of beef stew are tossed into the fire to burn clean.

"Remember the time I saved your life after that cottonmouth bit ya?"

"Remember how we used to catch perch with cigarette butts as bait, and then use the perch to catch catfish?"

"Remember all those chickens grandpa had, and those nasty poodles that would shit in the hall?"

The last of the driftwood is piled on the fire.

"Remember Sergeant Smith in Motor T?" Dave remembers. "You know he died, killed in a car accident."

"Do you remember the Highway of Death?" I ask.

"I'll never forget it. It was really fucked up. You know, I had a tough time readjusting," Dave says, adding, "I talked to a counselor for about a year after the Gulf War."

"Why didn't you come talk to me?" I ask. I'm hesitant to admit that I should have followed his footsteps. Instead I got married, divorced, engaged to Jenna, and became a depressed and verbally abusive workaholic. Yet my own blood suffered in his own world, pride and pain keeping his own experience to himself.

The huge pile of driftwood is reduced to a pile of glowing embers.

"You were too busy," he answers with peaceful honesty.

JULY 2003—HOLLYWOOD, CALIFORNIA—ONE MONTH BEFORE THE *BOTTLE ROCKET* LEFT FOR LAKE ITASCA

I needed to be with other vets. I needed to talk with someone who understood what few Americans could possibly imagine.

I joined the American Legion for sixteen bucks.

Through the elegant wrought-iron gates, past the WWI cannon, I wandered into the front door of Hollywood Post 43. I followed the sound of voices down a stairway into a subterranean cafeteria, where I met a hundred veterans. The average age was twice mine at least.

General Smith startled me with a loud, "Semper fi! How old are you, son? Have you considered joining the Marine Corps Reserves? You know, you'll be sixty one day and will have needs that the Marine Corps can provide. You should consider reenlisting." He led the way to the bar.

Paul bought me a beer. He had been a UDT (precursor to SEALS) team leader, conducting missions from subs in the Gulf of Tonkin during the early 1960s. Insertion and extraction began and ended from an air-filled bell under a submarine a mile offshore.

John, sitting at the bar next to me, bought me a meal ticket. John's army unit was stationed in Alabama in 1940, where they trained in the use of chemical warfare. He showed me scars from chemical burns on his arms.

Twice a month these veterans meet for cocktails and dinner. They enjoy the comfort of a loose military organization where they can tell stories and voice their gripes about politics and the VA.

"Dinnertime!" someone yelled.

I shuffled forward in the chow line to get my plate of pasta covered with beef stroganoff. The cook gave me a heaping pile. "Hey there, youngster. You look like you need a few extra pounds." Although I've gained a pound a year since the Gulf War ended, I was still relatively young and skinny compared to the majority of WWII vets quietly enjoying their meal.

On the other side of the cafeteria, Paul and John saved a seat for me. Before taking a seat, I volunteered to get them drinks, milk this time.

The post commander took the podium on a stage surrounded with flags of each of the armed forces. "Sergeant of Arms, place the POW/MIA flag on the empty chair," he barked, bringing the dinner mayhem to order. An old man shuffled to the center of the dance floor to drape the flag over the chair's plastic frame.

Another old man stood. "Vice commander reports that no one has died in the past month."

I was escorted to the stage along with two other veterans, one from the Vietnam War and another from WWII.

"We've got a few new members to swear in tonight," the vice commander said. Then he turned to speak to us. "Okay, you three, repeat after me." He guided us through the ritual of membership. The chaplain gave a prayer.

The commander barked, "Hand salute!"

"About face!" The expected clack of heels was replaced with the soft squeak of padded tennis shoes on a polished floor. We turned around to see the proud, dentured smiles of weathered faces. There is so much for me to learn from them all, so I listen. There's little for me to say.

Veterans are everywhere. Just pay attention to who's on the bus next to you. Millions more have joined the civilian ranks since the Iraq War began. If veterans wore their service on their faces, you would see their pride and frustration in wrinkled half-smiles, their eyes watering with camaraderie and bleeding with humility.

If you pay attention, you will see them—pumping gas, flying planes, doing time, building bridges, and sleeping under them.

16

GOING FOR BLUE

The marine in dress blues is perfect and sacred. The black jacket, with gold embroidered chevrons on red felt sewn meticulously on each shoulder, stands in contrast to blue pants with a blood-red stripe down the outside. Black shoes are polished to mirror perfection. A white belt and white cover, adorned with a golden eagle, globe, and anchor, are matched by bright white gloves. Across the chest are a few ribbons, including the orange-and-green striped Kuwait Liberation Medal. Above the right chest pocket are the crossed silver rifles, denoting marksmanship.

In dress blues you feel untouchable, like the surface of the sun.

DECEMBER 31, 2003—UNDER THE SUNSHINE BRIDGE—MILE 168 LM

"Hey, this place is a dump!" Jenna yells. She has returned to the *Bottle Rocket* for the final journey to New Orleans.

The sun has set behind the Sunshine Bridge, leaving little choice but to beach the raft in the next available space between grounded barges. There are hundreds of barges on either bank and entire fleets of them moored in the middle of the river. We circle around a dozen barges and discover a bare spot on the muddy bank. I seesaw the raft across the mud, using pieces of driftwood and garbage to support my weight in the muck, finally tying the *Bottle Rocket* to another rope holding an empty barge in place.

"I'm not kidding. It really is a dump."

Beyond a small rise between the river and the levee, there are countless piles of rubble from home construction projects. A pile of roofing shingles lies next to a pile of shattered bathroom tile. Abandoned refrigerators, stoves, washers, and dryers sit beneath the green vegetation that tries vainly to camouflage their white carcasses.

The Mississippi River is a sewer. Cans, bottles, millions of pieces of foam, and other bits of plastic debris are everywhere, as well as the occasional zip-lock bag of yellow liquid. There is more industry—chemical plants, refineries, and grain elevators—on the river between Baton Rouge and New Orleans than between northern Minnesota and southern Mississippi. Days ago, as Dave and I passed Baton Rouge, we floated by a barge being emptied of an unknown chemical that hovered on the surface of the river, creating a hazy mirage. With no place to hide, we covered our mouths and noses, but still suffered headaches and nausea for hours. The common designation of this stretch of the Mississippi River as "Cancer Alley" is easily understood.

Jenna and I celebrate the New Year in semi-slumber, with the intermittent barrage of fireworks on the levee. A horn blast from a towboat startles me to my feet. I look out the tent to discover the nearest barge moving.

"Hey, hey, wait a minute!" The rope anchor used by the grounded barge is now taut, and so is the rope from the *Bottle Rocket* I tied to it earlier. The corner of the raft is lifted a few inches off the ground.

"We're not going anywhere tonight," the captain reassures me. He doesn't seem to mind my raft tied to his barge. I don't mind either.

The following day is a gauntlet of barges and boats. They are everywhere, and the river has narrowed, making it fast and less predictable to navigate. Every few minutes one of us yells, "Barge check!" just to be sure. We ride the edge of the channel, cautiously staying clear of parked barges.

Bwamp! Bwaaaaamp! an escort tugboat lays on the horn. We're less than a quarter mile in front of a tanker ship that's howling downriver. It's enormous, with its empty hull riding five stories above the water. Traveling at more than four times the speed of a barge, a typical tanker, the length of two football fields, can travel as far north as Baton Rouge, requiring a forty-foot draft.

Bwaaaaaaaaaaaaammmp! It's right behind us.

"Paddle! Paddle! Paddle!" I yell to Jenna with panic in my voice. We squeak by and ride the bow waves toward the bank. In the minutes between barge checks, the tanker silently slipped around a bend.

"Barge check," I say to Jenna with a chuckle.

We pitch our tent on a grassy knoll above the muddy bank, under the watchful eye of the *Jean Lafitte* and *Jolly Rancher,* two towboats whose crews inundate us with groceries and good wishes. The *Bottle Rocket* is tied to a cypress stump and the corner of our tent.

The morning fog is thick and the temperature rises to seventy degrees—typical Louisiana winter. We hug the bank closely. On the marine radio we monitor discussions about our raft. Soon, a Coast Guard helicopter circles overhead for a closer look, then calls on Channel 16 to check that we have life jackets and an air horn.

A water tower rises above the levee and the trees. It reads

"Wallace" in big letters. We take a break from the fog, tying our raft to willows under the Gramercy Bridge. The town of Wallace consists of no more than thirty homes, with their roofs appearing out of the forest canopy like icebergs.

"How are you folks this morning?" Gerald says, meeting us on top of the levee while on his usual morning jog. We walk down to the abandoned buildings of Wallace Elementary. Gerald is glad to recite his history to an eager audience. Built in the early 1960s, Wallace Elementary was intended to desegregate the community by busing in whites from surrounding neighborhoods. Gerald helped build it. In 1963 he was the first black man to win a seat on the local school board, despite threats and a gun once thrust in his face.

"They tried bringing whites here, but it didn't work," he says. The social experiment couldn't break the tradition of separation. The school closed. A sign nailed high on a telephone pole in front of the school reads, "God Give Us Peace."

JANUARY 4, 2004—NEW ORLEANS—MILE 103 LM

"I've got some good news and bad news...." says the Coast Guard captain from the bow of his patrol boat.

Jenna and I have been riding the river effortlessly on a wave of homeward-bound anticipation. I know the river here. The Bonnet Carré Spillway, on the east bank, allows floodwaters to pour into Lake Pontchartrain. It's a great place to catch snakes. It's also where much of New Orleans comes to excavate new river sand to fill the holes that appear in the earth of the sinking city.

The Norco refinery appears next with its flaming spires burning unwanted gas. Once in a decade or so, Norco makes TV news when it blows up. There's the old match factory behind the levee, and the dock we used to jump off into the river as kids. There's the control tower for the New Orleans International Airport rising above the tree line.

The Coast Guard captain continues, "You've made it to New Orleans, but you can't go through..."

Under the Huey P. Long Bridge, past the Avondale Shipyard, beyond the Corps of Engineers building where my mother worked for twenty-three years, around Carrollton Bend, on the bank of the river beneath the Audubon Zoo, is where family and friends are waiting. Four and a half months since I dipped the pontoons of the *Bottle Rocket* into the cool waters of Lake Itasca, Minnesota, three months since Jenna first churned the paddle wheel in Dubuque, Iowa, we are finally here in New Orleans.

"...'cause we're on Orange Alert, and this is a security zone."

"My grandmother is waiting around the bend," Jenna says defiantly, adding, "DO YOU MIND?!"

She's bundled in multiple layers of fleece and rain gear, with a blue nylon cap, white rabbit-fur earmuffs, and her 1950s prescription glasses. She moves with short rapid gestures. Even I am afraid of her.

The journey down the Mississippi River is about to end for Jenna. She will soon return to Los Angeles and write about the river, the people, and three months of camping, arguing, dancing, and shivering with her ex on a junk raft.

I describe our adventure and destination to the Coast Guard captain as quickly as possible, while the current takes us along, and while Jenna turns red with anger. Nothing will stand between Jenna and her family. The captain stands in equal defiance, with two Coast Guardsmen behind him holding M16 rifles.

"This is so stupid," I think. Do they believe we're terrorists, on a raft of soda bottles? He's just doing his job. Perhaps he knows it's a façade, like the chain-link fence around the river locks and dams, when any boat, or multiple boats, can travel through them unchecked, or the hundreds of uninspected barges and container ships that arrive in our ports daily. I know the Coast Guard has a lot of coast to guard and has to show something for their effort. Today they keep two tired Americans on a bottle raft from infiltrating the strategic port of New Orleans. I can see Jenna's family waiting on the levee a quarter mile downriver. Debbie Pearson and other former coworkers of mine from the Audubon Zoo are waiting there with champagne to celebrate our arrival and to help lift the raft out of the water. The Coast Guard relents and escorts us in.

Jenna quickly forgets about the Coast Guard as her family descends the levee to the bank of the Mississippi. She is jumping in her seat. I tie the raft to rocks on the bank. Jenna walks away from the raft with noticeable hesitation, looking at me to make sure everything is secure.

She melts into the arms of her grandmother, cousin Melanie, aunts and uncles. She is amazing. She actually did it. I'm proud of her. I doubted her ambition. I doubted she would have the integrity to meet me in Dubuque. I doubted her perseverance to make it all the way. I always doubted her. Yet, she is here.

What I realize is that she is much greater than me, or this river. I can see it in the way she holds her grandmother's hand. She is a wonderful woman with an innate moral compass that always points lovingly. She abounds with compassion, integrity, and ethical virtue. She joined me on the river to support me, not for her story, and not for personal recognition. She came to support me. Her selflessness hits me like a ton of bricks.

JANUARY 19, 2004—POINT A LA HACHE—MILE 49 LM

My mother greets me with watering eyes and a comforting embrace. The worry washes down her cheeks. She has been terrified for my safety since I began. She retired from the Corps of Engineers three years ago. She's seen the torrent sweep untethered barges into disaster, witnessed swollen, discolored bodies being recovered, and once was lifted out of her seat by the explosion of a grain elevator directly across the river from her office.

For two weeks I sit in my childhood home telling stories to her about the river. She's so happy. It's so good to see her that way.

After I fix a few things around the house, my mother drops an unintentional hint, "Even in January I've got to cut the grass." She would cut it herself, but I insist on doing it this time. I push the lawnmower over and around the landscape of my childhood. There are depressions where trees used to stand. The sloping pit near the back door is where a large birch tree once held my tree house, lined with green shag carpet from a neighbor's remodeling project. I remember the oak tree where I hung homemade birdhouses with glass windows so I could watch the chicks. I remember the neighborhood kids twenty-five years ago, wrestling, pitching tents, and chasing chickens and dogs across the yard. I remember the huge fight my neighbor Ricky and I had with a couple of bullies. He hit one in the stomach with a baseball bat, resulting in a parent meeting and a neighborhood truce. Ricky and I would later have it out, resulting in my being chased by him with a butter knife in one hand and a raw egg in the other. A buried septic tank still stands as the highest point. In the back corner of the yard, I grew tomatoes and cucumbers. There was once a giant homemade pond in the middle of the yard, where I kept those ninety-six turtles—my first lesson in what not to do to animals.

Walking the neighborhood, I measure the passage of time by the growing girth of oak trees. I think about the river constantly. I'm not done.

"Welcome to New Orleans," I say to Tony, who's come here to complete his documentary of my trip down the Mississippi River.

Past New Orleans and beyond the Belle Chasse Naval Air

Station, all the way to the ferry crossing at Point a la Hache, is where the *Bottle Rocket* is reunited with the Mississippi River. It's thirty-nine miles to Venice, the last town on the river, and the literal end of the road at mile 10.

Without Jenna and her gear, the raft is lighter and more maneuverable. New Orleans was her final destination. Her seat is empty. It feels wrong that it is.

It's cool and cloudless. There's little industry, and the river is absent of the hundreds of barges that lined the bank from Baton Rouge to New Orleans. The only traffic is the dozen giant ships that speed by. An enormous ocean liner, cruising upstream, dwarfs my raft. The river is wide and straight, but there's still a swift current moving us along the vacant bank. Forty-two percent of the nation drains to this point of the Mississippi. There are no more tributaries leading into the river. This is it. Giant levees barricade the river, not from land, but from the marshes and lakes that connect to the Gulf of Mexico.

I accomplish eighteen miles to Empire, Louisiana, with few headaches. I meet Tony over the levee, where we gorge on a gift of satsumas and oranges from a kind Cajun's grove. We find a small sandwich shop with fried okra for Tony and a boudin po-boy for me.

It's cold camping followed by another day of warm sun and a calm steady current. We land in Fort Jackson, a star-shaped brick fort built in 1832 to protect the port of New Orleans.

"This place only saw action for a few days in the Civil War," Mike explains. He's the manager of the fort, and a preacher on weekends. Beginning on April 18, 1862, the Confederate army began to fire its cannons on Admiral Farragut and his Union fleet of forty-three ships. The fort fell in ten days. New Orleans surrendered soon after, and a century later Fort Jackson became a national historic monument, hosting the Plaquemines Parish Fair and Orange Festival every December.

After a walking tour of the grounds, we all sit in the bowels of the fort discussing religion, politics, and the river. Lee and Alvin, groundskeepers and old Cajun river rats, join the conversation. We pass around a bag of satsumas.

"Things aren't getting better, that's for sure," Mike says, referring to the state of small towns on the river. The Corps of Engineers battles the shrimp trawlers and oystermen for rights to redirect river water into the surrounding marshland.

"The marshland is sinking cause there ain't enough sand going into it," Mike explains.

"But you foul up the marsh and you kill the oysters," Alvin responds defensively, adding, "What do we do then?" Like most men in the Delta, his livelihood is tied to the fishing industry in some way. Alvin's worked off and on shrimping along the Gulf Coast for much of his life. "You can't get much for shrimp anymore unless you sell what you catch on the side of the road," he explains. Today, the industry is largely commercialized. Solitary fishermen can't compete with the giant trawlers that can deliver large quantities of shellfish to restaurants and wholesalers at lower prices.

The conversation meanders to politics and religion, the Iraq War, and the state of our nation. It's a blend of similar dialogues I've had with hundreds of Americans since Minnesota. After an hour-long debate, our consensus is that the path of our nation is not sustainable.

"America will change by revolution or renaissance," I suggest.

"Or reformation," the preacher adds.

I pitch my tent next to the moat, overlooking the portholes where cannons and rifles once fired. The temperature is down to the lower thirties. I fall asleep to the hoot of owls and wake to crows and blue jays. The sun shimmers on the water in the moat. The wind disrupts the reflection of giant oaks, their outstretched limbs adorned with long strands of waving Spanish moss.

JANUARY 21, 2004—VENICE, LOUISIANA—MILE 10 LM

Tony films the triumphant arrival of the *Bottle Rocket* at Venice, Louisiana. The west bank from Ft. Jackson is lined with boat docks and helicopter pads servicing the offshore oil rigs. Crew and supplies fly daily to and from Venice.

Without drama, I beach the *Bottle Rocket* on the rocky shore, quickly attending to the task of dragging the boat out of the water. There is no "Welcome Home" banner, marching band, or fireworks, just the river and me. It's an uneventful finale.

For the last five months I've dreamed of blue water in the Gulf of Mexico. Thoughts of watching the brown river blend with salty blue water lured me away from a thousand thoughts of surrender. I wanted to go all the way, but it's not practical. It would be impossible to make it to mile 0 at the Head of Passes because of the lack of return transportation upriver, against the current. I would be literally swept out to sea.

The drive back to New Orleans is quiet. I think about my aching body and the simple pleasure of being warm, dry, and fed. I feel older. I feel mortal, unlike the day I launched the raft in Lake Itasca five months ago.

My adventure down the Mississippi River is over. But it feels woefully unfinished.

JANUARY 28, 2004—GOING FOR BLUE—MILE 0 LM

At 3:30 a.m. Dave and I meet Anthony and Sam at a gas station in Slidell, Louisiana. It's like what we used to do twenty years ago, when we'd sneak out of the neighborhood to go catch snakes all day in the swamp. This time they're taking me to see blue water.

We're on our way to Venice to launch Sam's boat for a day of fishing on the Midnight Lumps. Roughly thirty miles into the Gulf of Mexico, there is a bulge in the continental shelf that brings the sea floor within two hundred feet of the surface in an otherwise five-hundred-foot-deep sloping shelf. There are plenty of fish that hang out there. We launch Sam's boat where the *Bottle Rocket* left the river. We're going for the blue water that eluded me a week ago.

Mile 0 is at the Head of Passes, where the river divides into three channels that connect ships to the Gulf. There are a dozen logs planted vertically on the rocky point, with horizontal logs bolted to them. The rising sun is beginning to glow. Above a raging torrent I hop off the boat and scoot along a log to the sign: "Mile 0. Head of Passes." After a few photos, I'm back in the boat. The river officially ends here, but not for us.

There is a lighthouse at the outlet of Southwest Pass, the westernmost channel to the Gulf. On the horizon there are dozens of oil-drilling platforms and a few ships. Otherwise, there is nothing. For five miles the water is still brown, then suddenly I notice a frothy line of debris demarcating the silt-laden fresh water of the Mississippi River from the blue/green seawater.

The Midnight Lumps are another eighteen miles away. I blissfully watch the water turn blue. Then we sit, bait our hooks, and pass the hours.

"Remember that cottonmouth that bit ya?" Sam says.

"That was a long time ago," I reply.

"How about those guard dogs at the junkyard behind the drive-in," Anthony remembers. "They kept us stuck on top of that truck until the cops came."

David catches a shark. We let it go.

"How about catching catfish at Lafreniere Park," Dave remembers. "We used to cook them with sticks and newspaper and put catsup on them." We all agree they tasted horrible, but we loved the idea of being self-sufficient.

"Hey, remember the horse at Woolworth's?" Sam says, causing a roar of laughter. We would race to the department store before opening hours with a coat hanger and a mouthful of bubble gum, stick the gum-laden hanger down the broken coin chute, and proceed to extract fifteen to twenty dollars in quarters from the mechanical horse.

I catch a red snapper. It's out of season. We let it go.

"What about those gallon cans of pears we stole from the St. Lawrence School cafeteria?" Anthony says, bringing more laughter.

Sam catches a huge grouper that fills the ice chest.

Anthony has the story of the one that got away. Something pulls his line hard. A bluefin tuna we imagine. It drags the boat around for fifteen minutes until it pops his eighty-pound test line.

We talk about our friendship. Then we don't talk about much for hours more. Just fishing.

"Friends till we die," Anthony says.

The day passes quickly. My trip down the Mississippi ends here, in the company of friends. I wouldn't have it any other way. There is nothing greater than us, here, now.

We are untouchable, like the surface of the sun.

AFTERWORD

Behold, I teach you the overman:
he is this lightning, he is this frenzy.
Friedrich Nietzsche, Thus Spake Zarathustra

MARCH 2004—LOS ANGELES, ONE MONTH AFTER
RETURNING FROM THE RIVER

"Can I help you guys set up?" I ask a man with a long gray
beard, green fatigues, and combat boots. He doesn't say anything—just hands me a white cross while he busily stretches a
tape measure three hundred feet across the beach. Today there
are 588 eighteen-inch by twelve-inch white crosses, crescents,
and Stars of David standing three feet apart in twenty-five rows.

Every Sunday a group of veterans—some with gray hair and
bifocals, others in sun-bleached olive drab Vietnam-era uniforms, and still others in Birkenstocks and wide-brimmed hats
—collect themselves on the sand before the Pacific Ocean, on
the north side of the Santa Monica Pier, to put grave markers
in the sand to create a memorial called "Arlington West." The
rows grow in length each week as more Americans die in Iraq.

I join Veterans For Peace for twenty-five bucks.

Mark King was a grunt in Vietnam. He remembers firefights,

calling in air strikes, and Vietcong bodies piled on trucks. He tells me his stories. He's still sad about them. He asks me about mine. "Where did you go? What did you do? How do you feel about that? Tell me that story again." And again. Every Sunday he's there putting crosses in the ground, and then asking me details about everything I did in the Gulf War. "How do you feel about it? Have you told your family? What are you doing about it now?"

I tell him everything. Every Sunday for more than a year I tell him all the stories, one by one. I show him the Iraqi dog tags I looted. I've never admitted this one story to anyone, not even Jenna. I think my shame was too great. I tell him everything, and he understands.

I meet hundreds of Iraq War veterans on liberty from Camp Pendleton or Fort Erwin. I sit with them on the beach, listening to their stories. A marine on liberty for the weekend stumbles upon the memorial, as I did. "You know...I walk around the shopping mall at home or down my street...there can be a thousand people around me and I...I feel so alone," he says. His memories of firefights in Falluja, dead civilians, and dead marines pour down his cheeks. I help him put the names of his fallen comrades on crosses.

By the end of the day there are mementos left on the crosses, Marine Corps insignia, ribbons, flags, an MP shoulder patch, and dozens of notes.

"Being so young, you did so much. Thanks."

"Hope you rained steel brother. Semper Fi. Report to heaven."

"Always loved by your family."

"You are a hero."

"We will end this madness that took your life!"

"While I was celebrating my birthday, you were dying. I'm sorry."

"He died too young. Bring the rest of the troops home— Now."

"Mahalo and Aloha—you'll be missed."

"Semper Fi Gunny. Fair winds and following seas."

"Bless you. Sorry you got caught up in all this crap."

MARCH 2005—LOS ANGELES, ONE YEAR AND ONE MONTH AFTER RETURNING FROM THE RIVER

Jenna and I lived together for almost a year after the river, but old wounds persisted. We argued like we argued when we were engaged, like when we were on the river. I tried to admit my past transgressions, but she only suffered further. I shamefully ended the relationship at the end of 2004.

I still go down to the beach every Sunday to build Arlington West. Mark King still pulls me aside to talk, and I sit with Iraq and Afghanistan veterans in the sand to listen.

"We've got to take this memorial on the road," someone suggests, followed by an impromptu unanimous vote to build a second memorial of a thousand crosses and travel to college campuses.

In the back of a homemade trailer, we carry the new crosses stacked on six handcarts, and boxes of free literature about VA programs, the VetCenter, and post-traumatic stress disorder (PTSD). Lastly, there's a three-foot-wide steel silhouette of the United States, which we use to write the updated daily total of Americans killed and wounded in the war in Iraq. All of this is towed behind my 1984 Ford Econoline van.

APRIL 5, 2005—"ARLINGTON WEST ON THE ROAD" LEAVES LOS ANGELES FOR NEW MEXICO STATE UNIVERSITY— LAS CRUCES, NEW MEXICO; UNIVERSITY OF TEXAS AT EL PASO— EL PASO, TEXAS; UNIVERSITY OF TEXAS AT SAN ANTONIO— SAN ANTONIO, TEXAS

Students pour from dorm rooms or the student union, hustling to morning classes with books in one hand, coffee cup in the other, and tired looks on their faces. Thousands of students and veterans stroll by the memorial set up in the quad. They grab literature and tell their stories.

"My brother's got shrapnel from that IED still stuck in him, and he's got hearing loss, so they made him a recruiter," one student says.

"I was in First Recon, near Baghdad," a marine says. "I'm not sure what I'm going to do once I finish school. There's Officer Candidates School or maybe I'll work for a private contractor or something." We talk at length about PTSD, and I give him information about Vet Centers.

Another student and I talk for a while. He was in the Marine Corps Platoon Leaders Course program for future officers, but resigned after realizing that he couldn't participate in the Iraq War, for ethical reasons.

Another vet pulls me aside to talk. "You ever get those dreams?" he says. "You know, the kind that make you think you're there again."

It is this generation that is most affected by the Iraq War, that's losing family and friends. Everyone seems to know someone who's either in Iraq, home from Iraq, or going to Iraq.

More than one million American servicemen and women have rotated through Iraq. Half of those are reservists or in the National Guard. Half of those are in college. That means approximately a quarter million veterans are on college campuses. We're in the right place.

"I didn't expect to see a cemetery here." Dexter was a marine in Iraq during the initial invasion into Al-Nasiriyah. He read and rewrote field reports from the platoon commanders fighting in the city. He confides in me one of the field reports he received.

"They found our MIAs later that day hung by their necks from lamp posts. They were in full uniform. You never hear about that stuff back home," he adds.

"How do you feel about all that?" I ask. He has my full attention.

"I think about it a lot," he says. "I took advantage of every chance I had to be a peaceful warrior. I remember an old man with a cane walking out of the burning city. When he passed our checkpoint, I gave him an MRE. He started crying and hugged me. I felt good for that moment. I don't know whether the war was good or bad, but I made my own choices to do what I thought was honorable. I could only control what I did, not the war."

Whatever these veterans gave, whatever they lost, they share the necessary desire to justify their experience with whatever rationale accounts for their service and suffering. Many still exude patriotism, loyalty to spangled banners, fondness for their respective uniforms and accompanying formalities; they are generous with their nationalistic praise, and might still sacrifice themselves without question to the whims of the elected.

APRIL 17, 2005—UNIVERSITY OF NEW ORLEANS— NEW ORLEANS, LOUISIANA

I stroll across the quad in front of the library, as I did as a student here, before and after the Gulf War. Today I'm planting a thousand crosses. I'll be here again in a few months when Hurricane Katrina inundates the city.

"Doc?" I say, slowly recognizing the man standing before our table. "Doc Clooney?" He was STA Platoon's corpsman in Kuwait fifteen years ago.

"What in the world are you doing here, Eriksen?" he asks jokingly.

"Doc Clooney!" I'm still joyfully amazed. "How have you been?" There's a handshake, a pat on the back, and a rapid round of formalities before we find an empty bench to warm.

"Remember when those first rounds of incoming landed?" Doc asks. "Suddenly I was digging a hole. I don't remember leaving the truck."

"We dug them just deep enough to get underground," I agree.

"Yeah. Then I had to go help the Iraqis." Doc recounts the

enemy wounded that came in dozens at a time. I remember them also. We talk about the hundred men sitting in rows, missing arms and legs. "They needed my help," he says, adding, "Every corpsman was ordered in." We both remember the artillery round that landed a hundred feet from there. We remember everything. I now have his perspective on that day, which has been relived in my head a thousand times.

Doc became a paramedic in New Orleans after the war. For ten years he witnessed the result of some of the nation's most violent urban crime, ". . . but nothing has compared to that day in Kuwait," he confides.

Suddenly, I realize that Doc, now pursuing a second career in engineering, is not the same man I knew years ago. I remember him youthful, in desert camouflage, with no gray hair, surrounded by sand and oil fires. How have the other men changed? Are they married, divorced, rich, or poor? Are they even alive? I don't know. For so long I've judged myself by the jury of my platoon as I knew them, but I don't know them anymore. I cannot predict what fifteen years has done to those men. Maybe they've changed their minds, or firmed their convictions. For the first time, I remove myself from their scrutiny.

When the day ends, Doc helps to take the memorial down. We were together in Kuwait on Hill 99. The day we left, we burned or buried whatever we couldn't take with us. We burned clothes, tents, furniture, and letters from home, and we buried countless AK-47s, flare guns, and American-made Iraqi weapons we planned to dig up someday. We left behind whatever innocence remained. We threw it all away and covered it with sand as if it never was, as if we were never there.

But the wind uncovers everything. And in time you're left with the task of putting it all back in order, in its proper place. You'll spend half your life in a dull-witted rampage, and the other half fixing what you broke.

We leave one cross under an oak tree. I write on the cross,

"On this day, April 17, 2005, 1557 Americans have died in the Iraq War."

Little did I know that in four and a half months, nearly fifteen hundred people in the city will drown when homes are torn apart and levees fail. I will meet my brother and mother in Tupelo, Mississippi, days after they escape from Hurricane Katrina. My brother's wife, a nurse still in the city, will describe patients on life support dying as power fails, as promises of evacuation turn from hours into days, and the last drops of fuel to power generators disappear. Dave's home in Slidell, Louisiana, though severely flood-damaged, will still stand, thanks to the two rows of destroyed houses that separate his home from Lake Pontchartrain. For three weeks we will rip out drywall, tear up carpets, and replace the roof on my mother's home. It will take several more months for overturned cars and boats in front yards to be replaced with FEMA trailers.

UNIVERSITY OF ALABAMA—TUSCALOOSA, ALABAMA

"Thank the Lord for George Bush!" screams some longhaired, double-chinned white guy in a dented pickup truck, as he flies by the memorial in a grassy field on the edge of campus at the University of Alabama. "Yaaaaah Hooo!" His squeal echoes long after he passes.

"Probably not a vet," I think. But throughout the day, between the intermittent rain and hail, I meet more veterans here than on any other campus.

An army ranger who served in Afghanistan and Iraq tells stories about his team capturing the fourth man in Bush's card deck of Iraq's fifty-two most wanted.

"You know, we knew what Afghanistan was about," he says. "We were gung-ho about it. But Iraq...We kept asking, 'Why are we here?'"

Hours later, a thin young man with shaggy blond hair comes to the memorial to toss a football with his toddler son. "I was a marine in Iraq last year," Daniel says. He describes the helicopter crash he survived, while four men in his six-man team died before his eyes. He raises his shirt to show his only scar from the accident. "I don't know why I made it," he exclaims. "I've been clean for four months now," he says, speaking of his addiction. "I've got no one here to talk to. No one understands. You know?"

For an hour we talk about Vet Centers, while his son plays among the crosses. Daniel talks about guilt, how much he loves his boy, and how hard his wife tries to keep things together and be good to him. He walks away from the memorial, but not before leaning over to kiss the top of a cross.

AUBURN UNIVERSITY—AUBURN, ALABAMA

"Are you guys some kind of a protest?"

"What's this demonstration about?

"You're antiwar, right?"

We are some kind of protest, at least in one respect. The degree to which we remind the country that the Iraq War continues to claim an average of two Americans and countless Iraqis each day is a protest against this administration's desire to have the public forget about it. Troops coming home in flag-draped caskets are censored from the news so viewers will forget. We are here as a reminder.

The atmosphere at Auburn is one of hostility toward any perception of anything antigovernment. After all, Bush landed his helicopter on campus last year to appease his voting base, and Cheney is due to give the commencement address in two weeks. Our memorial is restricted to the Free-speech Zone across from the football stadium.

I'm away from the memorial when two men in Army uniforms stop me with a handshake and a business card. The recruiters, assuming I'm a student, give me the sales pitch. I play along with a barrage of questions about their promises.

"So you've got this fifteen-month enlistment program, huh?"

I ask. "And after boot camp and infantry school, that leaves only a year, right?"

"No. Training isn't part of the fifteen-month commitment."

"Will I go to Iraq?" I ask.

"That's a strong possibility."

"Now if my unit gets activated on the fifteenth month of my enlistment—I'm sorry, the twenty-first month of my enlistment, including training—will I automatically get extended a year because of stop-loss?"

"That's also a possibility."

"So with boot camp, infantry school, fifteen months of service, and stop-loss, I'm looking at three years in your fifteen-month program."

"That's a possibility."

"Why didn't you just explain that in the first place?" I then explain our memorial and invite them to visit.

"I heard about you guys on campus. You're pro-military, right?" asks Captain Smith, the recruiter.

"No," I reply. "We're pro-troop."

"Why don't we work together? I can put my table up by your memorial, right?"

He wants to advertise the army with the backdrop of a field of a thousand crosses, covered with notes and mementos from grieving friends and relatives.

"Sure," I reply.

SALISBURY UNIVERSITY—SALISBURY, MARYLAND; AGNES SCOTT COLLEGE—DECATUR, GEORGIA

"I signed up to be a cook, now I'm in mortuary affairs, learning how to pick up body parts," Cody says. He explains, "Those recruiters still tell people that they're gonna be cooks or work in supply, but the recruiters know those jobs are outsourced to Filipinos and Pakistanis."

He joined after 9/11, when defending American interests made clear moral sense. "They don't need us cookin' food. Only the dirty jobs are left. Think about it, who's gonna sign up to bag and tag dead marines? They got us learning how to bury Iraqis facing Mecca and shit like that."

Thousands of students stroll by and through the memorial throughout the day.

"I'm so glad you all are here," says Brooke Campbell. She shares stories about her brother, Ryan, one of the first thousand American servicemembers killed in Iraq.

KENT STATE UNIVERSITY—KENT, OHIO

Four sets of pillars in a parking lot mark the spot where four students were killed exactly thirty-five years ago, when National Guard troops fired on them. We erect the memorial where the guardsmen stood. A candlelight vigil commemorates the anniversary of the shootings. Volunteers take turns through the night to stand at the four sites. The first shift is held by survivors and relatives of the victims.

"I was running away across the lawn over there between the trees when the gunshot knocked me down," Jim Russell says to me, pointing to an empty sloping hill a hundred yards away. "I saw him turn 180 degrees, aim, and fire." Jim is one of nine students who were hit by bullets. The lead round tore through his thigh, and a fragment lodged in his temple. The guardsmen were acquitted of any wrongdoing in the events that day, claiming that they only shot in the air to repel the mob of students that was threatening their lives.

"Threatened?" Jim replies to a young student's question. "Warning shots? He took aim! He deliberately fired on me as I ran away."

"I remember when my brother died," recalls Russ Miller, standing on the spot where his brother, Jeffrey Miller, fell. "I rushed home to the Bronx to be with my mother. In front of the house there was a limousine. When I walked in I saw my mother sitting with Governor Rockefeller. We all sat together and told stories about Jeffrey."

I begin to realize that what happened in this small college town had an enormous impact on the nation. It was a turning point in the antiwar movement and public opinion on the war in Vietnam. Kent State effectively moved the protest from college campuses to the streets across America, as people began to realize that the government was willing to turn its guns on its own citizens.

THE VIETNAM MEMORIAL WALL—WASHINGTON, D.C.

A low sloping hill rising from the Vietnam War Memorial is where I drive the first cross into the ground at 4:45 a.m., beneath fading stars and a golden sunrise blazing behind the Washington Monument.

"What the hell is this?" a suited man yells in my face. "Where are the crosses for the victims of 9/11? Where are the crosses for all the innocent Iraqis killed by the terrorists?"

"You're making a foolish assumption," I mumble in calm frustration. "We're a memorial to the fallen soldiers in Iraq."

More people visit our memorial today than in anyplace else. A steady stream of visitors walk from the Wall up the hill to our crosses. Hundreds of veterans bend our ears.

"I carried a flamethrower on Iwo Jima," Red says in a slow, raspy voice. Under his blood-red Marine Corps baseball cap is an eighty-three-year-old, tall, broad-shouldered man. He survived five Pacific campaigns in WWII. On Iwo Jima he was one of only three men in his platoon who walked away.

"I was too tall—a walking target. I don't know why I survived it." I walk with Red through the thousand crosses. "It's a shame. It's just a shame," he says. "I went to my local National Guard unit and shook all their hands before they left for Iraq." Then he leans toward me with conviction, his eyes dark like coal, and says, "That doesn't mean I agree with what's going on." Red continues, "It should be a constitutional law that if you've never served in war, you shouldn't be allowed to declare war. You know? Not unless you know the score."

When Smedley Butler wrote *War Is a Racket* in 1933, he suggested that the declaration of war should be put to a vote by the young men who would be sent to the battlefield to risk death for it. If that were the case, every American war since 1945 would likely never have happened.

The day ends quickly. Our permit does not allow us to accept donations, but another older veteran forces twenty bucks into my hand. I split it between two homeless men who help us take down the crosses. One is a Vietnam vet. We load the van and trailer, and finally visit the Wall ourselves. We watch our reflections pass 58,249 names etched in black granite. We leave one cross: "On this day, May 9, 2005, 1601 Americans have died in the Iraq War."

THE WHITE HOUSE—WASHINGTON, D.C.

Washington, D.C., is cold. It is a mausoleum littered with heavy stones scribbled with quotes and decorated with eagles, lions, and busts of ideologues. They are astonishing monuments to ourselves. We walk across the Potomac River to Arlington National Cemetery. I count 123 headstones for troops killed in Iraq. Endless perfect rows of quiet stone. Ryan Campbell's headstone is there, as his sister said at Agnes Scott College.

There are a hundred soldiers in uniform in front of the White House, performing a weekly army pep rally called the "Twilight Tattoo." There's a parade of American military costumes since the Revolutionary War and a band in red coats playing the army fight song. A few cannons, humvees, and dozens of flags make up the backdrop to the show. They perform every Wednesday.

Two Secret Service agents are patrolling outside the White House lawn. I remove a cross from my backpack and scribble across it, "On this day, May 11, 2005, 1610 Americans have died in the Iraq War."

I lean the cross against the black wrought-iron fence in front of the White House. I turn and walk away.

"Hey. You can't leave that there!" the agent yells, adding, "You gotta take it with you."

Another agent on a bicycle catches up with us. "What do you have there? Who are you? Where are you from?"

"I want to give the president a gift," I say, handing him the cross.

"You can't leave anything here."

"It's just a cross. Just a reminder."

"Give me your name." He takes out his notepad and asks for identification. I give him my VA card. He smiles.

GROUND ZERO—NEW YORK CITY, NEW YORK

The cavernous streets of Manhattan, with their vertical pillars of urban excess, conceal the massive pit where the World Trade Center once stood. How can you stand here and not feel a kind of anguish that makes you cry? I cannot begin to know the sound of people falling to their deaths, or the echo of fire-fighters' jackets beeping from their prolonged stillness. If you stand here and feel contempt for an arrogant nation that you think finally got what it deserved, then you're deprived of humanity. If you stand here and feel only anger and vengeance, then your grasp of the plight of humankind is as shallow as your empathy. How this happened is barely conceivable. Understandably, the question why is far more complicated. This was not the beginning.

There is a crucifix made from I-beams that did not fall when the towers did. A twisted sheet of metal drapes over the cross like cloth. We place one cross against the fence. "On this day, May 12, 2005, 1612 Americans have died in the Iraq War."

We turn and walk away.

It's time to go home.

I've sailed north to south, two thousand miles down America's greatest river, and driven coast-to-coast and back, 9,042 miles, to know my countrymen. I am American. I am home among American people. I identify myself with them, not with my government.

On the river and on the road, average Americans gave me food, shelter, and clothing, fixed my raft, towed my van, brought Thanksgiving dinner to my tent, blessed my journey, and helped me plant crosses and raise our flag. American people have always given to me. My government fails in comparison.

Private conversations with hundreds of people have led me to the affirmation that Americans are passionate and kind. We are good people, but we suffer from patriotic indoctrination, false security, and media magnetism. We bought a war that turned out to be a lemon. On the surface of every war is the rhetoric of freedom, nationalism, security of the homeland, and support for the boys on the battlefield. Warfare is painted with family values to ease the sacrifice.

Now we grow weary of the Iraq War, tired of the dying and frustrated by the lies. Veterans, students, bleeding hearts, and Demo-Repubs, progressives and conservatives alike, find a common enemy, one that has sold the spirit of our nation for a buck. Vietnam didn't teach our leaders to end the covert and overt wars on the third world, it taught them to intelligently streamline the government's business. The rules: Hit 'em hard and fast, under the public radar, and keep your voters morally satiated with domestic trivialities.

Our leaders are not great men. They are businessmen. As one Minnesota River rat once said, "Kerry and Bush... they both suckle from the same pig." The president is not our father or a moral authority. We are not children of the government, to be reprimanded for dissent. If anything, our elected leaders are our children, forever in need of our approval and direction, rightfully scolded when they misbehave.

Home is moral certainty.

I have yet to meet an intelligent person of moral integrity who does not believe that being responsible for the world of tomorrow is great service today. Personal sacrifice for the rights of others, regardless of their praise and gratitude, is moral authority. Sustainability is moral authority.

Home is forgiveness.

Forgiveness is making peace with yourself for what you've done, didn't do, or participated in against your will, or for lacking the courage to make the choices your conscience suggested. It's finding the ability to love yourself honestly and project it outwardly.

Forgiveness begins with sharing your past. It's talking with other vets who know you without knowing you. Telling your story releases the burden of horror and grief from your memory, makes your experience powerless in the present, so you can say, "Yes I did this. I can't change it, but I can be a better person today." Each time I tell a story about the corpses I looted, or the dead and dying Iraqi soldiers, it's like taking a brick off my back, giving it to the person I'm talking to, and watching them put it on the ground. Tell your stories to someone you trust. Tell them everything.

Home is like a house inside your head where your thoughts gather. You learn to love others in the living room where you let the light in. Some rooms will be dark places where your demons reside. Learn to control that darkness. Let those uninvited guests have their moments, then usher them out the door. You have forgiveness when the demons become powerless. They will always come back, but you have freedom when you become the keeper of the keys.

Home is always worth defending.

After you fight to understand why you were sent to an unjust war, and fight to quiet the demons that followed you back, become warriors with your fellow Americans to make things right again. Turn off your TV and lose the idea that your government can do no wrong. Ask of all politicians and media, "What information have you exaggerated, omitted, and invented?"

Sometimes patriotism requires that one be willing to protect one's nation from its own government. Become mentally prepared, factual and thoughtful, about principles of human rights and sustainability. Become a force of greater persuasion. Choose justice, choose your army, find your students, know your enemy, and then prepare yourself with clenched fists.

SUNDAY, MAY 22, 2005—SANTA MONICA, CALIFORNIA— THE END OF THE ROAD

It's a long drive from New York to Los Angeles. We left Phoenix this morning, rolling sluggishly along a wavering 107-degree asphalt highway, through vacant desert and brown hills peppered with black boulders of ancient volcanic basalt and blooming white flowers on saguaro cactus.

The end of Interstate 10 is soon ahead. At the end of the freeway, there is the Santa Monica Pier. Our other memorial is there on its usual Sunday display.

The first signs of urban life are the L.A. hip-hop radio stations that begin to outnumber the country stations and Bible-thumping talking heads. Then comes traffic, plowing through endless strip malls. The air is still boiling until the first green highway signs for Santa Monica appear overhead. The cool Pacific air stings my lungs.

We're only moments away from ending two months on the road, having built our memorial at nine college campuses, in a city park, and next to the Vietnam War Memorial in our nation's capital. We inch our way through four lanes of traffic moving less than five miles per hour.

"Is that a fucking joke?" a young man screams from the passenger seat of a blue Honda rolling slowly on my left. He sees the trailer filled with crosses and the metal silhouette of the United States listing the current number of troops wounded and killed in action. A young woman in the driver's seat, with deep concern across her face, is trying her best to keep the car parallel to mine.

"Is that some kind of a fucking joke?" he yells again, his face red with rage. "You think that's fucking funny?" he screams.

I hold back my agitation the best I can and say, "You're making the wrong assumption, pal."

He screams, "I lost five guys in Ramadi!"

I roll down my window all the way and lean out as far as I can with one hand still on the wheel and a foot on the brake. "I'm sorry for your loss." He's angry, tearful, but listening. "We're a traveling memorial going across the country to honor those who died in Iraq. We've been going to college campuses to remind people that there's still a war going on."

I watch him crumple into his seat, curl inward away from the window, covering his face. The young woman is trying to keep the car straight, while consoling him with her right arm. She's saying something to him. She's looking at the road. She's glancing over at me with pleading eyes. She wants me to leave.

I keep my van parallel to them, as a quarter mile of empty space opens between me and the traffic ahead in my lane. On the dashboard of my van there is still a stack of postcards describing the mission of our memorial. Leaning out as far as I can, I extend the card in my left hand. She motions to him to grab the card from me. The young man, young like the men I remember from STA Platoon fifteen years ago, leans out of his car to meet me halfway above the dotted white line between our lanes.

I can see the tears on his face as he strains to reach. Unnecessarily, he tries to apologize. I interrupt him, though not intentionally. As the card leaves my hand and the little blue Honda drifts away, I yell, loud above traffic, as clear as I can summon the words, "WELCOME HOME, BROTHER!"

It all happens in less than two minutes.

I take the next exit off the freeway and meander to the beach below the Santa Monica Pier, where thousands of people dressed for summer stroll along the boardwalk, past the Ferris wheel, carousel, and churro stands, to the steps leading to the shore.

"I hope that young marine comes to the beach one day to talk," I think, as I step into sand.

The Sunday memorial comes into view. I can see the older vets sitting in the shade, taking questions and engaging in conversations about the cost of war. "It's good to be back," I think. I want to tell them everything I've learned about my beautiful America.

Then I see the actual crosses.

A sea of white crosses stands in perfect rows above the white froth of the rising tide. Beachgoers on blankets under umbrellas surround the memorial.

Children chase the waves, running into the ocean and back again. From the security of land, they venture to the edge of America, coming home before the waves crash over them.

ACKNOWLEDGMENTS

Nothing I have done has been done alone. On the river, I must thank Tom and Denny, Terry and Miriam Smart, Terry Larson, Kevin Dyer, the Minnesota boy scouts of Troop 17, and the crews of the *J. S. Lewis* and *Jolly Rancher* for priceless help and hospitality. I'm grateful to the many friends I made at the National Mississippi River Museum and Aquarium and the St. Louis Science Center, to the Memphis Children's Museum for the gift of warmth and good food while the *Bottle Rocket* was on display, and to Debbie Pearson from the Audubon Zoo in New Orleans, who brought champagne when Jenna and I arrived.

Of the Marine Corps, I must thank STA Platoon H&S Company, 3/23 Marines (1990–91) for watching my back, especially Frank, Mauricio, and Calvin. I am grateful for my family's support, and to my brother, Dave, who gave up time to risk a few days on my raft with me. Tony Peck and Joe and Cherie Masters deserve acknowledgment for their documentary film work. I thank the many wonderful people I've met through Veterans for Peace. Beacon Press, especially my editor, Brian Halley, deserves gratitude for believing in this book.

I owe Jenna a debt of gratitude and atonement for everything she has given.

Printed in the United States
by Baker & Taylor Publisher Services